Word Work

Word Work

Practical Tools to Empower Language and Literacy Learning in the High School Classroom

Amber M. Simmons

NCTE

National Council of Teachers of English
340 N. Neil St., Suite #104, Champaign, Illinois 61820
www.ncte.org

Staff Editor: Cynthia Gomez
Manuscript Editor: The Charlesworth Group
Interior Design: Jenny Jensen Greenleaf
Cover Design: Beth DeWilde Designs
Cover Image: Beth DeWilde

ISBN: 978-0-8141-0131-5 (paperback); 978-0-8141-0133-9 (epub); 978-0-8141-0134-6 (PDF)

It is the policy of NCTE in its journals and other publications to provide a forum for the open discussion of ideas concerning the content and the teaching of English and the language arts. Publicity accorded to any particular point of view does not imply endorsement by the Executive Committee, the Board of Directors, or the membership at large, except in announcements of policy, where such endorsement is clearly specified.

NCTE provides equal employment opportunity to all staff members and applicants for employment without regard to race, color, religion, sex, national origin, age, physical, mental or perceived handicap/disability, sexual orientation including gender identity or expression, ancestry, genetic information, marital status, military status, unfavorable discharge from military service, pregnancy, citizenship status, personal appearance, matriculation or political affiliation, or any other protected status under applicable federal, state, and local laws.

Every effort has been made to provide current URLs and email addresses, but, because of the rapidly changing nature of the web, some sites and addresses may no longer be accessible.

Library of Congress Control Number: 2023935125

For all my children: those of my blood, Graham and Ivy Claire, and those of my classroom. May we always learn from each other.

Contents

Acknowledgments

This book would not have been completed if not for the support of my advisors, administration, and colleagues. I would like to express my gratitude to my former advisors from the University of Georgia: James Marshall, Ruth Harman, and JoBeth Allen. Your instruction and support were formative to not only this book but also to who I have become as an educator. I hope I have made you proud. Thank you to NCTE, especially Kurt Austin, for showing your faith in this project and keeping it alive despite a global pandemic. Finally, thank you to my school administration for supporting innovative language instruction and to my fellow educators for making me want to be a better teacher. I am in awe of you. Working with you has been the most rewarding form of professional development.

Recognizing the "Looting of Language"

1

"We die. That may be the meaning of life. But we do language. That may be the measure of our lives."

—Toni Morrison (1993, para. 21)

Toni Morrison, in her 1993 Nobel Prize speech, tells a proverb about a group of young people who attempt to play a trick on an old, blind woman. They ask her, "Is the bird I am holding living or dead?" Being blind, without having the bird in her own hands, it is impossible for her to know if the bird is alive or dead. The joke, cruel in its intention, is to mock her age and blindness. The old woman responds, "I don't know. . . I don't know whether the bird you are holding is dead or alive, but what I do know is that it is in your hands. It is in your hands" (Morrison, 1993, para. 7). Morrison goes on to craft a meaningful metaphor comparing the bird that is in the young people's hands to language. She explains:

> The systematic looting of language can be recognized by the tendency of its users to forgo its nuanced, complex, mid-wifery properties for menace and subjugation. Oppressive language does more than represent violence; it is violence; does more than represent the limits of knowledge; it limits knowledge. Whether it is obscuring state language or the faux-language of mindless media; whether it is the proud but calcified language of the academy or the commodity driven language of science; whether it is the malign language of law-without-ethics, or language designed for the estrangement of minorities, hiding its racist plunder in its literary cheek—it must be rejected, altered, and exposed. It is the language that drinks blood, laps vulnerabilities, tucks its fascist boots under crinolines of respectability and patriotism as it moves relentlessly toward the bottom line and the bottomed-out mind. Sexist language, racist language, theistic language—all

> are typical of the policing languages of mastery, and cannot, do not permit new knowledge or encourage the mutual exchange of ideas.
>
> (Morrison, 1993, para. 13)

When reading and analyzing this speech with my classes, I feel a huge sense of responsibility. Morrison is not only telling us to teach our children to read, write, and speak. She is reminding us—warning us, even—that we must teach our children to use language conscientiously and responsibly. As language arts teachers, it is our calling to show students the power they, and others, have over the bird that is in their hands—the future of our language. They have two choices: they can kill it, using language as an act of violence to disempower and harm others, or they can nurture and care for it, protecting it from those who aim to defile and pervert it to injure others. Eyes wide at Morrison's grotesque description of the violence of language, one student timidly asked: "How do you stop it? How can we change it? I can't even see it."

Over ten years ago, when I first began teaching, I had no answer to such a question. Back then, my understanding of language education was synonymous with prescribed grammar. I presented grammar, our usage of language, as "a set of rules representing a privileged language within a culture" (Amberg & Vause, 2009, p. 84) and had students complete grammar exercises from the grammar book. Then, I expected that these rules would be utilized in their own writing, leading to essays that were grammatically correct, complete with commas after opening adverb clauses and pronoun–antecedent and subject–verb agreement. Very straightforward: easy as one, two, three. After all, grammar *is* the math of the English classroom; follow the formula, and you are guaranteed success, right?

Wrong.

What I found was that the rules I taught and the lessons I crafted rarely led to students questioning their word choice or sentence structure, more grammatically correct writing, or students even remembering the lesson, causing me to repeat the same lesson over and over again expecting different results. Wasn't it Einstein who said such behavior is madness? Most importantly, my lessons did not investigate the relationship between language use and society. However, I wasn't aware of another way to teach it.

Reflecting, I realize that what I previously considered "language" education was really prescriptive grammar, and, as Humphrey (2011) stated, "the word 'grammar' conjures up memories of stultifying lessons in parsing analysis, red pen on a composition" (p. 4). I also remember myself as a student zoning out during these lessons, not paying attention, and not recognizing how these rules applied to my life, my writing, or my world. Learning the "rules" outside the context of my interests and my own writing made them irrelevant to me and just another brick in Pink Floyd's wall. So, why would what didn't work then work for my students now? How could I empower students to see that the *words* in their hands were powerful and could be wielded for good or for ill, just as they are in the texts they read? And how could I answer that bewildered student's anxious question? These questions ultimately led to my journey in search of a meaningful language education, resulting in the curriculum discussed in the following pages.

The Problem

Australian researcher Kristina Love (2006) accurately critiqued the United States when she observed that we are not encouraged to teach how one's language choices convey ideological stances and influence readers' attitudes. Indeed, when looking at the widely adopted 2010 Common Core State Standards (CCSS) and standardized tests, conceptualizing grammar as a system of choices that can be critically assessed, and not as a set of rules that must be followed, has not been fully accepted by American institutionalized education (Common Core State Standards Initiative, 2010). Consequently, grammar is viewed as prescriptive, and viewing grammar as a meaningful part of the relationship between language and society has not been fully explored as a way of teaching language in American classrooms (see Common Core State Standards Initiative, 2010). Table 1.1 provides a summary of the CCSS for English Language Arts (ELA), grades 9–10 and 11–12, in relation to language education.

As you can see, most of these standards perceive grammar and language as a set of rules rather than choices, and none asks students to investigate the relationship between these choices and society. However, later in the book, I will show you how a few alterations, supplemental materials, and scaffolded activities can help your students achieve the latter while also fulfilling the already-established standards.

Why So Much Prescriptive Grammar?

There are many reasons for the prevalence of prescriptive grammar and language education; however, a few are most relevant to my teaching situation. First, as shown from the focus in the CCSS, Standard English, the privileged discourse, conceptualizes grammar as a set of "rules" that need to be followed, and the ability to speak Standard English, particularly in the United States, gives learners opportunities they might not otherwise have if using another subform

TABLE 1.1. CCSS Language Strand for High School ELA (Common Core State Standards Initiative, 2010)

Standard Title and Number	Common Standard	9th–10th Specific Sub-Standards	11th–12th Specific Sub-Standards
Conventions of Standard English: CCSS.ELA-LITERACY.L.1	Demonstrate command of the conventions of Standard English grammar and usage when writing or speaking	A. Use parallel structure	A. Apply the understanding that usage is a matter of convention, can change over time, and is sometimes contested
		B. Use various types of phrases (noun, verb, adjectival, adverbial, participial, prepositional, absolute) and clauses (independent, dependent; noun, relative, adverbial) to convey specific meanings and add variety and interest to writing or presentations	B. Resolve issues of complex or contested usage, consulting references (e.g., *Merriam-Webster's Dictionary of English Usage*, *Garner's Modern American Usage*) as needed
Conventions of Standard English: CCSS.ELA-LITERACY.L.2	Demonstrate command of the conventions of Standard English capitalization, punctuation, and spelling when writing	A. Use a semicolon (and perhaps a conjunctive adverb) to link two or more closely related independent clauses	A. Observe hyphenation conventions
		B. Use a colon to introduce a list or quotation	B. Spell correctly
		C. Spell correctly	
Knowledge of Language: CCSS.ELA-LITERACY.L.3	Apply knowledge of language to understand how language functions in different contexts, to make effective choices for meaning or style, and to comprehend more fully when reading or listening	A. Write and edit work so that it conforms to the guidelines in a style manual (e.g., *MLA Handbook*, Turabian's *A Manual for Writers*) appropriate for the discipline and writing type	A. Vary syntax for effect, consulting references (e.g., Tufte's *Artful Sentences*) for guidance as needed; apply an understanding of syntax to the study of complex texts when reading
Vocabulary Acquisition and Use: CCSS.ELA-LITERACY.L.4	Determine or clarify the meaning of unknown and multiple-meaning words and phrases based on [grade level] reading and content, choosing flexibly from a range of strategies	A. Use context (e.g., the overall meaning of a sentence, paragraph, or text; a word's position or function in a sentence) as a clue to the meaning of a word or phrase	A. Use context (e.g., the overall meaning of a sentence, paragraph, or text; a word's position or function in a sentence) as a clue to the meaning of a word or phrase
		B. Identify and correctly use patterns of word changes that indicate different meanings or parts of speech (e.g., analyze, analysis, analytical; advocate, advocacy)	B. Identify and correctly use patterns of word changes that indicate different meanings or parts of speech (e.g., conceive, conception, conceivable)
		C. Consult general and specialized reference materials (e.g., dictionaries, glossaries, thesauruses), both print and digital, to find the pronunciation of a word or determine or clarify its precise meaning, its part of speech, or its etymology	C. Consult general and specialized reference materials (e.g., dictionaries, glossaries, thesauruses), both print and digital, to find the pronunciation of a word or determine or clarify its precise meaning, its part of speech, its etymology, or its standard usage
		D. Verify the preliminary determination of the meaning of a word or phrase (e.g., by checking the inferred meaning in context or in a dictionary)	D. Verify the preliminary determination of the meaning of a word or phrase (e.g., by checking the inferred meaning in context or in a dictionary)

Vocabulary Acquisition and Use: CCSS.ELA-LITERACY.L.5	Demonstrate understanding of figurative language, word relationships, and nuances in word meanings	A. Interpret figures of speech (e.g., euphemism, oxymoron) in context and analyze their role in the text	A. Interpret figures of speech (e.g., hyperbole, paradox) in context and analyze their role in the text
		B. Analyze nuances in the meaning of words with similar denotations	B. Analyze nuances in the meaning of words with similar denotations
Vocabulary Acquisition and Use: CCSS.ELA-LITERACY.L.6	Acquire and use accurately general academic and domain-specific words and phrases, sufficient for reading, writing, speaking, and listening at the college and career readiness level; demonstrate independence in gathering vocabulary knowledge when considering a word or phrase important to comprehension or expression	N/A	N/A

Note: English Language Arts Standards (grades 9–10 and 11–12) are presented in full on the Common Core State Standards Initiative website (see http://www.corestandards.org/ELA-Literacy/L/9-10 and http://www.corestandards.org/ELA-Literacy/L/11-12).

of English (e.g., various urban and rural vernaculars) (Fairclough, 1995). Therefore, many teachers feel the need to "fill" their students with knowledge regarding Standard English, neglecting to focus on how language positions the learner in the world. Raciolinguist Geneva Smitherman (2017) defined this as *linguistic miseducation*, "where teachers be obsessed wit teaching 'correct' grammar, spelling, and pronunciation rather than teaching students what language is and allows human being to do, the socio-historical formation of their language, its communicative and social functions . . . and master the power of language—which is about way more than whether yo verbs and subjects agree" (p. 6). Language analysis to deepen critical understanding of language's role in ideology, especially related to social class, is also missing (Freire, 1994).

In addition, students and teachers rarely have a collective metalanguage that provides them with the resources to discuss the social nature of language, and the metalanguage available is typically under-explained and inconsistently applied, which makes it of little long-term use to students (Christie & Macken-Horarik, 2011). This book is designed to be a step in remedying that deficit.

Another reason prescriptive grammar is alive and well is because state standards demand that students have knowledge of these "rules," and high-stakes tests assess for students' ability to recognize grammar errors, thinking that students' ability to identify "errors" means they will avoid making these errors in their own writing (Applebee, 1974; Haladyna, 1999; Pearson & Dole, 1987). With standardized tests asking students to identify the grammatical error in a sentence, I believe that we are encouraged to teach grammar as a set of rules and less as rhetorical choices made by an author. The current SAT test is a fantastic example of this. Many of the questions in Section 2 (Writing and Language) of that significant exam are focused on grammar rules. Here is an example excerpt from a practice exam available on College Board's website:

> 26. <u>Work, that is easily understood and appreciated, is supported</u>, while more complex work goes unnoticed.
> A) NO CHANGE
> B) Work that is easily understood and appreciated is supported,
> C) Work that is easily understood, and appreciated is supported
> D) Work—that is easily understood and appreciated—is supported,
>
> (College Board, 2016, p. 30)

Here, it is clear that they are testing students' knowledge of essential and non-essential adjective clauses (CCSS.ELA-LITERACY.L.1)—incredibly prescriptive.

Even though the current standards advocate that students are encouraged to use grammar as a stylistic tool in writing (see CCSS.ELA-LITERACY.L.3), what is suggested in the standard and what is tested do not line up, supporting the traditional instruction of prescriptive grammar. Macken-Horarik (2009) states that, "as the national tests have reminded us, traditional grammar is most often used to correct students' writing. It is a deficit model" (p. 63). Therefore, grammar education has become synonymous with punishment, red marks on papers, and drill and skill exercises. Furthermore, the tests value students' ability to "identify parts of speech in particular sentences, to correctly spell words in a sentence, to put quotation marks where they belong in direct speech, and so on" (Macken-Horarik, 2009, p. 56); therefore, educators teach to that aspect of the test (Freebody, 2007), focusing on memorization of grammar "rules." And why wouldn't we, if our students are at a disadvantage on exams if we don't? I know that I am preaching to the choir when I say that this "teaching to the test" is a much larger issue in education that can't simply be solved in these pages. However, I hope to show you how a linguistically based curriculum can support the skills on which students are assessed, fulfill the standards, *and* provide students with a nuanced understanding of the relationship between language and society.

Traditional grammar is also prevalent in the classroom because many teachers themselves aren't really comfortable in their knowledge about language. I know I wasn't comfortable with my own understanding of semiotics and linguistics until my curriculum, my students, and my goals put me in personal and professional crisis, forcing me to find a solution. According to Macken-Horarik (2009) reports indicate that new teachers lack the metalanguage and general language knowledge to have conversations with their students about how grammar and word choice constructs meaning in specific contexts and with particular audiences (Harper & Rennie, 2009). This was me, earlier in my teaching career. I was not confident in my own knowledge regarding grammar to teach it as a set of "rules," let alone discuss how grammar and language relate to society, especially power structures and relationships. This is a personal testament to the fear instilled in both students *and* teachers when grammar and language are broached in the classroom.

> *I argue for a linguistically informed approach that highlights the constitutive nature of language and encourages more linguistic conceptualization that primes students to better understand how words function to make meaning.*

In addition, Cranny-Francis (1996) suggests that students do not have as much practice thinking in critical terms because they have mostly been primed to understand the story of the text—the meaning of the words and not the meaning behind them (CCSS.ELA-LITERACY.L.4.D). Therefore, I argue for a linguistically informed approach that highlights the constitutive nature of language and encourages more linguistic conceptualization that primes students to better understand how words function to make meaning. We can do this by introducing tools that students can utilize to help them critique how language is used in the world around them and offer an ELA education that provides "a study of language that is inseparable from the study of life" (Hymes, 1977, p. 169).

> *If we can change our focus to discussing and analyzing the* why, *students will invariably get instruction on the* how.

Now, I understand that a comma has the power to change the meaning of a sentence and that understanding the basics of sentence construction is necessary for clear and intellectual communication, so please do not send me angry letters. But, as Smitherman (2000) reminds us, asking a student to "correct your grammar and resubmit" (p. 113) fails to help students "develop intellectually and linguistically by centering instruction on more fundamental features of student writing and thinking" (Durst, 2014, p. 63). What I *am* saying is that this prescriptive presentation answers the *how* but not the *why* of language use. If we can change our focus to discussing and analyzing the *why*, students will invariably get instruction on the *how*.

Conceptual Framework

In order to support an ELA curriculum that shows the relationship between language and society, the curriculum presented in this book is aligned with the goals of critical theorist Paulo Freire, critical discourse scholar Norman Fairclough, and theoretical linguist M. A. K. Halliday. Critical theory aims to uncover how oppression is perpetuated and how harmful ideologies and hegemony can be exposed in order to create a more just society (Rogers et al., 2005). The critical theorist Paulo Freire believed that the way to create a more just society is through dialogue. Freire (1970) stated that "dialogue is an encounter between [people], mediated by the world, in order to name the world" (p. 76). Dialogue is difficult because individuals must be open to other perspectives and to "even change their own perspective" (Allen, 2007, p. 68). Therefore, dialogue is utilized as a method for exploring and questioning our own perspectives and understanding the perspectives of others in my classroom and, therefore, in this book.

The critical linguist Norman Fairclough concluded that critical social science, which focuses on practices and beliefs in various spheres of social life (Chouliaraki & Fairclough, 1999) and the values of people (Fairclough, 2006), must be considered when conducting discourse analysis, for language is both at stake and the site of social struggle (Fairclough, 1989). Since critical language studies aim to "denaturalize everyday language" (Luke, 1996, p. 12), *critical discourse analysis* (CDA) sets up a dialogue between linguistics and critical social science (Chouliaraki & Fairclough, 1999) by providing an analytical and theoretical framework for inspecting the relationship between language and society. Halliday's *systemic functional linguistics* (SFL) is Fairclough's preferred language theory for performing CDA and creating *critical language awareness* (CLA) (Martin, 2000a). Hence, SFL is the socio-semiotic theory utilized in this book to analyze how language functions in society and specifically chosen fantasy, canonical (and classical), and nonfiction texts.

All of this brings me to my favorite language analysis system within the SFL framework. J. R. Martin's (1992) appraisal system, developed in the 1990s, is situated within SFL and provides a method with which we can evaluate attitudes by investigating an author's use of grammatical resources. These attitudes—categorized as *affect*, *judgment*, and *appreciation*—can be tracked and coded within a text, helping students identify how an author or character feels and allowing students to go deeper by questioning the purposes and effect of specific language choices. This system, along with the analysis of modality and identification, is focal to my language curriculum as it allows students to investigate the structural *how* and the critical *why*.

Advances in Language Education in the High School ELA Classroom

I do not claim to be the first or only person to recognize the deficits in the language curriculum, and many researchers and educators have made massive contributions in changing how students see and engage with language and grammar. In this section, I will introduce you to how theoretical approaches to linguistics have been successfully incorporated into the ELA curricula around the world, with the hope of convincing you of the benefits of having a linguistically informed curriculum in the United States.

Leaders in the use of SFL in the secondary school context to support CLA include the Australian pedagogical linguists Frances Christie, Mary Macken-Horarik, Joan Rothery, and Sally Humphrey. While these are not the only scholars to study the application of SFL with secondary-level students, the Australian national curriculum has taken bold strides in including standards and methods that value students' understanding of the social nature of language. Unlike the US CCSS, Australia's curriculum features a standard strand entitled "Language for Interaction" and includes the following two standards that are clearly missing and woefully needed in US ELA classrooms:

- understand how language use can have inclusive and exclusive social effects, and can empower or disempower people (Australian Curriculum, Assessment and Reporting Authority, 2020a)
- understand that people's evaluations of texts are influenced by their value systems, the context and the purpose and mode of communication (Australian Curriculum, Assessment and Reporting Authority, 2020b).

Crikey! Mind. Blown.

Australia *has it going on* when it comes to recognizing the importance of teaching students the relationship between language and society, and there is a lot we can learn from this approach. Indeed, I *did* learn a lot from it and will strive to relay the same to you. However, the first lesson is simply this: just because the language of the CCSS does not seem to value "language for interaction," it doesn't mean it is not important, valuable, or useful to us teachers or to our students. In fact, the National Council of Teachers of English's (1994) position statement on language study resolves that students should examine how language reflects social, political, and economic values, showing that teacher-led organizations welcome strategies and methods that could help us achieve this goal. For this reason, I am excited to show you the potential of a language study that values the interactive nature of language by introducing you to the work of the above-mentioned researchers. Their studies, which often focus on encouraging students to assess the relationships between culture, power, and language, served as inspiration for the curriculum presented in this book and are partly responsible for the remarkable results that have been achieved.

Particularly relevant to understanding how my curriculum has been developed is Rothery and Stenglin's (2000) analysis of how the appraisal system (Martin & Rose, 2003) can be utilized by students to write about and interpret literature. Their study provided a hypothetical scenario on how an appraisal analysis could help students utilize an author's language choices (affect, judgment, and appreciation words) to support the student's interpretation of the text. Rothery and Stenglin argued that, because students did not have the discourse analysis tools necessary to deconstruct the language of the text, they were limited to writing a synopsis of the plot and were stunted in their critical growth as they were not able to question traditional interpretations of literature. How many times have you had to remind a student that they are not writing a book report and had to reteach summary versus analysis? One million? Two zillion? My own experiences (let alone those of all of you) in the classroom validate Rothery and Stenglin's claim.

When performing an appraisal analysis on the narrative *CLICK* by Judith Stamper, Macken-Horarik (2003) focused on the coercive nature of the text through its use of affect and judgment words. Macken-Horarik suggested that an appraisal analysis of narratives can teach students how to recognize the "intersubjectivity (a capacity to 'feel with' a character) and supersubjectivity (a capacity to 'stand over' a character and evaluate his [sic] actions ethically)" (p. 287). Here, appraisal concepts not only helped students identify grammatical language features but also played a role in building empathy and questioning the ethics of social norms. Powerful stuff. Maune and Klassen (2014) build off Macken-Horarik's work on using the appraisal system to support the CCSS in middle schools, showing how appraisal helps students identify the characteristics of different text types, especially personal narrative and character analysis.

Christie and Derewianka (2008) also recognize how appraisal analysis can be beneficial when students write character analyses, showing how students can critique "positive appreciation of the characters and of the way they hold our interest" (p. 72). By focusing on attitudinal values, students are better able to not just interpret what a text says but what it shows—between the lines, so to speak—about a character, rather than just provide a plot summary of a character's actions.

Through their research, Humphrey et al. (2011) found that the linguistic resources of *modality* and *contrast and concession* helped students, as writers, negotiate their position with their readers and provide more nuanced analytical texts. Focusing on the interpersonal metafunction (which will be further explained in Chapter 2) can result in the development of students' CLA both as they read and write texts. Humphrey et al. (2011) wrote an amazing book, *Working Grammar: An Introduction for Secondary English Teachers*, which is full of resources to help teachers (especially those teaching to the Australian standards) implement functional grammar in their classrooms. May the education gods bless them and keep them. Amen. Humphrey's (2018) more recent work further explores how "the discourse semantic system of appraisal provided language to discuss and interpret how explicit and implicit values in a text construe ideological positioning" (p. 50), focusing on the critical benefits of a linguistically informed curriculum and how it helps fulfill that second standard, mentioned above, of the national Australian curriculum (Australian Curriculum, Assessment and Reporting Authority, 2020b).

Recently, despite the fact that the CCSS standards do not focus on the relationship between language and society, American educators have found ways to make language education more relevant and engaging for secondary students without the use of SFL. For example, *Grammar to Get Things Done* by Crovitz and Devereaux (2017) helped teachers apply grammar to everyday contexts, encouraging teachers to move away from skill-and-drill exercises. Focusing on intent, Myhill (2010) argued that, when people focus on the accuracy of their grammar and punctuation, they are less likely to see how grammar can be used as a tool to create "rhythm and dynamics in text" as well as shape "nuances of mood and meaning" (p. 173). Therefore, instead of looking at language as a set of rules to be followed, some educators have focused on building students' appreciation of language's power to move and manipulate the reader (see Haas, 2011; Love, 2006; Noel, 2011).

Many ideas have been published that share such a view of grammar and language, and even encourage students to question the validity of grammar "rules." For example, Anderson (2006) encouraged teachers to have students look at grammar as a way of creating, not fixing. He stated that teachers should provide students with good examples of authors who use elements of grammar effectively and have students pull examples from their reading to teach grammar in context. Lindbolm and Dunn (2006) stated that having students look at "grammar rants" à la Dear Abby or Bill O'Reilly allows students to debate how "proper" and "improper" English are socially constructed. In addition, Flynn (2011) addressed how dialects are a cultural practice and had students examine their own generational language as well as those of other communities, comparing them to Standard English and recognizing that each variety has its own rules and value. And, in an extremely bold move, Keely (2011) had students research derogatory terms in order for them to understand their history and power so that they could intellectually "fight back" when such terms are used. While these exercises all assess how we view grammar, they also support critical literacy by relating grammar to society and power. Each of these examples is a step in the right direction in terms of developing language education norms. However, I think we can build on this progress by situating a linguistically based approach within an established socio-semantic theory. Like Toto from *The Wizard of Oz*, we can pull back the curtain and reveal the wizard, so to speak.

Many of the language studies cited above not only looked at grammar in a generally functional manner, but they also had critical goals. Fairclough also believes that such a curriculum helps students become critically aware of how language affects social practices and perceptions of knowledge. Harman (2008) has also suggested that SFL—especially an emphasis on cohesion, transitivity, and modality—could increase students' awareness of how language functions and improve their writing. As Bhatt and Jones-Martin (1995) stated, while some ambitious teachers may use language-awareness materials to "create an atmosphere of tolerance and 'civilized respect' in their class" (p. 291)—but actual historical and social analyses as to the cause of intolerance are often ignored—the actual *questioning* is absent. Therefore, Fairclough (1989) believes that it is important to teach CLA to help students "overcome their sense of impotence by showing them that existing orders of discourse are not immutable" (p. 244). Furthermore, Clark (1992) stated that performing such practices in the classroom gives students the chance (and I would say the courage) "to challenge existing conventions and the right to offer alternatives in order to help shape new conventions" (p. 124) outside of the classroom.

Ivanic and Simpson (1992) advised that a classroom focused on critical awareness would have to *recognize* that certain types of language leave people out and that the language variety an individual chooses to use is a part of their identity. The teacher then needs to teach students *how to use* language to "look after their own interests and maintain their identity" (p. 315). This can be done by turning awareness into action by (a) challenging the view that the standardized English variety is better than any other, and demanding one's right to have their preferred variety respected; (b) gaining awareness of how some groups dominate others by silencing them; (c) rejecting the role of the "ideal reader" and learning to critically question texts; and (d) recognizing the power relations at work when entering into different discourses (Janks & Ivanic, 1992). Each of these examples led students to critical recognition and encouraged action by flouting language conventions that dehumanize particular members of society, providing "an intervention in the apparently natural flow of talk and text in institutional life that attempts to interrupt everyday common sense" (Luke, 1996, p. 12). Such assignments that focus on CLA can be enhanced by the linguistically informed approach presented in these pages.

The Goal of This Book

As you can see, while important work has been done on assessing classroom texts (see Coffin, 1997; Fang, 2006; Schleppegrell, 2004; Schleppegrell & de Oliveira, 2006) and investigating classroom discourse (see Chouliaraki, 1998; Davies, 2003; Rymes, 2009), there is little research on teachers doing SFL *with* students, especially in the high school arena (see Accurso & Gebhard, 2020). This is disappointing, as this type of language study supports the growth mindset of learning and counters the idea that reading and writing is an inherent skill. Language and rhetoric, going all the way back to Aristotle, is an improvable art, a part of the Greek idea of *dynamis*, which can be defined in its broad usage as "ability" or "potential." In a world that likes to label people as "good" or "bad" readers, writers, speakers, etc., the emphasis of language use as a teachable art has been lost, or at least overshadowed. A linguistically based curriculum provides an opportunity to grow students' linguistic and analysis toolbox so as to improve their understanding of and ability to use language, countering the false labels of *good* versus *bad* and changing them to *beginning* versus *developed* users of language, allowing for growth and movement between the two as learners gain experience.

In a world that likes to label people as "good" or "bad" readers, writers, speakers, etc., the emphasis of language use as a teachable art has been lost, or at least overshadowed.

Investigating how students react to the instructional use of linguistics when analyzing texts can "broaden students' ability to use language more expertly across a variety of social and academic contexts" (Gebhard et al., 2007, p. 421), supporting the idea of language as a teachable art, and enhance students' CLA, making visible the ways in which authors use language to manipulate an audience. In fact, in a recent literature review of over a hundred studies, Accurso and Gebhard (2020) found that continued focus on how "privilege and power intersect with meaning-making" (p. 17) influenced teachers as much as students. They claim that SFL-based professional development (and books such as this one, I boldly add) supply four-pronged support for teachers by providing increased semiotic awareness, pedagogical knowledge, critical awareness, and confidence in literacy teaching.

The work and curriculum presented in this book is meant to serve as a means to provide the above-mentioned support for teachers and show how the introduction of linguistic theoretical approaches can enhance your own as well as students' CLA when reading texts of varying levels of familiarity and difficulty. However, the goal is not to generalize these results or create a lockstep curriculum but, instead, to support educators by presenting strategies that can help everyone in their classroom use metalanguage and discourse analysis tools to support a critical analysis of various literary texts. In other words, I hope that sharing my curriculum and revealing how my students responded to using linguistic tools can provide a model for creating your own. You do not have to have a linguistics degree to do this, my friends. I hope that you use this book as a way to reflect on what is and isn't working in your language and grammar instruction and to build a curriculum that uses the methodology and terminology of socio-semiotic linguistics in a way that is approachable for your students. I'll break it down like DJ Lance, y'all (it's embarrassing that most of my pop culture references are limited to *Yo Gabba Gabba!*, *Daniel Tiger*, and *Power Rangers*, but there it is, folks), and in the process will answer the following questions:

- How can SFL provide a metalanguage for teachers and students to discuss the linguistic choices authors are making? How can this metalanguage enhance educators' and students' ability to articulate the social meaning behind authors' language choices?
- How can this instruction be scaffolded for student success?
- How do students respond to a linguistic analysis of various genres of text, such as student-valued, canonical/classical, and nonfiction texts? Are there differences in students' engagement with each genre? If so, what accounts for those differences?
- How does introducing a linguistically informed approach into the classroom allow a teacher to guide students toward language awareness? How does that awareness deepen, and is it reflected in students' written and oral analyses of texts?
- How can linguistically informed instruction support student achievement on high-stakes tests?
- How does a linguistically based approach fulfill the requirements of the CCSS?

Overview of Chapters and Organization of the Book

The chapters in this book are organized to guide you through the theory, practice, curriculum, context, and outcomes in order to best help you understand the "how," "why," "in what way," and "to what end" of this curriculum. At the beginning of each chapter, I will provide a condensed version of the major takeaways, what I am calling a "Guiding Gist": a summary of knowledge I hope will guide you while reading the chapter. Each chapter will end with some Reflection Questions to help you think about the following: your relationship with language, your practice, what you want for your students and classroom, how this curriculum can best serve your students, and how you can apply this new knowledge to your already-established curriculum.

Because CDA is both a theory and a method (Gee, 2004; Jorgensen & Phillips, 2002), Chapter 2 aims to familiarize you with the theoretical framework that provides the underpinnings for this curriculum and explains why I advocate for a social semiotic theory as an approach to teaching English. It provides the foundation of what we are doing in Chapter 3, which is building your linguistic repertoire, or language analysis toolbox, and introducing and practicing different analysis methods. The language study presented in this curriculum hinges on students' use of modality, appraisal, and identification analyses in order to determine an author's attitude and assess the relationship between language and society. Therefore, Chapter 3 defines each type of analysis, providing a review of each's aims and purposes. It also gives examples of each analysis being performed and provides a discussion of what is learned by doing the analysis, effectively walking you through how to conduct each type of analysis so that you can model it for students. In addition, there are some workshop exercises so you can try your hand at utilizing these analysis tools.

Chapter 4 outlines the pedagogical context of the language curriculum, which is based on the theories of Freire and Fairclough and moves students through the following stages: description, interpretation, explanation, and problematization. Here, I will show how my linguistically informed approach also supports the tenets of critical literacy, engages in CDA, and helps students develop CLA—another objective of my pedagogical practice. Chapter 4 also discusses the primary texts that were the focus of the language study and how they are related thematically and scaffolded to lead to a critical orientation to the text. Details of the projects and writing assignments in which students engaged are also discussed. For each text, students engaged in practice with coding and discussing the results of discourse analyses, a project that included dialogue and a written essay response to a high-stakes exam. In other words, this chapter reveals the details of what I do in my classroom, how it is scaffolded, and how it fulfills a variety of standards.

Chapter 5 is my favorite chapter because it is where I get to tell you about my kids (they're so great, you're going to love them), community (equally amazing), and classroom (described as "noisy" and decorated like a Hogwarts common room). I'll expose the context of my language study curriculum and introduce my school, community, and student participants who will serve as examples of how this curriculum functions in the classroom. Chapter 5 also discloses that the construction of my curriculum was dependent on state and district standards (CCSS), College Board requirements, and the standards of teacher-led organizations such as the International Literacy Association (ILA) and the National Council of Teachers of English (NCTE). It details how it fulfills each of these organization's requirements. Chapter 5 also reveals the necessary specifics of my data collection methods as well as multiple discourse analyses methods and coding systems used to explore student work and dialogue presented as examples throughout the book.

Chapter 6 reveals the results of a discourse analysis on students' use of discourse analysis tools to determine their level of comfort when coding language and making critical observations about language use. Spoiler: the results show that, as students had more opportunities to utilize discourse analysis tools, their use of low-modality verbs decreased and their use of high-modality words increased. The goal of Chapter 6 is to document and show how students gained confidence in talking about the relationship between language and society and using metalanguage as they progressed throughout the curriculum.

Through the use of focal events, Chapter 7 shows how students' discussion of coding and discourse analysis of texts provided a means for them to assess how language was positioning participants and to critically examine the choices behind such language choices. When discussing each text, students relied on the results of their analyses to support their claims while also using personal experiences to challenge the role of the "ideal reader."

Chapter 8 reveals how the use of students' language analysis toolbox and CLA manifested itself in students' writing for high-stakes tests. While students did not necessarily use discourse analysis methods when writing high-stakes essays, our discussions that stemmed from our language study played a role in determining the topics on which students wrote. Furthermore, students' understanding of how writers manipulate an audience's emotions through language was evident in their mimicking the same persuasive elements. In addition, students' responses mirrored the scaffolding intended by the spiral curriculum. Analyses of students' essays and a comparison of essays before and after the language study reveal that, when students did use language analysis tools, their responses were more focused on how authors' language use supported their purpose for writing and less on plot summary.

Word work—*language study and use*—*is, in my opinion, the most direct and comprehensive way to produce a more just society, create respect and equality between human beings, build empathy so we can understand more than our own lived experiences, and develop citizens who can heal our wounded world.*

In Chapter 9, I summarize the major benefits and takeaways of this curriculum and the outcomes. Chapter 9 also outlines the specific limitations of this study and reiterates that success will look different depending on the classroom. It speculates, too, on how you might choose to build on the language study presented or adapt it to better fit the needs of your students. It also provides examples of variations to the curriculum, showing how it can be applied to a variety of texts and grade levels with similar positive results.

The Appendix, or "the bonus chapter" as I like to call it, is a collection of reproducible resources such as charts, practice sheets, and graphic organizers that I used throughout the language curriculum that worked for my students and might work for yours too. The resources provided in the Appendix can either be copied and directly used or revised to support your specific focus or classroom goals. Seriously, do what you want with them.

But, before I end this chapter, and we get started on the work, I want to leave you with a quote from Toni Morrison (1993) that inspired the title of this book: "Word-work is sublime . . . because it is generative: it makes meaning that secures our difference, our human difference—the way in which we are like no other life" (para. 20). This statement, in and of itself, is the best reason and argument I can give for including linguistically informed practices in our classrooms.

It is a big ask of language arts teachers. The weight of the work is crippling at times. But it is also sublime, and I can't think of a better use of my time on earth than guiding youth, including my very own children, to use language in a way that is generative, creative, and productive.

Reflection Questions for Chapter 1

1. Remember yourself as a student. How were you taught grammar? What was your relationship with grammar and language instruction?
2. How has your experience with grammar and language instruction influenced how you teach it to your students?
3. Think about your students. What are their demographics? How is society's use of language working for them or against them? How could their recognition of this change their relationship with language or their perspective on the relationship between language and society?
4. What are the "nonnegotiables" of your curriculum—things that you absolutely will not teach or things you refuse to give up? For example, you'll pry *Heart of Darkness* from my cold, dead hands before I stop teaching it. It provides oodles of opportunities for CDA and meaningful discussions about the impacts of imperialism. In the same breath, *Ethan Frome*? Vomit. The snow is symbolic. I get it. Keep this in mind as you read the following book, and focus on how these practices can enhance what you are already doing and the lessons you love.

Theoretical Frameworks That Inform This Approach

2

Guiding Gist

- SFL sees language as a set of choices, not rules, that have social consequences.
- Language is organized through *stratal* layering (embedded in one another like Russian nesting dolls in the following order: context, semantics, lexicogrammar, phonology, and phonetics) or *metafunctional* layering (ideational, interpersonal, and textual metafunctions that are all equal ingredients in a recipe, interwoven and working simultaneously).
- *Genre*, *text*, *context*, and *register* are elements of this semiotic approach that organize and link language to social process, both macro and micro, to help us interpret the meaning of language and how it functions as a system.
- The *interpersonal metafunction* (residing in the register of tenor) is the primary focus of this curriculum and considers the relationship between the author and the audience that helps determine point of view, mood, and attitude.

You might be tempted to skip this chapter. It is weighty and arguably the most technical and dense in the whole book. I'm not really selling it, am I? A basic understanding of these theories and terms is necessary to build a foundational understanding of the theoretical underpinnings of this curriculum as well as develop your own metalanguage, which is exactly what we will be asking students to do. However, I will provide some alternative definitions, metaphors, analogies, and synonyms for these concepts to make them easier to introduce to students. Furthermore, by reading this chapter, I hope that you come away with why I advocate for a social semiotic theory as an approach to teaching ELA. This understanding will allow for a discussion of how the theoretical approaches to linguistics should inform ELA teaching in the United States. But we can't do that if you skip this chapter. So, stick with me.

SFL

Halliday defined *systemic functional linguistics* as a functional or "natural" grammar that focuses on how language is designed and used. In other words, "grammar should not be seen as a stand-alone set of rules and definitions" (Knapp & Watkins, 2005, p. 40) but, rather, as a set of choices with social consequences rather than rules (Macken-Horarik, 2004). This hearkens back to Toni Morrison's point that language is something with which to create something new or meaningful, not a method of punitive judgment. In order to discuss particular elements of language, the SFL metalanguage that "can help us articulate principles of progression" (Schleppegrell, 2011, p. 199) is discussed below.

Stratum and Metafunctions

Most theories within linguistics have established that there are multiple layers to language use. This is because, as Martin and Rose (2005) point out, "texts are bigger than the clause and smaller than the culture" (p. 3). SFL considers two types of this layering: stratal and metafunctional. *Stratal layering* sees language as Russian nesting dolls: the whole is made up of smaller components that are embedded within one another (see Figures 2.1 and 2.2.). Appreciate and analyze the outer doll, crack it open, and you will see another doll to appreciate and analyze, and so on and so forth until you get to the tiniest unit.

If we continue using the Russian nesting dolls analogy, stratal layers would include the following: *context*, *semantics*, *lexicogrammar*, *phonology*, and *phonetics* (Berry, 2017) (see Figure 2.3).

Stratal layering is typically considered a hierarchical system, so context would the highest and phonetics the lowest.

Context influences and shapes our language culturally, socially, and specifically. It encompasses larger cultural practices as well as institutionalized practices and considers things such as our gender identity, age, and socio-economic status. It also considers the nature of an interaction; for example, formal or informal. When considering context, we realize that these larger elements impact our language use and must be considered when analyzing language (Humphrey et al., 2011).

FIGURE 2.1. Russian nesting dolls in individual units example

FIGURE 2.2. Russian nesting dolls encased within one another example

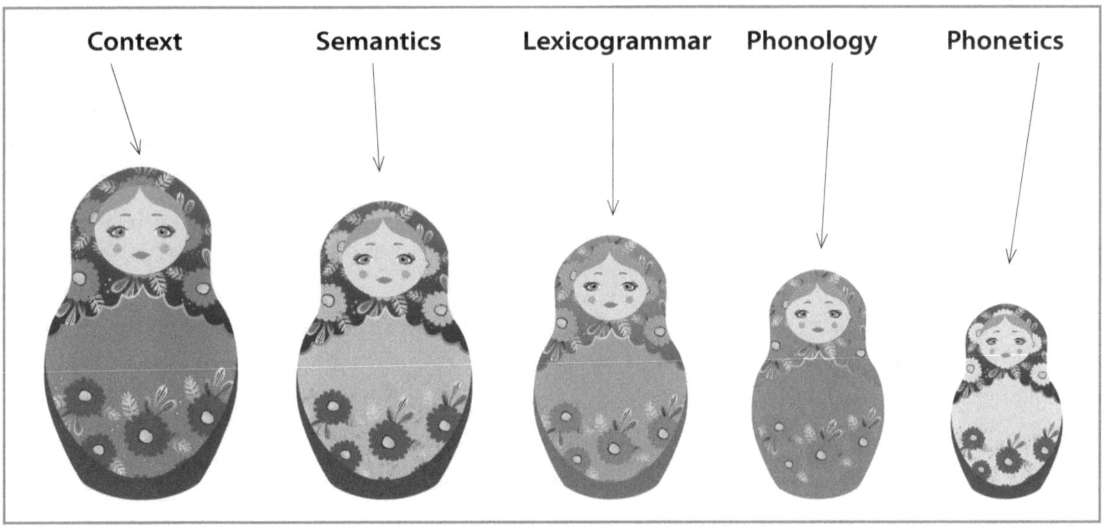

FIGURE 2.3. Stratal layers within the nesting doll analogy.

The next layer is *semantics*, a level that studies how we understand meaning and interpret words, signs, and sentence structures. Semantics are not stationary and depend on context, the previous stratum. *Lexicogrammar* encompasses syntax and vocabulary (Halliday & Matthiessen, 1985/2014). The approach that I present in this book is especially concerned with these three stratums and how language is a network of systems, not structures, which is much more nuanced because, as Berry (2017) points out, the boundary between semantics and lexicogrammar is not always clear, making SFL's interpretation of stratum as one that creates "interrelated sets of options for meaning-making" (Halliday & Matthiessen, 1985/2014, p. 15). While the Russian nesting doll analogy is imperfect, what it does capture is the "dynamic relationship" (Cafferal, 2009, p. 890) that provides opportunities for English language arts teachers in the classroom.

Language is a network of systems, not structures.

Phonology is the units of patterns that create meaning, and it "regulates the pulse of the spoken language" (Halliday & Matthiessen, 1985/2014, p. 15). In other words, it is the relationship between patterns of speech that deals with systems of sound. Halliday uses the example of the foot being a unit of rhythm in the English language as a phonological example. Finally, there is *phonetics*—often considered a subset of phonology—that deals with the level of sound production (syllables, pronunciation, etc.). To simplify, we can say that context is cultural and/or situational; semantics is meaning; lexicogrammar is wording and syntax, and phonology (and phonetic subset) is sound pattern.

Now let's take a look at the *metafunctional layering*. Halliday utilized three *metafunctions* that name the social purposes that language accomplishes: they are the *ideational*, which represents experience; the *interpersonal*, which is involved with understanding and representing relationships, and the *textual*, which is concerned with the organization of the text. Unlike the stratal hierarchy (illustrated by the Russian nesting dolls), all metafunctions are interpreted as equal in importance and are all interwoven and work simultaneously throughout a text. We can think of the metafunctions as ingredients in a recipe. For example, flour, sugar, and eggs are all needed to bake a cake (see Figure 2.4), and they all work together to construct the whole.

Again, this illustration isn't perfect, but what it demonstrates is that no one metafunction is considered more important than the other, because, without all three, there is no cake. There is just . . . I don't know . . . a lot of cursing that you

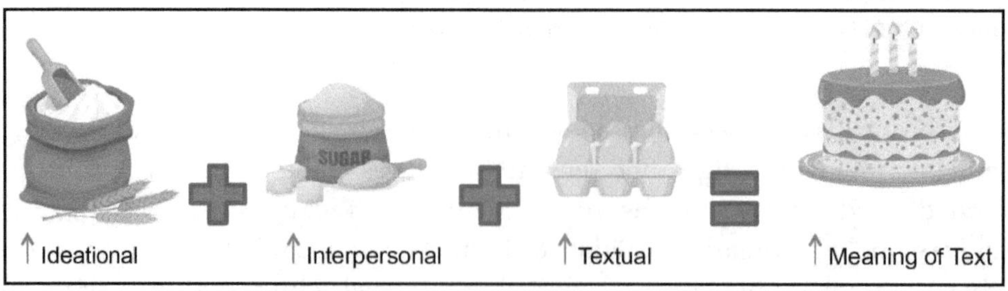

FIGURE 2.4. Metafunctional layering cake analogy

started a recipe without having all the ingredients and now you have a big mess that is a complete waste. Okay, maybe that is just very specific to me, but it's my analogy, so we'll go with my baking experiences.

Halliday saw the metafunctions as a reflection of how language functions and how it has evolved in making meaning. An ideational analysis would be concerned with the writer's relationship with the subject, what the text is about, and the language that is being used to talk about the world. For example, an ideational analysis of the Harry Potter books would consider the actual construct of the fictional fantasy world, the purpose of that construct, and the language Rowling uses to express the ideological beliefs of the wizarding world's society. An evaluation of the interpersonal would explore the writer's mood, attitude, and/or relationship with the subject matter being discussed. Using Harry Potter again, because it is a work of fiction, we would consider characters' attitudes toward one another, power relationships, and structures, and consider the author's intentions and mood toward her subject matter through such a presentation. When looking at a text from a textual perspective, we would look at how the text is organized, the means of communication, the role of language, and the connective tissue that holds it together. A textual analysis would look for points of departure, patterns, and omissions. Therefore, in a textual analysis, we would consider the organization of the Harry Potter books, the shift from narrative to dialogue, and what is directly said (and how) and omitted, looking for patterns in grammar structure and vocabulary, and so forth.

Genre, Text, Context, and Register

There is some additional terminology that we need to consider before you have a general understanding of SFL and how the social semiotic approach is beneficial in helping students analyze, question, and interpret the meaning of texts.

Genre

The most well-known definition of *genre* in the language arts classroom is that of an organization system for literature as originally devised by Plato and Aristotle. However, in SFL, *genre* goes beyond the categories of poetry, drama, and prose. According to Martin (1984), a genre is "a staged, goal-orientated, and purposeful social activity that people engage in as members of their culture" (p. 25). This definition, adopted by the Sydney School, including theorists such as Frances Christie, J. R. (Jim) Martin, and Joan Rothery, see genre as the system through which texts are produced and are classified according to their social purpose (Knapp & Watkins, 2005); for example, narrative, recount, account, argument, and explanation (Schleppegrell & Achugar, 2003).

Text

Texts are language in use (Halliday & Hasan, 1985) that are "tied closely to particular social actions and interests in the contexts of particular social institutions" (Luke, 1996, p. 15). According to Halliday (1994), text is meaningful because it is the "actualization" (p. 366); it is the "meaning-producing event" (Knapp & Watkins, 2005, p. 13) that comes from a social occasion. For example, a text can be a novel, what we traditionally consider text, or it can be a billboard, speech, phone conversation, or a conversation between a patient and a doctor. In other words, a text can be written or spoken (Fairclough, 1992b) so long as it is a part of a social process. Remember, with SFL, we consider language as choices that create meaning within a social context.

Context

In order to conduct an SFL analysis, one must consider the context of culture and the context of situation. The *context of culture* is the environment in which language is somehow involved (Halliday, 1999), and it refers to the social practices that surround the text and the full range of systems of situational contexts that the culture embodies on a macro and a micro level (Christie & Unsworth, 2000). Macro structures include value systems, ideology, power, prestige, and the status quo, while micro structures include the purpose, process, and structure of the text as well as an organizational concept for cultural practices (Freadman, 1994). Humphrey et al. (2011) describe it as "the broad cultural practices associated with different countries or ethnic groups but also to the institutionalized practices within groups such as schools, sporting associations, or internet chat groups" (p. 5).

Context of situation was coined by Malinowski (1968) and refers to the immediate context in which the language is used. Halliday defined the context of situation as a "coherent pattern of activities . . . from which the discourse gains its relevance" (Halliday & Matthiessen, 1985/2014, p. 22). In other words, context of situation comprises "what is going on, who is taking part, and what speech acts are designed to achieve" (Halliday, 1994, p. 365). An example of context of situation could happen in a classroom. Learning and investigation of specific content is "going on," students and teachers are "taking part" with deference toward the teacher, and the spoken inquiry of question, answer, and teacher response generally takes place as "speech acts" to achieve the learning and investigation.

Register

In order to evaluate the linguistic construal of context of situation, Halliday refers to a concept known as *register*. In my opinion, Eggins (1994) gives the best definition of the purpose of register: she describes it as the schematic structure for how context gets into text. Halliday organizes this structure into metafunctions that include the context of field, tenor, and mode. The *field* encompasses ideational choices that address how the writer/speaker presents ideas and experiences. The *tenor* comprises interpersonal choices and examines the mood and attitude of the writer/speaker through how they express their relationship with others and their stance on the topic being discussed. The *mode* covers textual choices such as organization, structure, and conjunctions (Eggins, 1994; Knapp & Watkins, 2005; Thompson, 2004; Wallace, 2003).

Derewianka's (1990, p. 19) genre model is helpful in showing how each of these concepts depend on and are embedded with one another. Let's look at how an excerpt from *Harry Potter and the Sorcerer's Stone*, Chapter 7: "The Sorting Hat," fits into this genre model (Figure 2.5):

> "The Sorting Ceremony will take place in a few minutes in front of the rest of the school. I suggest you all smarten yourselves up as much as you can while you're waiting."…"I shall return when we are ready for you," said Professor McGonagall.
>
> (Rowling, 1997, p. 114)

As depicted in Figure 2.5, we can see how cultural and situational contexts inform how macro and micro structures will be represented and why. This is because how we ask, explain, and do things with words are a cultural doing within specific situations related to that cultural context. In addition, Figure 2.5 allows us to visualize how context of situation is situated within context of culture and is determined by register, and how within both is text, which is language in use that can be classified according to register, genre, and context. By looking at how each concept envelops texts, we can examine the relationships between genre, register, and language, and how it is functioning in a particular culture (Christie & Unsworth, 2000). Halliday does a much better job explaining this than I have by using a comparison of weather and climate; for example, *weather* shifts from day to day while *climate* is more of a constant that we can use to plan long term. Text similarly interacts with the system. We can argue that the text (weather) influences the system (climate) or that the climate (system) determines the weather (text) (Martin & Rose, 2005). The fluid and intricate nature between the text and the systems makes language meaning incredibly nuanced and delicate.

In order to show the complexity of the system, and show how each metafunction is dependent on the others, let's identify the metafunctions in a text utilized in the present study: Obama's (2009) speech delivered at Cairo University in Egypt. When performing an ideational reading, I would focus on

Context of Culture
The secret wizarding world and the cultural and ideological practices within it

Genre
Explanation with some imperative use

Context of Situation
____________Sorting Ceremony____________

Register
Field: ideational analysis of the Sorting Ceremony experience. Here, it plays the role of establishing students' identity within the school and serves as a rite of passage, personality test, and labelling
Tenor: interpersonal analysis—maybe an appraisal analysis—that establishes students' obligatory, expected, anxiety-ridden feelings toward the event and society's attitudes (culturally and socially expected) regarding the Ceremony
Mode: textual analysis—maybe an identification analysis—that could look at the grammatical choices that could reveal potential power relationships (teacher–student, adult–child)

Text (aka "meaning-producing event"—McGonagall's speech to the students waiting to be the subject of the Ceremony)

FIGURE 2.5. Representation of "The Sorting Hat" excerpt in Derewianka's (1990) genre model

The fluid and intricate nature between the text and the systems makes language meaning incredibly nuanced and delicate.

determining Obama's (and the USA's) representation of the East in terms of the social construction of East versus West, knowledge of Eastern politics and culture, and history with the specific issues being addressed in the speech (globalization of terrorism, for example), and the social action that is taking place (an American giving a speech/lecturing on Western–Eastern relationships in an Eastern country).

When analyzing the text from an interpersonal perspective, I would consider how Obama's language reveals not only his knowledge but also his attitude about the East and the topics being discussed, and how his language choices reveal the power relationship between the East and the West. When performing a textual analysis, I would look at how the speakers are using language to negotiate the interaction to organize the text on a micro to macro level based on the social context. While each metafunction looks at a different aspect of the same language event, they are still very much interwoven. For example, in order to perform an analysis of Obama's attitude and relationship with the audience (interpersonal), you have to understand the content of the discourse (ideational). Furthermore, in order to determine Obama's attitude, you can rely on a textual feature, such as a participant identification analysis (the tracking of participants), to track how he identifies or names countries and people from the East and the West.

The Interpersonal Metafunction

While all three metafunctions are interwoven and work in tandem, bringing meaning to each other, this curriculum deals specifically with the interpersonal metafunction working within the register dimension of tenor. Therefore, I will be forgoing an in-depth discussion of the ideational and textual metafunctions and the various types of analyses that can be utilized to investigate those discourse systems. The interpersonal metafunction directly relates to the language classroom, in that it can "help readers gain insights into how an author positions and persuades readers in particular ways, an understanding that is important to the development of critical literacy" (Fang & Schleppegrell, 2010, p. 592). Understanding how to use analysis tools that help interpret the interpersonal meaning in text can help achieve critical literacy because

> Competent writers and speakers are able to distribute both explicit and implicit interpersonal meanings through the whole text so that the audience is "positioned" toward a particular point of view or interpretation of the content. The rhetorical effect on this distribution of interpersonal meanings is that the interpretation or point of view of the speaker/writer will seem "natural" to the reader.
>
> (Rothery & Stenglin, 2000, p. 240)

In essence, analyzing interpersonal meanings can help students develop language awareness through the use of discourse analysis tools and metalanguage in order to achieve conscientization and problematization (Freire, 1970/1986), encouraging them to denaturalize and critically assess language. Macken-Horarik (2009) also noted that the interpersonal function makes us address issues such as point of view and "how the text positions us to see, feel, judge, and appreciate what happens" (p. 64). With that being said—and here is where it becomes evident that all three metafunctions work together—I will also present some analysis methods that would technically fall into the "textual" metafunction (identification analysis, for example) that can also help in determining (or give textual evidence of) how a text is using language as a creative or coercive tool to position readers.

SFL is a view of language use as an unfolding process that is configured organically depending on the context of culture and situation, which is such a different view than the emphasis on correct standard grammar. It is dynamic, unfolding, and pliable—just like our lives.

What is unique about SFL is that it sees language as bidirectional. We move fluidly between context, a thought, and wording, considering each as we construct meaning. We can start with the context to see how it influences the thought that shapes the wording or vice versa. This approach to language study makes the entry point into language analysis incredibly wide for students as they can engage with texts at any (or all) level(s). Furthermore, SFL is a view of language use as an unfolding process that is configured organically depending on the context of culture and situation, which is such a different view than the emphasis on correct standard grammar. It is dynamic, unfolding, and pliable—just like our lives. This complex intertwining of context, thought, and wording conjures the image of the three Greek Fates, knitting the mortal thread of all humanity. It is divine; it is responsible for both the good and the evil we see in the world. Giving students the permission and tools to unravel this thread has the ability take away the fatalistic interpretation of language as "set in stone" and to see it as generative and as powerful as their ability to wield it.

Reflection Questions for Chapter 2

1. Take the time to identify the theoretical underpinnings of your current curriculum and educational philosophy. If you had to create a mission statement based on this, what would it be? How do/would you achieve it?
2. How would you define the relationship between language and society? What are you currently doing in your classroom to make students aware of this relationship?
3. Think of one text that you teach and apply Derewianka's (1990, p. 19) genre model. How would you describe the context of culture? The context of situation? What is the relationship between the register, genre, and context?
4. Thinking of that same text (or a different one—you do you), which metafunction might provide the most fruitful analysis and in which register does it reside?

3

Building a Linguistic Toolbox

Guiding Gist

- An *appraisal analysis* evaluates the attitudinal choices of an author, looking at how affect, judgment, and appreciation words directly and indirectly position both their subject and their readers' interpretation of a text.
- A *modality analysis* can reveal the commitment level or confidence of a writer or speaker, or how strongly they feel about something, based on the polarity of the modal operator and their use of hedges and boosters.
- *Hedging* is vague language that can be used to analyze texts as well as an analysis tool to gauge your students' confidence and growth when using discourse analysis tools.
- An *identification analysis* is a way to track participants in a text and to evaluate how an author classifies a person or group and is useful in determining power relationships and the author or speaker's feelings toward the participant.
- Introducing the analysis of *contrast and concession* along with *citations* can help students not only recognize supporting content but also examine the author or speaker's relationship with the audience, focusing analysis on the purpose of the language.

Now that you have a working knowledge of the tenets of SFL, this chapter will introduce you to the main analysis tools used in my approach that shows how a linguistically informed curriculum can give students the metalanguage necessary to denaturalize language and question the author's purpose/effect as well as use it effectively to achieve their own writing purposes.

Appraisal Analysis

J. R. Martin first introduced the appraisal system at a presentation to the Sydney Linguistics Circle at Macquarie University in 1994 (Rothery & Stenglin, 2000). According to Martin and Rose (2003), *appraisal* is "concerned with evaluation: the kinds of attitudes that are negotiated in a text, the strength of the feelings involved, and ways in which values are sourced and the readers aligned" (p. 22) and it "offers one linguistic system that allows us to track patterns of attitudal choices in interactions" (Love, 2006, p. 224). This makes appraisal analysis ideal in revealing the evaluative positioning of an author because it helps divulge how an author feels about a subject or person. It also provides linguistic and grammatical evidence of how they are trying to manipulate the emotions of the reader. It offers the proof for the claim(s) students may intuitively sense but lack the evidence to substantiate.

In order to introduce students to appraisal and not overwhelm them with metalanguage as they attempt to perform analyses, I limit students' vocabulary, introducing them to only the basic terms needed to conduct analyses, such as affect, judgment, appreciation, modal, polarity, and naming.

In the appraisal system, Martin and Rose (2003) define three types of attitude:

1. *Affect* deals with emotions. People can express positive or negative feelings directly or through implication.
2. *Judgment* shows our personal or moral admiration or criticism of people.
3. *Appreciation* looks at how things are portrayed in a positive or negative light through the use of amplified words.

Now that I have provided working definitions, I will describe how these three terms function in analyzing text. First, though, it is important to note that appraisal values can be both *inscribed* (explicit) or *invoked* (implicit). To simplify, we can say *directly* and *indirectly*. We will see this as we look at examples of affect, judgment, and appreciation words.

Affect

Since *affect* deals with emotions, affect words can be inscribed directly (e.g., "I am embarrassed") or be invoked indirectly (e.g., "I couldn't make eye contact with him"). In the first statement, the feeling of embarrassment is directly expressed—there is no ambiguity. However, in the second example, the reader must rely on their understanding of the relationship between facial expressions, feelings, and social norms to understand the emotion being expressed, recognizing the fact that I wouldn't make eye contact with him *because I was embarrassed*. Affect also relies on the reader having emotional responses to the selected language, so, when performing an appraisal analysis on texts, students can code words that reveal emotion, evoke an emotional response in themselves, or feel emotionally charged as *affect*. This often depends on the genre of the text.

Examples of Inscribed and Invoked Affect

Before moving on and looking at *judgment*, on your own, try to think of one or two examples of inscribed (direct) affect and invoked (indirect) affect that you have seen at play in your own life experiences or in a text that you teach.

Inscribed (Direct) Affect	Invoked (Indirect) Affect
1.	1.
2.	2.

Judgment

Judgment shows our personal and moral admiration or criticism of people with respect to social norms. This also can be inscribed directly (e.g., "He was guilty"), or be invoked indirectly (e.g., "He thought he was above the law"). "He was guilty" is a direct judgment because the word *guilty* is culturally associated with proven wrongdoing, whereas "he thought he was above the law" only suggests an attitude of superiority that might lead to wrongdoing. Regardless, both judgments are negative and critical of the individual being discussed. When coding for *judgment*, students can look for words that show social approval or censure with regard to a person's actions, ideas, or beliefs.

Examples of Inscribed and Invoked Judgment

Similar to our exercise with *affect*, try creating some of your own examples here:

Inscribed (Direct) Judgment	Invoked (Indirect) Judgment
1.	1.
2.	2.

Appreciation

Appreciation evaluates products, processes, and other systems of social value through gradations that express compositional qualities and portray them in a positive (e.g., "It was a very serious matter") or negative (e.g., "It was a ludicrous proposal") light through the use of amplified words. The amplified words "very serious" and "ludicrous" in the examples enhance, heighten, and clarify the positive or negative feelings toward the product, process, or system being discussed.

People can also be evaluated using appreciation by focusing on an aesthetically related reaction (Martin & White, 2005). For example, in the sentence "He had a handsome face," the appearance of his face is being evaluated, not his behavior, making it appreciation and not judgment. Students can differentiate appreciation from judgment by determining whether it is a person's behavior or disposition that was being evaluated or their appearance. Students also can code words that reveal one's attitude about non-human or abstract entities as *appreciation*.

Examples of Appreciation

For your practice with *appreciation*, try creating a few examples that differentiate appreciation of a product, processes, or systems with that of an aesthetic appreciation so that you can see the difference between aesthetic appreciation and judgment.

Appreciation of a Product, Process, or System	Aesthetic Appreciation
1.	1.
2.	2.

Appraisal at Work

Let's look at the following examples from the opening pages of Rowling's (1997) *Harry Potter and the Sorcerer's Stone* that I often use (e.g., Harman & Simmons, 2014, p. 85) to introduce appraisal analysis (affect is in *italics*, judgment is **bolded**, and appreciation is <u>underlined</u>):

> Mr. and Mrs. Dursley, of number four, Privet Drive, were *proud* to say that they were <u>perfectly</u> **normal**, thank you <u>very</u> much. They were **the last people you would**

> **expect to be involved in anything strange or mysterious**, because they **just didn't hold with such nonsense**.
>
> Mr. Dursley was the **director of a firm** called Grunnings, which made drills. He was a <u>big</u>, <u>beefy</u> man with <u>hardly any neck</u>, although he did have a <u>very large</u> mustache. Mrs. Dursley was <u>thin</u> and <u>blonde</u> and had <u>nearly twice the amount</u> of neck, which came in <u>very</u> useful as she spent <u>much</u> of her time craning over garden fences, **spying** on neighbors. The Dursleys had a <u>small</u> son called Dudley and in their opinion **there was no finer boy anywhere**.
>
> (Rowling, 1997, p. 1)

These two paragraphs provide us with much to analyze. First, Rowling uses many appreciation words to physically describe the Dursleys' appearances—otherwise known as *aesthetic appreciation*. This is common enough when we are being introduced to new characters, a pattern that might be worth pointing out to students when teaching direct and indirect characterization. However, what I find most interesting about this appraisal analysis is what we learn through the affect and judgment words. We get both inscribed (direct) and invoked (indirect) judgment words for the Dursleys. The family judges themselves as "normal," which begs the question: what is normal? This is followed with the indirect judgments of "the last people you would expect to be involved in anything strange or mysterious" and "just didn't hold with such nonsense." These indirect judgments help give context to what Rowling is trying to establish as "normal." Not only that, the direct affect word "proud" indicates that they are boastful of their perceived normalcy.

The next paragraph provides us with judgments of the individuals. Mr. Dursley is a "director of a firm," an indirect judgment that suggests that he is in a managerial position, having power over others. Mrs. Dursley is associated with spying. Here, "spying" is coded as a negative judgment because we have very clear social connotations with spying: you should not do it. It is rude, intrusive, and indicates that you might be a nosy person. Finally, in reference to Dudley, "there was no finer boy anywhere." However, we must consider the context of that judgment—it is from his biased parents.

Looking at how these words create meaning, both directly and indirectly, we can already get a glimpse of the Dursleys' view of the world as well as Rowling's. To dig deeper into evaluating these attitudes, I ask my students the following questions in order to not only help them analyze their meaning but also to see the relationship between language and society:

- Based on your findings, how does Rowling (and our society) view the relationship between language and society's social expectations?

- According to the analysis, what can be said about the expected social roles of men and women?
- Based on the analysis, what do you think are Rowling's feelings toward society's view of "normal"?
- Why is she establishing this so early in the text? What could be the purpose?

The appraisal analysis (and the critical questioning, but more on that later) provides a deeper understanding of a text's purpose and the author's attitude toward social structures by looking at her use of language when presenting characters for the first time. This is a good example of how identifying parts of speech, the "how," helps us understand the "why." This takes the CCSS standard (CCSS.ELA-LITERACY.L.1) to a more advanced and meaningful level. The analysis goes beyond the typical "character analysis" that is asked of students because it requires them to use evidence from the analysis to support an argument as to *why* and *how* the characters are being presented in such a way, not just that they are. If students were now requested to write a paragraph on the characterization (CCSS.ELA-LITERACY.R.1) of the Dursleys, the appraisal analysis has provided oodles of material with which to analyze the family (CCSS.ELA-LITERACY.R.3), not just describe them.

Modality Analysis

A *modality analysis* can add to our understanding of authors' and characters' feelings and enhance our understanding of the power relationships that guide such feelings. According to Halliday (1994), modality represents a speaker's "judgment of the probabilities, or the obligations, involved in what he is saying. A proposition may become arguable by being presented as likely or unlikely" (p. 73). In other words, modality "refers to the area of meaning that lies between yes and no—the intermediate ground between positive and negative polarity" (Halliday, 1994, p. 356). Therefore, modality gives a speaker room to determine how far they want to commit themselves to a claim or statement, or, conversely, distance themselves from it (Fairclough, 1992b). Analyzing modality in texts is important because "writers and speakers can alter or modulate meanings of possibility to temper their opinions about how likely something is. They can also temper meanings of obligation or 'mustness' so that their recommendations do not appear too strong" (Humphrey et al., 2011, p. 87).

While there are many modal operators, Halliday focused on select verbs and where they fall on a polarity scale of *high*, *medium*, and *low*:

- high—must, ought to, need to, has to, is to
- medium—will, would, shall, should
- low—may, might, can, could

(Halliday & Matthiessen, 1985/2014, p. 363)

I like to present modality as a Likert scale (Figure 3.1) or as a thermometer (Figure 3.2):

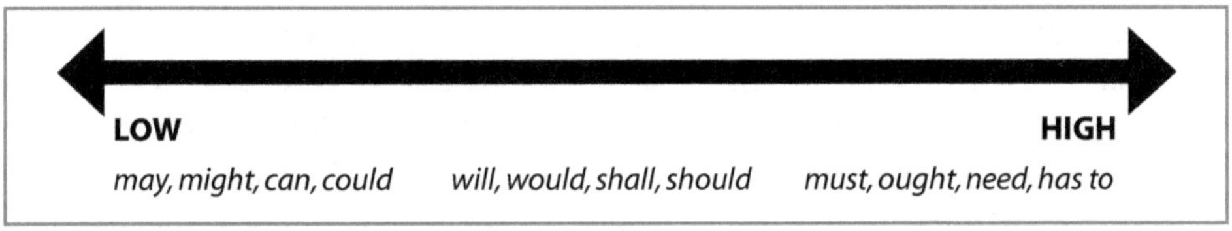

FIGURE 3.1. Modality represented as a Likert scale.

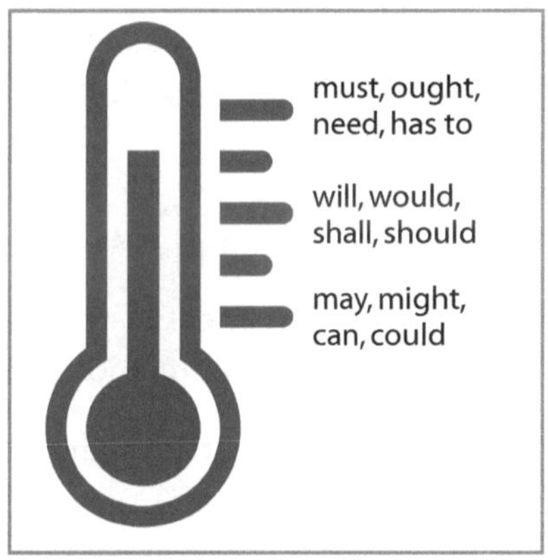

FIGURE 3.2. Modality represented as a thermometer.

Using Figures 3.1 and 3.2, you can show students how modality shows strength of certainty, or how speakers/writers can use modality to metaphorically "turn up the heat" (CCSS.ELA-LITERACY.L.2). You could also use this continuum to create an "attitude line" to determine the strength of affect words when doing an appraisal analysis (Schleppegrell & Moore, 2018).

When looking at these scales, it is important to remind students that *high* and *low* do not translate to *good* and *bad*. It is not that kind of grading scale. All modal operators are appropriate in specific contexts. What we want students to do is look at how others are using modal words to express their degree of confidence, commitment, obligation, or power. We can then analyze what that means and reveals about the social situation or character. For example, if I say, "I must go see the new *Star Wars* film," I am strongly committed to going. If I said, "I might go see the new *Star Wars* film," you would be less confident in my dedication to see the movie. Neither example is "good" or "bad" modality because one is high and the other is low—the modal choice just reveals my commitment level—it is *appropriate*.

Now, here is where things get nuanced. I know I just said that there are no good or bad modal operators. However, a person's modal choices can have positive or negative effects on others or reveal constructive or harmful power relationships. Let's look at some student–teacher interactions in *Harry Potter and the Sorcerer's Stone* that I use to confirm this (see Harman & Simmons, 2014, p. 85). Here is a statement from Professor Snape:

> "I **can** teach you how to bottle fame, brew glory, even stopper death—if you aren't as big a bunch of dunderheads as I usually **have** to teach."
>
> (Rowling, 1997, p. 137)

Geesh. Teaching IS NOT Snape's calling. How do we know? First, let's look at the low modal word "can." How invested is Snape in teaching his students these skills? Not very. He *can* do it, but will he? I'm not convinced. Snape is an example of a teacher who is holding knowledge hostage. (I *hate* that with every fiber of my being. Like it belongs to him. . . whatever, Snape. Go jump in a lake.) In this way, we already see him establishing a negative power relationship with his students; it is a verifiable abuse of his power as a teacher, in my opinion. Next, we look at his high modal word "have." He is obligated to teach these kids. Is he excited about it? Does he want to? I think it is safe to say his use of the insult "dunderheads" indicates that he is not thrilled with the prospect.

Example Modality Analysis

How could we change Snape's modality to create a positive teacher–student power relationship? Give it a go.

Rewrite Snape's dialogue here:

Here's what I came up with:

"We **will** learn how to bottle fame, brew glory, even stopper death—if you are like the other stars I usually **get** to teach."

This phrasing suggests I will not give up until students have the skills they need and that teaching is something I have the pleasure of doing—that I want to do. Notice how I also changed the subject from "I" to "we" and shifted "teach" to "learn." Considerably small changes that dramatically change how I express how I see learning—as something we do together.

We can look at an interaction between Dumbledore and Harry that shows a completely different teacher–student power relationship. Here are a couple of excerpts of dialogue from Dumbledore in Chapter 12, "The Mirror of Erised":

> "Now, **can** you think what the Mirror of Erised shows us all?"
>
> . . .
>
> "The Mirror **will** be moved to a new home tomorrow, Harry, and I **ask** you not to go looking for it again."
>
> (Rowling, 1997, pp. 213–214)

Dumbledore does a lot in this situation to give power to Harry yet also establish himself as a wise mentor (see Simmons, 2018). He does not put pressure on Harry by demanding an answer (e.g., "Tell me") but instead uses the low modal "can" to give Harry permission to answer or not, and he suggests that a correct or an incorrect answer would be accepted. This is extremely different to how Snape uses "can" in the previous example. Here, I am trying to make clear how modal words must be considered in the context of the social situation before we can determine their purpose and effect. Same word, two very different outcomes.

In the second Dumbledore example, we see him establish his authority with his highly modal statement that the mirror "will" be moved—this is not up for negotiation. However, in the same breath, he "asks" Harry not to look for it; he does not tell him or demand it. This balances the power in the relationship and allows Harry to maintain his agency. It is a request that he hopes Harry will follow, but, ultimately, it will be Harry's decision whether or not he goes looking for it. As teachers, we can learn a lot from Dumbledore about how to speak to students, encourage their curiosity, and value their independence.

An analysis of modality, associated with the amplification of feelings (Martin & Rose, 2003), also plays a role in identifying the author's attitude. For instance, consider the following example from *Harry Potter and the Deathly Hallows* (see also Harman & Simmons, 2014, p. 85):

> He **would have** found Kreacher, with his snout-like nose and bloodshot eyes, a distinctly unlovable object even if the elf had not betrayed Sirius to Voldemort.
>
> (Rowling, 2007, p. 191)

"He would have found Kreacher": the inclusion of the words "would have" suggests the probability of Harry liking Kreacher under different circumstances. In this case, the medium modality shows a change in Harry's opinion of Kreacher to be not impossible but unlikely. Looking at such language choices is important because, when analyzing language critically, modality helps form a character or speaker's self-identity and therefore their relationship with others. This is because modality has the ability to give agency or to take it away (Fairclough, 1995, 2003). In the case of Harry and Kreacher, a critical look at the modality of the language reveals that Rowling has put Harry in a position of power: he has the right to feel something about Kreacher and express those feelings. Kreacher does not. We then have to ask—why?

Hedging

Hedging is another way people modulate their commitment or degree of belief in what they are saying. Hodge and Kress (1988) included *hedges* as a variety of verbal modalization to determine the "speaker's degree of commitment" (Fairclough, 2003, p. 171). Therefore, hedging is an element of low affinity modality that allows one to distance themselves from a claim (Fairclough, 1992b). Hedging is vague language that can also be used to mark politeness (e.g., "Nothing personal, but I disagree with your opinion") or to soften a request (e.g., "Kindly hold your applause until the end of the performance") (Yates, 2010). You will see how I use this type of analysis later in the book.

> *Performing a hedging analysis is especially useful when determining degrees of certainty in oral discourse, and is therefore one way to measure your students' confidence and growth in using language analysis tools.*

While usually associated with colloquial speech (Swales, 2001), hedging also occurs in academic oral discourse. In fact, academic speech combines elements of both colloquial language and academic discourse generally found in academic writing (Biber, 2003; Csomay, 2006; Meyer, 1997). Hence, performing a hedging analysis on students' oral discourse during their analyses that were performed in an academic setting would help me identify when and how students wobbled in their certainty or understanding of SFL or critical observations (e.g. race, class, and gender construction).

First coined by George Lakoff (1972), *hedging* is a way to modify a statement in order to make it "fuzzy" or "less fuzzy" (p. 195). Later, Brown and Levinson (1987) explored how hedges are often markers of politeness in social discourse. Since hedging plays a role in social discourse, when considering language critically, Fairclough (1992b) determined that hedging often occurs when an individual is (a) not sure of the accuracy of their claim, (b) reluctant to make a claim, (c) expressing a lack of power, or (d) lacking conviction in their knowledge. Taking Brown and Levinson's (1987) discussion of hedging into account, Wilamová (2005) modified their current hedging classification system in order to show the function of these language markers (Svarova, 2008). Table 3.1 presents a summary of Wilamová's (2005) classification system.

TABLE 3.1. Wilamová's (2005) Classification System.

Classification	Hedging Example	Purpose
Clausal mitigators	pseudo-conditionals such as "if you say so" or "but" clauses	generally used as a face-saving tool
Subjectivity markers	pragmatic expressions such as "I guess," "I hope," or "I don't know"	show the statement to be the speaker's personal belief, opinion, or judgment
Downgraders	usually seen in negative politeness statements such as "just in case," "a bit," or "rather"	serve as self-protection for the speaker against any backlash from the addressee.
Tentativizers	phrases or clauses that are intentionally vague, such as "kind of" or "I don't know"	to show uncertainty
Performative hedges	most often marked by the inclusion of "just" or "must"	tend to give the listener time to adjust their response
Pragmatic idioms	words such as "please," "kindly," "perhaps," or "maybe"	indicate that the speaker is supplying a request or suggestion
Hedges on politeness maxims	conventional adverbial expressions such as "to tell you the truth," "unfortunately," or "nothing personal"	generally used in refusals or criticism

In the context of this book, an analysis of hedges was done on transcribed students' protocol analyses, which were oral interactions, to determine their level of certainty and comfort when utilizing discourse analysis and linguistic tools, as well as their commitment to their observations, analysis, and beliefs. In essence, it helped me measure each student's commitment to their statement.

However, I am aware that hedging cannot be simplified as just "feeling comfortable" with what one says, feels, or thinks. Hedging can be used for multiple purposes other than to show uncertainty or discomfort. In her study on the language use of English language learners, Neary-Sundquist (2013) showed how comfort with the English language, not just the content, can affect a student's use of hedges. Additionally, scholars have discussed the differences in the hedging patterns of men and women, determining that the genders differ in how, when, and why they use hedging phrases (Holmes, 1995; Lakoff, 1975). For example, according to Holmes (1995), women often hedge to express warmth and build rapport, which is not necessarily an indicator of tentativeness.

Furthermore, hedging can be affected by communication apprehension or lack of familiarity with a partner, meaning the frequency of hedging can change depending on the power relationship between the two discussants (Lakoff, 1975). With this in mind, it is important to note that, although I have rapport with my students and they have been in my classroom for a year, the teacher–student power relationship may cause an increase in their hedging. Therefore, I have provided examples as to which hedges were coded in order to guard against interpreting a pragmatic idiom hedge that was uttered out of politeness (e.g., "Maybe we should move on to the next analysis") as a hedge showing uncertainty (e.g., "Maybe the word should be coded as appreciation and not as an affect").

Example Hedges

Before learning about identification analyses (i.e., the next section), can you think of any hedges that you commonly use or hear your students use? Can you classify them based on Wilamová's (2005) classification system?

What are some common hedges that you use or hear from your students?

Intentional Hedging in Academic Writing

It should be noted that hedging can also be used intentionally for academic purposes. There is a large body of research that shows that hedging is very important in academic writing to show diplomacy, anticipate reader doubt, and craft dialogically balanced views (Hyland, 1994, 1998, 1999; Hyland & Jiang, 2016). In fact, studies have found that, as students move from secondary to college writing, hedging consistently appears in more proficient papers (Aull & Lancaster, 2014; Brown & Aull, 2017). These students use hedges to balance *boosters*: expressions of conviction that strengthen claims and shut down alternative voices (Hyland, 1999). Examples of boosters include adverbs such as "certainly," "undoubtedly," "definitely," and "obviously," verbs like "prove" and "know," and absolute terms such as "always" and "never."

Interestingly, Hyland and Jiang (2016) revealed that the use of boosters in academic writing has been on the decline since 2015. Instead of using traditional boosters, Zhang and Cheung (2018) revealed, through their study, that many academic writers are relying on graduation to reveal the strength of implications of their research, with the use of words such as "numerous," "most," "preferred," and "a wide range of" to suggest strength of certainty and commitment to findings. Therefore, the shift from declarations of certainty to possibility shows that hedging in academic writing can be a sign of a balanced and thoughtful writer, not necessarily an uncommitted one. For that reason, many scholars view hedging as a linguistic resource for student writing—and indeed it is, if it is being used intentionally by students for the above-listed reasons.

Finally, it should be noted that the hedging that is analyzed in this study is not in the context of student academic writing. The hedging analyzed herein takes place in controlled protocol analyses and during classroom discussion, meaning students' use of hedges and boosters were spontaneous and not necessarily strategically chosen when considering (and reconsidering) a sentence as one does while writing. This spontaneity is critical to the evaluation of students' initial and growing understanding and use of linguistic resources.

Identification Analysis

While determining that the polarity of words can help ascertain the feelings of an author or participants in a text, conducting an *identification analysis*, tracking participants in the text (Martin & Rose, 2003), can also play a role in examining power relations and feelings between participants. Furthermore, "classification and description provide a means of making specific the type of participant *being talked about* and of giving information about a participant's characteristics or features" (Jackson, 1990, p. 108).While an identification analysis is technically a method of determining an author's textual choices, how an author chooses to refer to an individual can help determine their attitude about that person. Thus, this is an example of how all three metafunctions support one another: I will be using a *textual* resource to determine *interpersonal* meaning.

Let's take a sentence from the passage quoted earlier in this chapter (see also Harman & Simmons, 2014, p. 85) to show what we can learn about Rowling's attitude toward Kreacher (nouns and pronouns describing Kreacher are underlined):

> He would have found Kreacher, with his snout-like nose and bloodshot eyes, a distinctly unlovable object even if the elf had not betrayed Sirius to Voldemort.
>
> (Rowling, 2007, p. 191)

An identification analysis confirms the claim that Harry Potter does not view Kreacher as worthy of respect and courtesy. While Rowling mentioned Kreacher's proper name, which is generally a sign of respect, he is referred to with a pronoun once, as an "elf" once, and once as an "object." The author is constantly reminding the reader of Kreacher's lesser status—that of non-human—by using such words to identify him and by making his proper name a version of the common noun "creature."

Example Identification Analysis

Look at this passage from Chapter 5, "Diagon Alley":

> "That's Hagrid," said Harry, pleased to know something the boy didn't. "He works at Hogwarts."
>
> "Oh," said the boy, "I've heard of him. He's sort of a servant, isn't he?"
>
> "He's the gamekeeper," said Harry. He was liking this boy less and less every second.
>
> "Yes, exactly. I heard he's sort of a savage—lives in a hut on the school grounds and every now and then he gets drunk, tries to do magic, and ends up setting fire to his bed."
>
> (Rowling, 1997, p. 78)

Now that you've read it, circle all of the words (nouns and pronouns) that are used to identify Hagrid and list them here:

List the nouns and pronouns used to describe Hagrid here:

Now, in this case, the repetition of pronouns is not incredibly revealing. However, the name is the most proper noun, and a person's refusal to use it in regard to someone else is incredibly telling about how they are trying to position them. More importantly, we see Malfoy doing something similar with the titles he gives Hagrid: "servant" and "savage." It is Harry that uses Hagrid's name and proper title. Here, Rowling is giving us insight into the "pure-blood" society's attitude toward those in service to wizards. We can now make predictions about Malfoy's character and his future relationship with Harry based on Harry's affection and respect for Hagrid and Malfoy's dismissal of him as a "savage."

All of this is also setting us up for the larger themes of othering and inequality that will be presented throughout the series (see CCSS.ELA-LITERACY.RL.2).

Hopefully, you can see that by utilizing language and analysis tools derived from SFL and discourse analysis, students can conduct a critical analysis on texts, allowing them to see how participants' language choices reveal their feelings about institutions and groups of people, or even themselves, allowing them to better recognize the purposes behind such positioning.

Contrast and Concession

After students have a firm understanding of the above-discussed analysis methods and have had ample opportunities to show proficiency, I then introduce contrast and concession and citations as further useful analysis methods for nonfiction texts. According to Humphrey et al. (2011), *contrast and concession* is effective because it positions the speaker as open minded and willing to negotiate by first *conceding* to the opposing side about an issue, but then the speaker immediately provides a *contrast* to support their own position. This device is made visible through the use of concessive conjunctions (however; but; still; yet; while; nevertheless; although; even though; whereas) and prepositional phrases (in contrast; on the other hand; in spite of; one could also say; despite; instead of). Let's look at an excerpt from the nonfiction text that I use as an example throughout the rest of the book, Barak Obama's (2009) speech given at Cairo University, Egypt:

> Now, much has been made of the fact that an African American with the name Barack Hussein Obama could be elected president. **But** my personal story is not so unique.
>
> (para. 12)

In this example, the concession is "much has been made of the fact that an African American with the name Barack Hussein Obama could be elected president," because Obama recognizes that his election is a monumental first in US history. The contrast is "my personal story is not so unique." Here, while he concedes that he is the first, he contrasts with popular belief that he is an exceptional case by appealing to the common man and American experience. He uses the concessive conjunction "but" to signal this shift in perspective. Helping students recognize these "signals" helps them identify when an author is conceding to their audience before introducing a contrary opinion or perspective that might not be as readily received. If students can identify them, then they can discuss the purpose and effect of such statements.

Example Contrast and Concession

To practice, identify the concession and the contrast, and the grammatical resource used to transition between the two, in the following excerpt from the same speech:

> And I consider it part of my responsibility as president of the United States to fight against negative stereotypes of Islam wherever they appear. But that same principle must apply to Muslim perceptions of America.
>
> (Obama, 2009, para. 10)

Concession:	Contrast:	Grammatical Resource:

Reciprocity is the key purpose of this contrast and concession. Obama concedes his part when he says, "I consider it part of my responsibility as president of the United States to fight against negative stereotypes of Islam wherever they appear." Using the grammatical resource "but" he then presents his contrast "that same principle must apply to Muslim perceptions of America," indicating that the East must reciprocate by fighting against negative stereotypes of America in the East.

Citations

Citations are used to strengthen arguments by providing supporting evidence or evidence that challenges an alternate position. They can serve as quotations from, or references or allusions to, religious texts, historical or political documents, literature, statistics, or results from scientific research. Persuasive speakers often use these to provide additional support for or proof of their argument. Here is an example from Obama's speech:

> There must be a sustained effort to listen to each other; to learn from each other; to respect one another; and to seek common ground. As the Holy Koran tells us, "Be conscious of God and speak always the truth." (*Applause.*) That is what I will try to do today—to speak the truth as best I can, humbled by the task before us, and firm in my belief that the interests we share as human beings are far more powerful than the forces that drive us apart.
>
> (Obama, 2009, para. 6)

Here, Obama cites the Koran, the religious text of Islam. However, it is not enough for students to just be able to identify when an author is doing this; they must be able to explain the purpose and the effect that the citation has on the audience. This is the first citation that Obama makes in this speech, and it is first for a reason. Obama knows the values and beliefs of his audience, and he cites the Koran to appeal to them. Before the citation, Obama reveals that he is going to speak on some subjects about which the Unites States and Egypt might not see eye to eye, but he reiterates that he is going to do his best to speak on those issues honestly and with the goal of establishing a dialogue of trust between the two nations. In order to reiterate this, he cites the following passage from the Koran: "Be conscious of God and speak always the truth." The effect? Applause. Why? Because he respects and reminds his audience that their religion supports truth and honesty, making them more open to the coming dialogue, even if it might be a difficult one.

By analyzing how an author uses citations, students can more fully discuss why the author makes the particular choice to do so and the social and persuasive effect of that choice.

Example Citation

Let's do a deep dive on another quote from the speech to practice this skill:

In the middle of the Cold War, the United States played a role in the overthrow of a democratically elected Iranian government. Since the Islamic Revolution, Iran has played a role in acts of hostage-taking and violence against US troops and civilians. This history is well known. Rather than remain trapped in the past, I've made it clear to Iran's leaders and people that my country is prepared to move forward. The question now is not what Iran is against, but rather what future it wants to build.

(Obama, 2009, para. 41)

Citation	Purpose *(to support or challenge)*	Status of source	Effect

Here, Obama cites the Cold War and the Islamic Revolution. The *status* of the source would be historical events/wars. The *purpose* here is to challenge, not support, the actions of the past and suggest a new path forward when it comes to the relationship between the East and the West. The *effect* is that the audience recognizes that acts of violence against each other has not worked for either side in the past and encourages them to agree with Obama that peace and cooperation are the only ways forward.

Conducting an analysis of contrast and concession as well as citations along with appraisal, modality, and identification analyses can provide more resources for students to draw from in order to discuss the social purposes behind language—especially with nonfiction texts.

Reflection Questions for Chapter 3

1. Have you ever found yourself recognizing how authors were expressing their feelings or manipulating their readers using elements found in appraisal, modality, or identification, but lacked the metalanguage to systematically express what you were seeing? Give an example.
2. What texts in your current curriculum could benefit from an appraisal, modality, identification, contrast and concession, and/or citation analysis?

3. How could applying these analyses to specific texts help students see how language is being used and help them articulate their observations in order to construct an argument?
4. Do you ever find your students hedging? How does it impact the strength of what they are saying? Your opinion of their argument? How can making this apparent to them through instruction (not correction) possibly change their language habits?

4

Scaffolding a Critical Language Study

Guiding Gist

- The goal of *critical literacy* is to investigate, expose, and change the way harmful ideology and hegemony are perpetuated in order to create a more just society.
- A critical-oriented mindset is developed through *conscientization* and *problematization*, and the best way for this to happen authentically is through *dialogue*.
- Moving students through three stages of *Critical Discourse Analysis* (*description*, *interpretation*, and *explanation*) develops *Critical Language Awareness* and provides a platform in which conscientization and problematization can occur.
- A *spiraled curriculum* of three texts that are thematically linked and represent fantasy, fiction, and nonfiction is the best way to scaffold students' use of discourse analysis tools as well as to develop a critical orientation to the text.
- Students will remain in the zone of proximal development by following a *learning cycle* that focuses on the stages of *deconstruction*, *joint construction*, and *independent construction*.

Now that we have gone through the analysis tools used in this curriculum to reveal authors' attitudes, I will now introduce the theories of Freire and Fairclough and explain how my linguistically informed approach also supports the tenets of critical literacy, engages in CDA, and helps students develop CLA. In this chapter, I will also discuss details such as the primary texts that are the focus of my language study and how they are related thematically and scaffolded to lead students to a critical orientation to the text. The chapter also introduces the projects and writing assignments in which my students engage and that will be used as examples throughout the rest of the book. After reading this chapter, I hope you can conceptualize what I do in my classroom, how it is scaffolded, and how it fulfills standards while also building students' CLA.

As I established in Chapter 1, when reviewing state and federal educational standards and mandates, we can see that critical literacy is not reflected as a main value in American language arts classrooms. In fact, there is no standard in the language arts curriculum that requires students to question the ideologies and hegemony that are perpetuated in our society through text. Indeed, there are people who (if given the opportunity) would criminalize it. (I am giving these people the benefit of the doubt here when I say that this desire must stem from their misunderstanding of the goals of critical literacy, or lack of knowledge about it, because *surely* they do not want to perpetuate inequality and injustice? Right? But I digress.) In my home state, the closest statement in support of critical literacy is in the introduction of "The Common Core Standards for English Language Arts and Literacy in History/Social Studies, Science, and Technical Subjects." It states that students should be able to understand the author's message but also question the speaker's assumptions and logic, appreciate other cultures, seek to learn about other cultures through reading and listening while engaging with peers of other backgrounds and evaluate their point of views "critically and constructively," and experience other worldviews "vicariously" through "great classic and contemporary works of literature" (Common Core State Standards Initiative, 2010, p. 7). While the language suggests elements of critical literacy, the fact that it is in the introductory material and not in the actual standards suggests that it can be overlooked and that teachers and students will not be evaluated on their ability to perform such tasks. Considering my student body—middle-class teenagers who are embedded in the dominant culture—"vicarious" experiences through characters in novels must be supplemented with discussion in order to critically and constructively evaluate point of view.

For this reason, Paulo Freire's concepts have been adopted by many teachers in order to fill this gap in the educational experience, because they work toward emancipatory education and support the critical progression of students. Conveniently for me, they also mesh well with newer techniques that may develop or enhance students' critical awareness of the world. Norman Fairclough's usage of CDA infused with SFL in order to support CLA provides a way to use grammar and language as a tool to support critical literacy and expose ideology and hegemony.

CDA, CLA, and SFL are promising ways to engage students in critically assessing language, and, through scaffolding, provide students with a repertoire of tools with which to evaluate and achieve a variety of social and political purposes (Harman, 2008). Furthermore, as Wennerstrom (2003), points out, it allows learners to "take control of their own language development" (p. 3) while also developing awareness of how ideologies are socially constructed and how a community culture produces discourse to support it. It hands the reins to the students, giving them the tools to analyze meaning and control the development of their own awareness.

Freire and Fairclough, an early contributor to CDA, were both influenced by many of the same theorists and advocate for the same goal: emancipatory education. Since Fairclough's (1995) first and foremost aim is to promote critical goals, I align him with Freire's goal of intellectual emancipation, allowing for a curriculum that supports language education based on questioning, dialogue, and respect.

Critical Literacy: A Brief Review

The Frankfurt School, which was "given to intellectual acts of resistance" (Willinsky, 2007, p. 1), is credited for the creation of critical theory, as scholars from multiple disciplines came together to investigate how oppression was perpetuated and how harmful ideologies and hegemony could be exposed in order to create a more just society (Rogers et al., 2005). (Hold on a minute. Isn't that just the coolest? From now on, I want to be referred to as a daughter of the Frankfurt School who engages in "intellectual acts of resistance." There. I've retitled myself—back to the book.) To Freire (1970/1986, 1997, 1998a, 1998b), *ideology* is a domesticating force that deforms the truth to make it seem as though there is no struggle between the interests of the dominant culture and the oppressed. It standardizes norms through the manipulation of unsuspecting, less dominant cultures.

Developing a critical consciousness is not easy to do because it takes daily attempts at de-mythologizing our world and critically looking at our role in it. This can be difficult, uncomfortable, and, at times, heart breaking.

Christie and Mission (1998) stated that "ideology infiltrates our minds in particularly subtle and multifarious ways" (p. 12), and even having an understanding of it does not necessarily free us from its grasp. In other words, ideology is the unspoken set of norms and way of thinking that is supported *by* the dominant culture to *benefit* the dominant culture. Therefore, critical theorists aim to expose unequal power structures and the ideologies that perpetuate social injustices and inequality (see Habermas, 1972) so that we can consciously work against them in emancipatory ways. Developing a critical consciousness is not easy to do because it takes daily attempts at de-mythologizing our world and critically looking at our role in it. This can be difficult, uncomfortable, and, at times, heart breaking. And, if it is hard for grown-ups to do, you had better believe it is hard for students to do.

A recent example would be the revitalization of the #BlackLivesMatter movement instigated by the death of George Floyd by police and the #MeToo movement stirred by Christine Blasey Ford's accusations of attempted rape by Brett Kavanagh. These events have provided many examples of protestors exposing cultural ideology that subtly supports systemic racism and gender inequality/patriarchy. Figure 4.1 presents reproductions of slogans commonly seen on protest signs during marches related to these movements.

These signs show how protesters are fighting back against the normalized language that is used against those who fight or speak out against their oppression.

According to McLaren (2009), *hegemony* is when domination is maintained because the oppressed unknowingly participate in their own oppression by participating in consensual social practices. Individuals adopt the social practices of the dominant culture and begin to view the world, and themselves, according to the ideology of dominant groups (Freire, 1985). Hegemony's function is to make the less dominant class feel inferior, and the dominant class wants "to maintain the differences and keep its distance and to recognize and emphasize

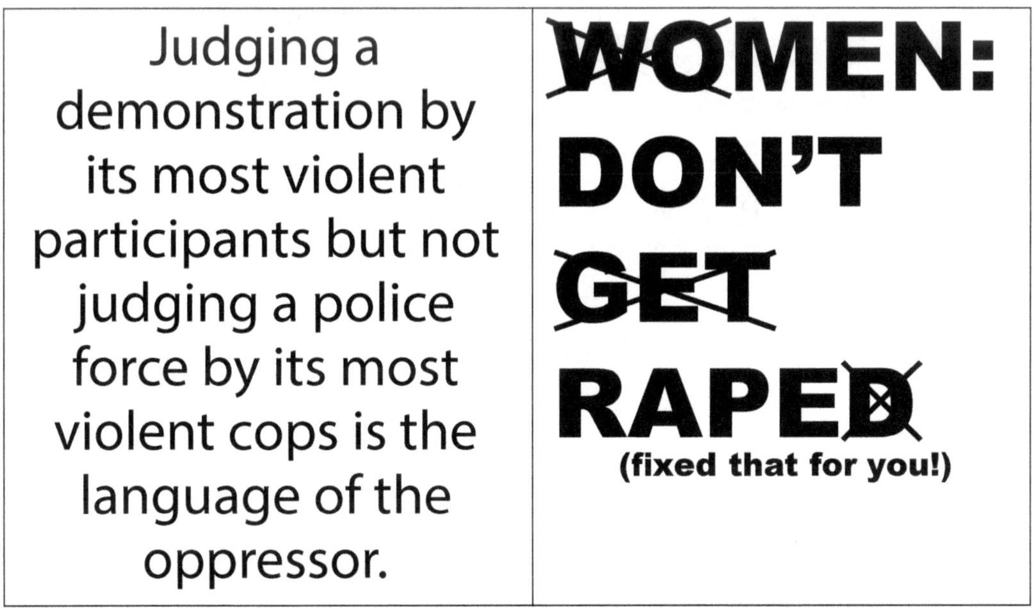

FIGURE 4.1. The language of protest signs questioning language use by a dominant ideology.

in practice the inferiority of those who are dominated" (Freire, 1997, p. 71). This is important, as Giroux (1985) stressed, for critical literacy to be effective, educators must "first be aware of the form that domination takes, the nature of its location, and the problems it poses for those who experience it as both a subjective and objective force" (p. 22).

In keeping with our examples of the #BlackLivesMatter and #MeToo movements, we can see many examples of hegemony acknowledged and challenged (Figure 4.2).

Pease's (2020) post was a popular social media share because it was quick to point out white privilege and the fact that Black people who stick by the mantra "all lives matter" in order to make white people more comfortable perpetuate racial hegemony. In the second example, we see how men and women hurt themselves by adhering to the social gender dichotomy of masculinity and femininity—ignoring gender fluidity and at times supporting toxic masculinity. Gender norms and expectations are so ingrained in our culture that we rarely question the wardrobe of our babies: dominant blue for boys, pink for girls.

If you're a white person who thinks all this racism talk is getting out of hand, and you're quick to post a video of a famous Black person agreeing with you, but won't read a book from a Black person with a PhD in the field disagreeing with you, then you aren't trying to learn, you're just weaponizing Black voices to confirm your own bias.

(Pease, 2020)

How come a girl can wear guys' clothes and look cute or wear a suit and look hot, but when a guy wears a dress or a skirt it is weird?

Because our society thinks it's degrading to be feminine.

Whoomp, there it is.

(thegayby_2015, 2016)

FIGURE 4.2. Social media posts and memes addressing hegemonic racial and gender structures (Pease, 2020; thegayby_2015, 2016).

Giroux (1987), like Freire (1970/1986), went on to suggest that if individuals can name and identify oppressive ideological conditions and hegemony, then there is a possibility of transforming them to create a critical democracy. Through critical literacy, new, affirming ideologies can be put in place, for, as McLaren (2009) reminded us, if we have been made to think in a particular way, then our way of thinking can be "unmade" or "remade" (p. 80). Freire and Macedo (1987) used the term "cultural production" to refer to the act of "confirming the mutual ideological elements that emerge from and reaffirm their daily lived experiences" (p. 142). In order for healthy cultural production to occur and for critical literacy to be successful, Freire believed that participants must obtain a critical consciousness, be willing to question their own beliefs and the world around them, and participate in dialogue—which is one of my goals for the classroom.

Conscientization and Problematization

According to Freire and other critical theorists, a critical-oriented mindset can be developed through conscientization and problematization. The term *conscientization* (*conscientizacão*) "implies overcoming 'false consciousnesses'" (p. 46) by obtaining a critical consciousness that enables one to demythologize reality (Freire, 1970/1986). Once one obtains a critical consciousness, they obtain "awareness of oneself as a knower" (Berthoff, 1987, p. xiii) and are able to act against oppressive systems (Freire, 1970/1986). Taking action comes in the form of *problematization*: adopting a challenging attitude by asking questions (Coutinho, 1970), codifying reality in order to alter harmful forces (Goulet, 1973), and reflecting on social, economic, and cultural conditions by looking at the self as the first object of knowledge (Aronowitz, 1998).

However, Freire (1970/1986) said it best when he stated that problematization leads to a problem-posing education that "bases itself on creativity and stimulates true reflection and action upon reality, thereby responding to the vocation of [people] as beings who are authentic only when engaged in inquiry and creative transformation" (p. 71). This problem-posing education requires literacy learners to ask "What? Why? How? To what end? For whom? Against whom? By whom? In favor of whom? In favor of what?" and "to focus on the substantiveness of things, their reasons for being, their purpose, the way they are done" (Freire & Macedo, 1998, p. 7). However, for this problem-posing education to take place, one must be willing to participate in dialogue.

Dialogue

Paulo Freire (1970/1986) believed that *dialogue* was a "humanizing pedagogy" as it "ceases to be an instrument by which teachers can manipulate the students because it expresses the consciousness of the students themselves" (p. 56) and allows individuals to "name the world" (p. 76). In order for true dialogue to occur, one must love humankind and the world and be willing to humbly project one's ignorance. According to Freire (1970/1986), the classroom is a place for students and teachers to be in in equal positions of power to construct knowledge, everyone simultaneously being both the teacher and the student as authoritative titles are shed and we learn from each other. With this framework in mind, authentic learning only occurs when the topic is related to the reality of the student, and teachers and students break the "culture of silence" by "looking critically at his world in a dialogical encounter with others" (Shaull, 1970/1986, p. 13) and exploring what we can learn from each other, questioning ourselves as participants in the world, and gaining an understanding of the consequences of that knowledge (Aronowitz, 1998). In sum, when in dialogue, participants can disagree, and even try to convince and convert one another (Freire, 1973); however, each voice must be respected (Berthoff, 1987), and it is important that participants enter into dialogue with an openness to having their perspectives altered when receiving the perspectives of another. One way of doing that is to ask questions, especially questions regarding one's own views.

CLA

Fairclough (1989) defined *critical language awareness* as an understanding of the "orders of discourse of [our] society" (p. 239). The word *discourse* has many meanings, but my approach utilizes Fairclough's (1995, p. 7) definition: "use of language seen as a social practice." However, it cannot be awareness for awareness's sake. Students must also develop the ability to knowingly produce and interpret discourse. Fairclough argued that this is the only way that language education can be emancipatory. CDA and SFL are tools that can be utilized in providing students a metalanguage to discuss the functions of discourse, enabling them to wield and recognize its many attributes.

In order to understand how CLA can promote dialogue and a curriculum based on questioning, it is pertinent to understand Fairclough and Freire's views on ideology and hegemony, as these two elements play a central role in the oppression of less dominant cultures and their language practices. This section focuses on defining ideology and hegemony in relation to language use and gives examples of how elements of CLA, CDA, or SFL can play a role in revealing ideology and hegemony and aid in changing discourse. Another goal is making the oppressed aware of how language works against them, yet revealing how it also has the ability to work for them. Talbot (1992) sums up the effects of CDA on ideology by explaining how CDA denaturalizes and "makes strange" (p. 174) language that seems perfectly natural to dominant discourses, making us more sensitive to their effects and purposes and empowering us by giving us greater control over how we use and interpret language. Using SFL to assist in CDA can also enhance this sense of empowerment because people are able to become linguists through utilization, giving them the authority to attach meaning to particular language choices.

While this may be empowering, it is also frightening, because, as Freire (1970/1986) reminded us, it takes courage to demythologize reality when one has been submerged in that very reality. To rejoin the world with a critical awareness means questioning everything once thought to be natural and common sense; however, this awareness, which can be supported by CDA and SFL, is one method of de-clothing ideology's disguise. Therefore, practices that have become universal have been developed through "coercion or consent" (Fairclough, 1989, p. 33), and the only way to reveal and change these naturalizations is through problematization. Freire (1970/1986) stated that this means the oppressed must recognize the "culture of silence" (p. 33) in which they were functioning and obtain a voice so as to reveal "different forms of being, of thinking, of expression" (p. 33). Once this recodification occurs, reflexive action becomes social struggle (Chouliaraki & Fairclough, 1999). This struggle can take form in refusing to participate in a harmful ideology and becoming a part of "structuring of different social formations, particularly those that are related to gender, age, race, and class" (Giroux, 1985, p. xxi) in order to transform society.

> *To rejoin the world with a critical awareness means questioning everything once thought to be natural and common sense; however, this awareness, which can be supported by CDA and SFL, is one method of de-clothing ideology's disguise.*

Once a pattern is recognized, it can be problematized, and, if all parties are open to dialogue (Freire, 1970/1986), a "transformatory practice is most likely to develop" (Fairclough, 1992b, p. 90) through the establishment of democratic discourse. By *democratic*, Fairclough (1992b) meant "the removal of inequalities and asymmetries in the discursive and linguistic rights, obligations, and prestige of groups of people" (p. 201), and a Freirean view would perceive democratic as more dialogic and therefore more humanizing and productive.

CDA

Influenced by Michel Foucault's insight on the relationship between power and discourse (Foucault & Gordon, 1980), Fairclough's work looks at how discourse functions in society and constructs social subjects and their perception of knowledge (Fairclough, 1992b). Fairclough argued that, by performing *critical discourse analysis* with the use of Halliday's SFL, citizens can become critically aware of discourse's power in modern society, allowing them to recognize that discourse is socially conditioned through ideology and hegemony (Blommaert & Bulcaen, 2000). In turn, by making discourses transparent, individuals will become empowered to intervene in the perpetuation of harmful social practices mediated by discourse and "expos[e] power abuse, and mobiliz[e] people to remedy social wrongs" (Blommaert & Bulcaen, 2000, p. 449). According to Fairclough (1992c), this awareness is necessary for democratic citizenship and should be developed within children as they proceed through the education system.

Fairclough criticized traditional linguistic studies and discourse analysis because, "by itself, textual analysis is limited" (Fairclough, 2003, p. 14), and, in order to make meaning out of a textual analysis, "one needs to look at interpretations of texts as well as texts themselves, and more generally at how texts practically figure in particular areas of social life" (p. 15).

Therefore, Fairclough concluded that critical social science, which focuses on practices and beliefs in various spheres of social life (Chouliaraki & Fairclough, 1999) and the values of people (Fairclough, 2006), must be considered when conducting discourse analysis, because those who typically produce and interpret those texts often do not naturally see the perpetuation of harmful ideologies or power relationships (Fairclough, 1995). In other words, CDA is critical because it "sets out to explain, not simply describe, the discourse of society" (Lancaster & Taylor, 1992, p. 256) and focuses on exposing hidden connections and causes while intervening by providing the disadvantaged with resources to change it (Fairclough, 1992b).

In order to perform CDA, Fairclough (1989, 1992b) set out three stages: description, interpretation, and explanation. *Description* looks at the formal properties of the text; *interpretation* focuses on recognizing those properties as socially produced; and *explanation* is concerned with the social effects in an effort to "denaturalize the givens of a language system, to problematize its conventions" (McKensie, 1992, p. 226) and create awareness of a community's discourse conventions and their effects so that they can no longer manipulate students (Clark, 1992). Because learners are a part of the practice, once conscious of the ideologies and power relations that shape it, language can become a site of struggle. It can "be constructed and deconstructed" (McKensie, 1992, p. 226) to better serve those who are victims of the "alienating and disabling effects" (Fairclough, 1995, p. 89) imposed on them. Fowler et al. (1979) agree that language is the site of the struggle and argue that, when critically analyzing discourse, we should be concerned with not just the political nature of language but also the diaphanous intricacies of meaning-making in general. In essence, through CDA, learners develop CLA, which "equip[s] them with the capacities and understanding which are preconditions for meaningful choice and effective citizenship in the domain of language" (Fairclough, 1992a, p. 54), which becomes emancipatory when the awareness is turned into action (Janks & Ivanic, 1992). Martin (2000a) pointed out that CDA and Halliday's SFL have been interconnected since Fairclough's (1989, 1992, 1995) groundbreaking work in critical linguistics.

Although some of my students might have experienced hardship at some point in their lives, few, if any, have experienced hunger or neglect. In fact, many of those eligible for free and reduced lunches still live in houses within the affluent community, drive their own car, and even enjoy trips overseas. Therefore, due to their privileged experiences, it is my goal to expose my middle-class students to the struggles of those outside of their community and outside of their experience. However, we must take into account that some students are resistant to questioning ideologies of which they are a part and perpetuate through their daily interactions.

As I have argued before (Simmons, 2011), some middle-class students may choose to ignore critical issues of inequality because they have latched on to the idea that everyone is an individual and "equal." I call this "Kumbaya syndrome," which stems from the repetition of experiences and discourse that focus on the romanticized attitude that we should "all just get along" and oversimplifies the struggles for equality. They often fail to recognize that, in the game of life, not everyone is given the same equipment or are even starting the game on the same ball field. It also must be considered that "kids are resistant to theories that are incompatible with their own opinions" (Appleman, 2000, p. 126). With this in mind, it can be expected that students might resist the idea that they participate, consciously or unconsciously, in anything resembling inequality. I mean, grappling with that reality is a major bummer.

Therefore, it is necessary to scaffold students (Rothery, 1986) into recognizing the harmful power structures perpetuated through language so that students become thoughtful analysts of language, learning how it functions at a pace that eventually leads them to a critique of how language is used in the world around them. Again, this can be difficult, because most of my students could become powerful and successful in the current, unchallenged rhetoric, making it more difficult for them to recognize oppressive language, and, consequently, making it even more important to help them develop a CLA so that, once they *are* in a position of power, they do not perpetuate it, unintentionally harming others.

A linguistically informed language study is a way to address my critical goals through the use of grammar—an element of language that is highly assessed and valued in the educational system—as a tool to systematically "prove," through language, that inequality exists and encourage students to question why and how language creates unequal power relations. In this way, students can learn the metalanguage to express how texts are structured to promote dominant ideologies and illicit particular responses from the reader (Love, 2006). It is my belief that a linguistically informed curriculum can lead privileged students, and indeed all students, to a CLA that will allow them to openly criticize injustice, social inequity, and harmful dominant ideologies as they are exposed in the language of various texts.

Pedagogical Context

The pedagogical context of this curriculum is influenced by Fairclough and Freire's stages of critical analysis and development. In order to perform CDA, one must go through Fairclough's (1989, 1992b) stages—description, interpretation, and explanation—in order to eventually denaturalize and problematize language, making us systematically aware of the social effects of language choices:

1. *description* looks at and identifies the formal properties of the text

2. *interpretation* focuses on recognizing those properties as socially produced
3. *explanation* is concerned with the social effects in an effort to denaturalize and problematize language to create awareness.

> *In doing so, it is the goal of this curriculum to instill in students a critical consciousness that develops a more empathetic conscience, creating citizens who exercise language in responsible, respectful, and meaningful ways to construct a more just society.*

Figure 4.3 illustrates how I interpret Fairclough and Freire's processes in the context of this curriculum.

This pedagogical process allows students to progress through each stage while engaging with each text in hopes of developing a non-threatening curriculum that will encourage students, especially those of the dominant class, to assess how language can negatively affect members of society, particularly the most vulnerable. In doing so, it is the goal of this curriculum to instill in students a critical consciousness that develops a more empathetic conscience, creating citizens who exercise language in responsible, respectful, and meaningful ways to construct a more just society.

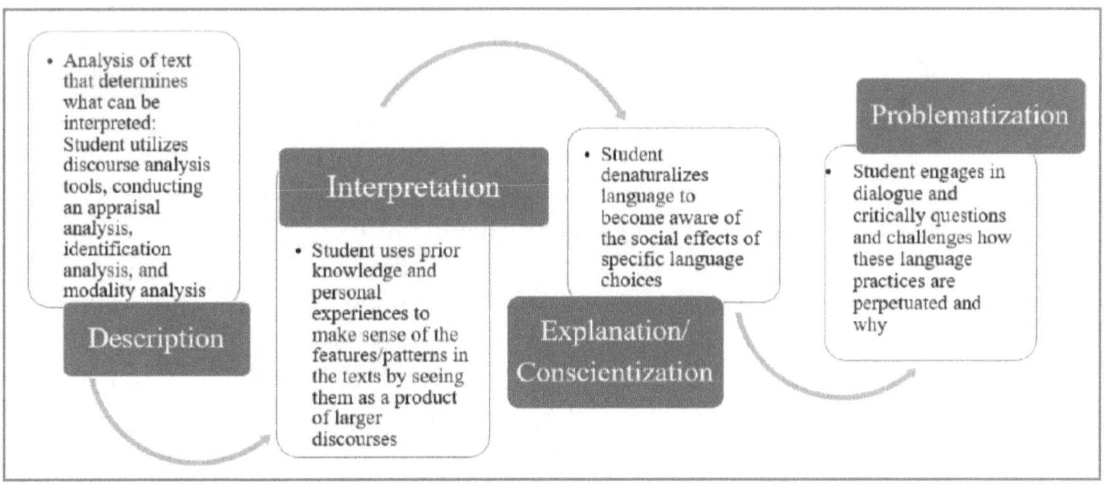

FIGURE 4.3. CDA evolution from *description* to *problematization* (adapted from Simmons, 2016c, 2018).

Literature Selections: Fantasy Fiction, Canonical Classics, and Nonfiction Current Events

I choose to focus on three specific texts because I believe that they represent various aspects of students' literacy experiences, and I want to provide students with three separate opportunities to use discourse analysis tools. I use Rowling's (1997, 1998, 1999, 2000, 2003, 2005, 2007) Harry Potter series, Shakespeare's (ca. 1604/2002) *Othello*, and Obama's (2009) speech in Cairo, Egypt, to represent the literary genres of fantasy fiction, canonical/classical fiction, and nonfiction, respectively. While the texts seem relatively unrelated, I connect them thematically, focusing on the othering and otherness within each text. According to Weis (1995), *othering* is the "process [with] which to mark and name those thought to be different from oneself" (p. 18). Once an individual is marked as an "other," social distancing occurs and the individual is alienated (Rana, 2009). In other words, othering is a way of excluding those who are outside the norm. Based on this explanation, I organize Harry Potter, *Othello*, and Obama's Cairo speech under the theme of "othering" in order to critically unify the texts.

Because the Harry Potter books were the largest-circulating fantasy fiction novels (Rymes, 2008) when I was developing this curriculum, English educators were finding ways to capitalize from the current popularity of fantasy literature, incorporating it into the ELA classroom (see Chappell, 2008; Cherland, 2009; Frank & McBee, 2003; Simmons, 2011, 2016a, 2016b). However, according to Williams (2000), children's literature has not been regularly utilized as a means for addressing how language functions in text. This can be due to the fact that children's literature, especially fantasy literature, is framed in the culture of, well . . . children. Since it is meant to be understood by the young, some criticize it as moralistic "fluff" (Thomas, 2003, p. 60) that does not contain any valuable material for analysis. However, Harry Potter provides a fantasy environment in which to approach the theme of othering as there is a distinct hierarchy of magical creatures throughout the series. This being stated, an interpersonal analysis of the magical hierarchy in Harry Potter can reveal the blatant and subtle abusive power relations that are perpetuated through fantasy literature.

In addition, children's fantasy literature, especially well-known novels such as those in Rowling's Harry Potter series, can serve as student-valued texts that provide the prior knowledge necessary to serve as a beginning venue to address how language is often used to support hegemonic structures. This is why, in order to facilitate students' language analysis development, I model how to conduct an appraisal analysis, identification analysis, and modality analysis using examples from Harry Potter. If you are not a Harry Potter fan, other fantasy novels that have similar hierarchal structures include *The Hunger Games* trilogy (Collins, 2008, 2009, 2010), the *Divergent* series (Roth, 2011, 2012, 2013), and, if you want to get really controversial, Philip Pullman's (1995, 1997, 2000) *His Dark Materials* trilogy. I provide a more comprehensive list of possible texts for this curriculum in Chapter 9 (see Table 9.1).

Unlike modern texts, the cultural context of Shakespeare's (ca. 1604/2002) *Othello* is far removed from that of my students. However, it is a CCSS requirement to teach a Shakespeare play each year of a student's high school career (CCSS.ELA-LITERACY.RL.1 and CCSS.ELA-LITERACY.RL.4), even in a course titled American Literature. Located in the heart of the British English canon, Shakespeare's work is associated with the academy, seemingly unrelated to twenty-first-century teenagers. However, the themes of racial discrimination and gender inequality that run throughout *Othello* are injustices with which they are familiar. Othello's racial difference makes him an outsider to his community, effectively othering him. A discourse analysis helps students sift through the difficult Elizabethan language to identify the ideologies that perpetuate inequalities in the text.

Delivered June 4, 2009, then-President Obama's speech in Cairo, Egypt, represents how political discourse can portray those who are not members of Western society as outsiders. Including this speech in the curriculum also serves to address the CCSS value of nonfiction argument/opinion texts (CCSS. ELA-LITERACY.RI.1-10). While complimenting the educational and religious institutions of Egypt, the language used within the speech also creates a dichotomy of "them" versus "us." In order to maximize students' understanding of this dichotomy, I introduce Said's (1979) *Orientalism* as a supplementary text to relate such language to the historical othering of the East. Spoken by a recognized liberal and progressive leader of the free world, a discourse analysis shows that, regardless of political party, politicians in the United States encourage people around the world to adopt American values.

Spiraling of Texts

In order to slowly build on students' CLA and linguistic skills, I adopt Jerome Bruner's (1963, 1968) pattern of a *spiral curriculum*, which posits that students are successfully able to advance to more complicated levels of understanding when building off previous knowledge. Rothery (1996) utilized this concept when teaching the narrative genre of writing and declared that creating a spiraled curriculum helped students cumulatively develop in their abilities and understanding of more difficult concepts. Doing so allows students to first draw on their own experiences before continuing to more advanced levels of understanding. Similarly, Macken-Horarik (1996) used this concept to "deploy linguistic and structural features that correspond more closely to everyday language use than more specialized academic discourse" (Harman, 2008, p. 36), eventually resulting in critical reflection on social practices.

Therefore, my map (see Figure 4.4) begins with utilizing student-valued texts within popular culture that I qualify as previous knowledge: fantasy literature. By performing a CDA that illuminates the hegemonic and harmful constructs in an unthreatening setting that oppresses fictional creatures in a world that does not exist, students are able to practice analysis tools in a context in which they are familiar and knowledgeable due to the novel's status in popular culture. As students became accustomed to the metalanguage and analysis tools that potentially exposed hegemonic power structures as well as harmful ideological and unjust concepts, they then begin working with more complicated texts. Canonical/classical works that are far removed from students' experiences but are set in our own world are addressed next, eventually spiraling to nonfiction with which students interact and are affected by on a daily basis, either because of their historical significance or relationship to current events. By spiraling these concepts, students learn to "read the world and the word" (Freire & Macedo, 1987) by developing a "critical consciousness" (Freire, 1970, p. 19) of how language has the power to position people to think and behave in a particular way that benefits the dominant class at a pace that allows for them to become accustomed to such ideas.

Figure 4.4 serves as a map to show how each text is built on the previous, showing how Bruner's (1963, 1968) spiraling method begins with prior knowledge, the popular fantasy literature which is removed from reality, and moves to texts that are closer to students' lived experiences.

This type of spiraling slowly encourages students to use their newly acquired linguistic knowledge to critically assess texts that reflect their own ideology.

Theory of Learning

At its core, my pedagogical practice, and that of many other educators who include SFL-inspired methods in their curriculum (Macken-Horarik, 1996; Rothery & Stenglin, 1994), is informed by Vygotsky's (1978) theory of learning. Since I view language as a social process, Vygotsky's social constructivist view of learning and zone of proximal development (ZPD) are the basis of my pedagogy. Vygotsky (1978) described the ZPD as "the distance between the actual developmental level as determined by independent problem solving and the level of potential development as determined through problem solving under adult guidance, or in collaboration with more capable peers" (p. 86). In other words, my goal is to

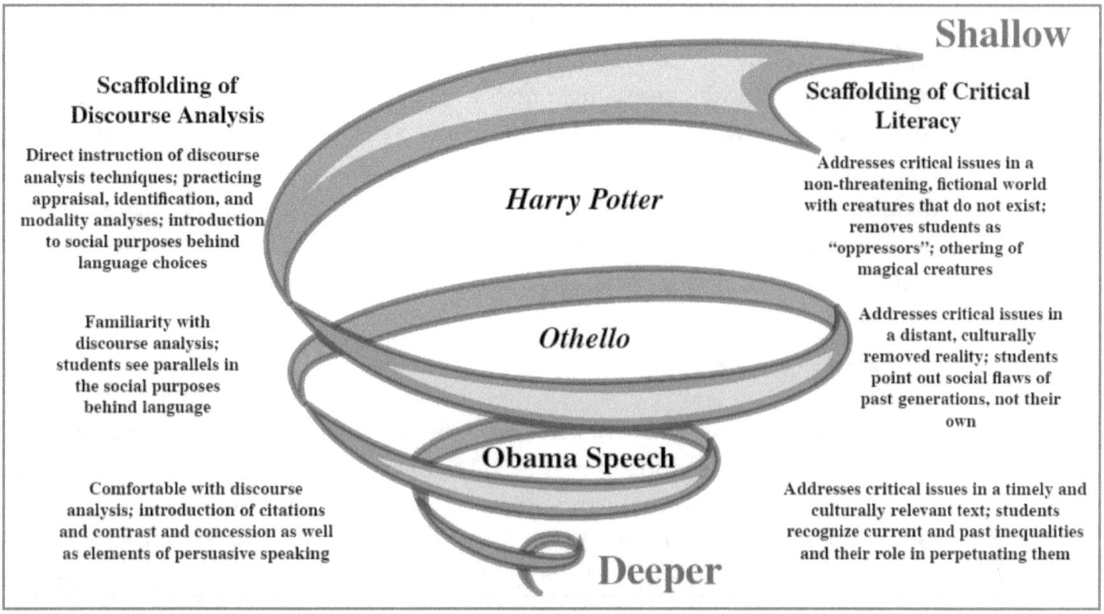

FIGURE 4.4. Scaffolding of SFL and critical literacy by text (adapted from Simmons, 2016c, p. 196, 2018, p. 80).

scaffold student learning so that they are continually challenged to complete more difficult work over time, building on previous knowledge through teacher and peer support. Rothery and Stenglin (1994) created a model to help visualize how SFL and genre theory help establish effective ZPDs (Martin, 2000b). Figure 4.5 articulates how this model looks when applied to my curriculum.

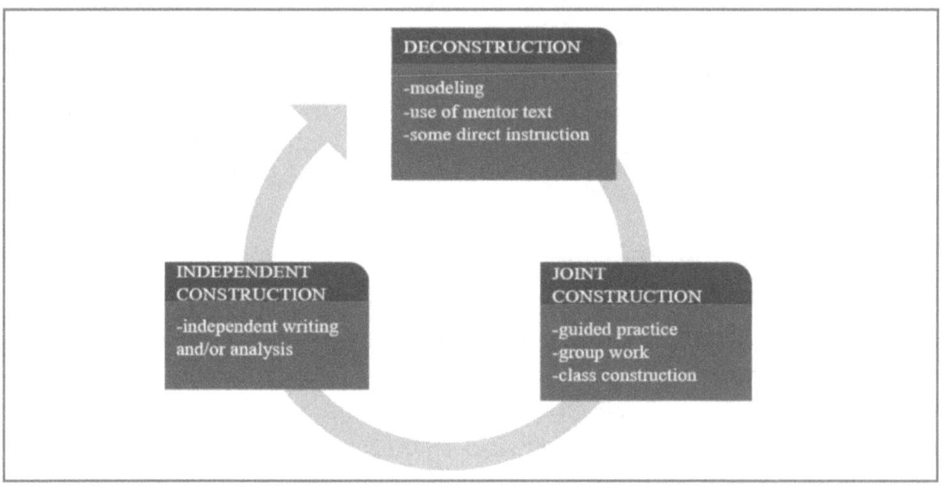

FIGURE 4.5. Teaching and learning cycle.

This cycle shows how students are continually scaffolded from classifying and framing the context and purpose of a genre through *deconstruction* to creating and critically assessing a text through *joint construction* and *independent construction*. As the model shows, a teacher can enter the cycle at the point of the student's current ability in order to remain in their ZPD. As this book progresses, I will be referring back to Vygotsky's theory of learning and Rothery and Stenglin's (1994) model in order to describe my students' development in their use of discourse analysis tools and critical awareness.

The Assignments

As I discuss the assignments in this section, please note that you can find handouts, directions, and supplemental materials re-created in the Appendix of this book. First, as indicated in Chapter 1, our investigation into language and word work begins with Toni Morrison's (1993) Nobel Prize acceptance speech (see also Table 4.1). In this phase of the curriculum, we do a close reading of the text and a Socratic seminar. Oftentimes, when students see that the teacher has put the desks in a circle, they inwardly groan (and sometimes outwardly express their displeasure). But, put the desks in a circle enough times, and, as students become practiced, a Socratic seminar becomes conducive to a dialogic classroom, because it focuses on asking questions and listening to multiple perspectives with the goal of listening and understanding rather than debating and trying to persuade others.

Next, as indicated in Table 4.1, I introduce SFL/CDA with a presentation that defines discourse analysis and its purpose. This presentation is followed by approximately a week of direct instruction and teacher modeling of how to perform the various discourse analysis tools: appraisal, identification, and modality. Again, many of these materials can be found in the Appendix. After direct instruction, students participate in discourse analysis practice, CDA projects that utilized discourse coding and analysis skills, and a written assignment.

Practice Leads to Perceptiveness

After reading each text but before performing a discourse analysis on the text, students practice their discourse analysis skills on a teacher-selected passage from the text in order to go over definitions and concepts and give students a chance to ask questions about the process of textual analysis before they are asked to critically analyze the text based on their discourse analysis (Table 4.2).

TABLE 4.1. Teaching and learning cycle.

Order of Activities
Read and discuss Toni Morrison's (1993) Nobel lecture
Introduction to SFL/direct instruction
Read *Harry Potter* (Rowling, 1997)
Harry Potter SFL practice
Work on *Harry Potter* projects
Harry Potter project presentations and discussions
In-class timed essay: Malcolm X (Murphy & Rankin, 2002)
Read *Othello* (Shakespeare, ca. 1604/2002)
Othello SFL practice
Work on *Othello* projects
Othello project presentations and discussions
In-class timed essay: Animal testing (Ehrenhaft, 2010)
Read Obama (2009) speech
Obama SFL practice
Work on Obama projects
Obama project presentations and discussions
In-class timed essay: "Drabble" (College Board, 2008)
In-class timed essay: "Shadd Cary" (College Board, 2008)
In-class timed essay: "Owls" (College Board, 2001) redo with SFL knowledge
AP Language and Composition exam

In order to help students organize their analysis and to ensure that each student's analysis is documented consistently for easy comparison, I adapted charts from Humphrey et al.'s (2011) *Working Grammar.* This step is essential because it gives students an organized format in which to practice performing appraisal, identification, and modality analyses in a large-group setting with teacher support before attempting it in smaller groups. It also provides them with an example to look at as they work on their project and the confidence to attempt such an analysis on their own.

After conducting a discourse analysis on a practice passage, students are asked to reflect on what their analysis ultimately reveals about the text (see Table 4.3). The questions on the reflection assignment model the type of questioning desired when students begin their projects, providing an outline to help them critically question their findings.

TABLE 4.2. Harry Potter Appraisal Student Coding Practice

Appraisal Analysis Exercise	
• affect—words that focus on *feelings* of characters, narrators, and/or readers • judgment—words that focus on the *judgment* of characters, narrators, and/or readers • appreciation—those that focus on *assessing feelings* about objects, setting, and appearance	
Appraisal Category	**Code**
affect	**bold**
judgment	underline
appreciation	*italics*

From *Harry Potter and the Sorcerer's Stone*, Chapter 12: "The Mirror of Erised":

"So—back again, Harry?"

Harry felt as though his insides had turned to ice. He looked behind him. Sitting on one of the desks by the wall was none other than Albus Dumbledore. Harry must have walked straight past him, so desperate to get to the mirror he hadn't noticed him.

"I—I didn't see you, sir."

"Strange how nearsighted being invisible can make you," said Dumbledore, and Harry was relieved to see that he was smiling.

"So," said Dumbledore, slipping off the desk to sit on the floor with Harry, "you, *like hundreds before you*, have discovered the *delights* of the Mirror of Erised."

"I didn't know it was called that, sir."

"But I expect you've realized by now what it does."

"It—well—it shows me my family—"

"And it showed your friend Ron himself as head boy."

"How did you know—?"

Appraisal Category	**Positive**		**Negative**	
affect (feelings of characters, narrators, and/or readers)	Harry	Dumbledore	Harry	Dumbledore
judgment (judgment of characters, narrators, and/or readers)	Ron			
appreciation (assessing feelings about objects, setting and appearances)	Mirror of Erised			

Excerpt source: Rowling (1997, pp. 212–213).

TABLE 4.3. Example of Practice Assignment with Critical Reflection

<table>
<tr><th>Modality Practice</th></tr>
<tr><td>"I don't need a cloak to become invisible," said Dumbledore gently. "Now, can you think what the Mirror of Erised shows us all?"
Harry shook his head.
"Let me explain. The happiest man on earth would be able to use the Mirror of Erised like a normal mirror, that is, he would look into it and see himself exactly as he is. Does that help?"
Harry thought. Then he said slowly, "It shows us what we want . . . whatever we want. . ."
"Yes and no," said Dumbledore quietly. "It shows us nothing more or less than the deepest, most desperate desire of our hearts. You, who have never known your family, see them standing around you. Ronald Weasley, who has always been overshadowed by his brothers, sees himself standing alone, the best of all of them. However, this mirror will give us neither knowledge or truth. Men have wasted away before it, entranced by what they have seen, or been driven mad, not knowing if what it shows is real or even possible.
"The Mirror will be moved to a new home tomorrow, Harry, and I ask you not to go looking for it again. If you ever do run across it, you will now be prepared. It does not do to dwell on dreams and forget to live, remember that. Now, why don't you put that admirable cloak back on and get off to bed?"
Harry stood up.
"Sir—Professor Dumbledore? Can I ask you something?"<br>"Obviously, you've just done so," Dumbledore smiled. "You may ask me one more thing, however."
"What do you see when you look in the mirror?"<br>"I? I see myself holding a pair of thick, woolen socks."
Harry stared.</td></tr>
<tr><td>On the polarity scale, are the words that the characters use mostly high, medium, or low?
Harry:

Dumbledore:

Why do you think this is?</td></tr>
<tr><td>Can a power relationship between the characters be determined based on your analysis? Explain.</td></tr>
<tr><td>Overall, what does this analysis reveal and how does it determine how we continue to read the text/series?</td></tr>
</table>

Excerpt source: *Harry Potter and the Sorcerer's Stone* (Rowling, 1997, pp. 213–214).

Projects

In my previous work (e.g., Simmons & Page, 2010), I had success in promoting a democratic environment and motivating students using William Glasser's (1986) model for student groups. Glasser believed that student groups:

1. create a sense of belonging
2. provide healthy peer motivation to work harder
3. provide a way for struggling students to be a part of a high-performing team
4. give strong students an opportunity to share their knowledge
5. make students less dependent on the teacher
6. help oppose social cliques outside of the classroom by encouraging students to build friendships through academic pursuits.

Therefore, for each project, students engage in CDA as a group, relying on one another to build understanding. As shown in my scaffolding map (Figure 4.4), I begin with Harry Potter. For the Harry Potter project, students are asked to choose a critical essay based on their interests.

List of Essays Used in the Curriculum

- "The Fallen Empire: Exploring Ethnic Otherness in the World of Harry Potter" (Anatol, 2003)
- "Hermione and the House-Elves: The Literary and Historical Contexts of J. K. Rowling's Antislavery Campaign" (Carey, 2003)
- "Cinderfella: J. K. Rowling's Wily Web of Gender" (Gallardo-C. & Smith, 2003)
- "Accepting Mudbloods: The Ambivalent Social Vision of J. K. Rowling's Fairy Tales" (Ostry, 2003)
- "Class and Socioeconomic Identity in Harry Potter's England" (Park, 2003)
- "Reading Harry Potter: Popular Culture, Queer Theory and the Fashioning of Youth Identity" (Nylund, 2007)
- "Sneaking Out after Dark: Resistance, Agency, and the Postmodern Child in J. K. Rowling's Harry Potter series" (Chappell, 2008)

- "Harry's Girls: Harry Potter and the Discourse of Gender" (Cherland, 2009)
- "Harry and the Other: Answering the Race Question in J. K. Rowling's Harry Potter" (Horne, 2010)
- "J. K. Rowling's Ambivalence towards Feminism: House-Elves—Women in Disguise—in the Harry Potter Books" (Kellner, 2010)
- "'The Less You Lot Have ter Do with These Foreigners, the Happier Yeh'll Be': Cultural and National Otherness in J. K. Rowling's Harry Potter Series" (Rana, 2011)

After reading the article, students make notes on the author's major claims. Students then return to the primary text, *Harry Potter and the Sorcerer's Stone*, and find examples that reflect or are relevant to the author's claims. Students then conduct a discourse analysis using an appraisal analysis, identification analysis, and modality analysis to see if J. K. Rowling's language supports or disproves the author's claims. Students then present their finding to the class using PowerPoint, Google Slides, or Prezi to stimulate discussion (see also Table 4.4).

Students' *Othello* project (Table 4.5) asks each student group to conduct an appraisal, identification, and modality analysis on one of the five acts, ensuring that all acts are analyzed (see also Table 4.6).

In addition to posing discussion questions to the class, the class is able to pose questions to the group regarding its interpretation of the data.

TABLE 4.4. Harry Potter Discourse Analysis Project

STEP 1: Read your selected critical article. Make notes on the major claims the author is making about the series and the examples they are using to make those claims.
STEP 2: Find examples from the book that are relevant to the author's claims. Perform a discourse analysis using an appraisal analysis, identification analysis, and modality analysis to see if J. K. Rowling's language supports or disproves the author's claims.

STEP 3: Present your finding to the class to stimulate discussion.
Requirements for the Presentation Your presentation should provide: 1. A synopsis of the author's claims. 2. Your original reaction to the author's claims. 3. If your author is working within a particular theory (feminist, queer, critical race theory, etc.), provide an overview of how the author defines the theory. 4. For each claim, choose one or two examples from the text on which to perform a discourse analysis. Please use all three types of analysis: appraisal, identification, and modality. You do not have to use all three on each example; choose the analysis for each example that you think will best support or disprove the author's claim. However, you need to have performed all three by the end of your presentation. 5. Show your work. When you do an appraisal analysis, create a code that shows the different elements: affect, judgment, and appreciation (see examples from your notes). Then, create a chart like we did with the examples. When you do an identification analysis, underline all nouns and pronouns used to refer to the individuals in question. Create a chart that lists each name per character and how many times it occurs in your selected passage. When you do a modality analysis, underline the words and identify where the words fall on the polarity scale. 6. Discuss with the class what each analysis reveals. Some examples of what you can talk about include: • What does the analysis mean? • How does it affect your views or interpretation of the novel? • What does it mean for the larger genre of children's fantasy literature? • What message is being taught? • How can it be changed?
You can also address other questions that come up.

TABLE 4.5. *Othello* Discourse Analysis Project

1. Each group will be **assigned an act (1–5).** 2. Each group will **perform an identification analysis, appraisal analysis, and modality analysis for their act.** There are many ways you can divide the work: for instance, by type of analysis, by scene, by character (for identification analysis), or by appraisal mode (affect, judgment, and appreciation). 3. Your group will **create the appropriate charts** and share them via Google Docs. 4. After conducting their analysis, your group will **make a handout** summarizing the results and give a brief interpretation of their meaning. The handout must include: • a summary of the identification analysis and a critical interpretation of what it means • a summary of the appraisal analysis and a critical interpretation of what it means • a summary of the modality analysis and a critical interpretation of what it means • three Socratic discussion questions for the class, based on your findings. *Note*: "Summary" DOES NOT mean copies of all of your charts for everyone. Synthesize your data. What are the most obvious or most important findings?
Make sure your handout is clear and easy to read. *It must be confined to one page front and back (so two pages front only).*
Your data will be presented during a Socratic seminar, so be prepared to informally share your data.

TABLE 4.6. Obama Speech Discourse Analysis Project

1. Each group will be **assigned an issue that is discussed within the speech**. 2. Each group will **perform an identification analysis, appraisal analysis, and modality analysis, contrast and concession analysis, and citation analysis for their issue**. 3. Your group will **create and complete the appropriate charts** and email them in to Ms. Simmons. She will make copies of your completed analysis/charts for each student in the class. 4. After conducting your analysis, your group will need to present your findings, informally, to the class, referring the class to their copy of your completed charts that support your analysis. 5. Think about our discussion questions and reflection topics. Was there anything in your results that helped you address, question, or answer one of those questions/topics? If so what and how? Explain to the class and encourage the class to share their interpretation of your results.
Choose to discuss three of the following reflection and discussion questions on Barack Obama's (2009) speech at Cairo University:
1. Does your identification analysis show a dichotomy of "them" versus "us"? Explain your findings and their effect on your feelings toward the subject and people being discussed.
2. Citations are used to strengthen arguments by providing supporting evidence that challenges an alternate position. How does Obama use citations to strengthen his argument? Do his citations play a role in how the audience views the West and the East? Explain.
3. Contrast and concession is effective because it positions the speaker as open minded and willing to negotiate by conceding to the opposing side about an issue, but then the speaker immediately provides a contrast to support the speaker's own position. Does Obama utilize this effectively? How does it impact you as an audience member?
4. Does Obama's modality assist in his persuasive goal to make arguments by laying out the facts of "how it is"?
5. Does Obama use language to suggest that the "Muslim world" (a term he uses to refer to over forty-five countries with little in common aside from the fact that the majority of the population identifies as "Muslim") is a whole different "world"?

continued on next page

6. Based on your SFL analysis, does Obama label Western values as "human," "modern," "civil," and all things "good"?
7. Based on Said's list of harmful "Oriental" stereotypes, looking at your analysis, does Obama's language—and even talking points—majorly support or counter such stereotypes? Does it do both? Does he focus on some more than others? Intentionally or unintentionally? Explain.
8. How does Obama use language to align the West with all that is "rational" and the East with the "irrational"?
9. How does Obama identify Muslim communities in America? What is the implication and effect of this linguistic choice?
10. Ambiguity is a key aspect of political speeches, because it allows the orator to avoid obvious contradictions with what they have said before. Are there places in this speech where Obama is intentionally ambiguous? Why?
11. Often, "what is 'said' in a text always rests upon 'unsaid' assumptions, so part of the analysis of texts is trying to identify what is assumed" (Fairclough, 2003, p. 11). What are some unsaid assumptions in this speech?
12. Is there a *universal* logic or science that allows all "humans" to be able to sit down at a table and discuss issues through "objective" reasoning that is untainted by cultural norms/ assumptions of good, bad, etc.?
13. One could say that *globalization* is the "widening, deepening, and speeding up of worldwide interconnectedness in all aspects of contemporary social life, from the cultural to the criminal, the financial to the spiritual" (Crossley & Watson, 2003, p. 53). A colleague of mine once said, "To be blunt, while education and media in the Muslim world has been dramatically Westernized over the last twenty years, I have to ask how Western education/media have been changed to reflect Muslim or 'Eastern' values in the last twenty years for us to accept this interpretation of 'mutual' global exchange?" As a student in a Westernized culture, do you think your education has been "globalized" to reflect Muslim or "Eastern" values?

14. How does Obama define "progress"? How does he suggest that "tradition" opposes "progress"?
15. Obama is giving a speech that, while primarily addressed to "Muslims around the world," will be heard by the non-Muslim population of the planet as well—not unimportantly, US citizens: how does this simultaneous addressing affect his language choices?
16. Obama is often attacked for "over-identifying" with the "East" and not being "American enough" (birth certificate, middle name, etc.). Based on your analysis of this speech, with whom does he identify most: the "West" or the "East"? How does he make this evident through his language choices?

Essays to Explore Evidence and Execute High-Stakes Writing

After utilizing discourse analysis tools to critically analyze texts and engage in critical dialogue about language use, students write an academic, AP exam-style essay, so I can determine if students applied their critical awareness and/or discourse analysis skills to their own writing. As previously mentioned, it is necessary for me to incorporate standardized writing assignments in order to prepare students for what they will encounter on the AP exam and other high-stakes writing assignments. For the sake of this book, I did not prompt students to think or read with a critical lens or use discourse when writing the essay. The purpose of the writing assignments was to see if students viewed text more critically and/or relied on discourse analysis skills to develop arguments about language use in texts *on their own*. In essence, I examine how students apply what they are learning through independent instruction to a seemingly unrelated assignment.

After students complete their Harry Potter project, they write an AP-style essay that asks them to:

> Carefully read the following autobiographical narrative by Malcolm X excerpted from *The Autobiography of Malcolm X* (1965). In a well-constructed essay, identify the author's purpose and intended effect and analyze the rhetorical strategies and techniques he employs to achieve this.
>
> (Murphy & Rankin, 2002, p. 212; see also X & Haley, 1965)

This excerpt focuses on Malcolm's experience as a boy being told by his teacher that he couldn't be a lawyer because he was Black. The excerpt provides multiple opportunities to utilize SFL analysis tools to assess how Malcolm used language to achieve his goal—encourage his readers to feel his anger at being discriminated against because of the color of his skin and join him in the fight against racism and inequality.

The essay that students write after their *Othello* assignment is defined as a *synthesis essay*. In a synthesis essay, students are expected to read multiple sources and use appropriate sources to support their argument. The purpose of this kind of essay is to test students' ability to utilize and organize multiple sources to create a cohesive essay that achieves a single persuasive goal. The prompt for this particular synthesis essay deals with the controversial issue of animal testing and asks students to:

> Read the following sources carefully. Then, in an essay that synthesizes at least three of the sources, take a position that supports, challenges, or qualifies the claim that animals should not be used in research.
>
> (Ehrenhaft, 2010, p. 232)

Sources that students can use to support their argument include statistics, opinion articles, graphs, and scientific reports from both sides of the argument. Using discourse analysis tools, students can question how the author of each source uses language to manipulate readers to take their position. Also, the students themselves can use the same techniques in their writing to persuade their readers to also adopt their position as well as support their analysis, interpretation, and use of the provided sources.

The essay students write after they finish their Obama project provides a provocative and controversial statement and asks students to agree, disagree, or modify the statement based on their beliefs and experiences. In essence, this is a *persuasive*-style essay, asking students to convince the reader that their interpretation of the quote is correct and provide examples as to why. For this particular essay, the prompt reads:

> In 2001, *The American Scholar* published an excerpt from a talk given by English author Margaret Drabble. In her talk, Drabble claimed that "Our desire to conform is greater than our respect for objective facts." Using appropriate evidence from your reading, observation, and/or experience, write a carefully reasoned essay defending, challenging, or qualifying Drabble's assertion about conformity.
>
> (College Board, 2008, p. 24)

Because this prompt allows students to use examples from their readings and life experiences, it provides them with an opportunity to cite critical examples. Figure 4.6 shows how practice, projects, and writing assignments of this curriculum align with the teaching and learning cycle.

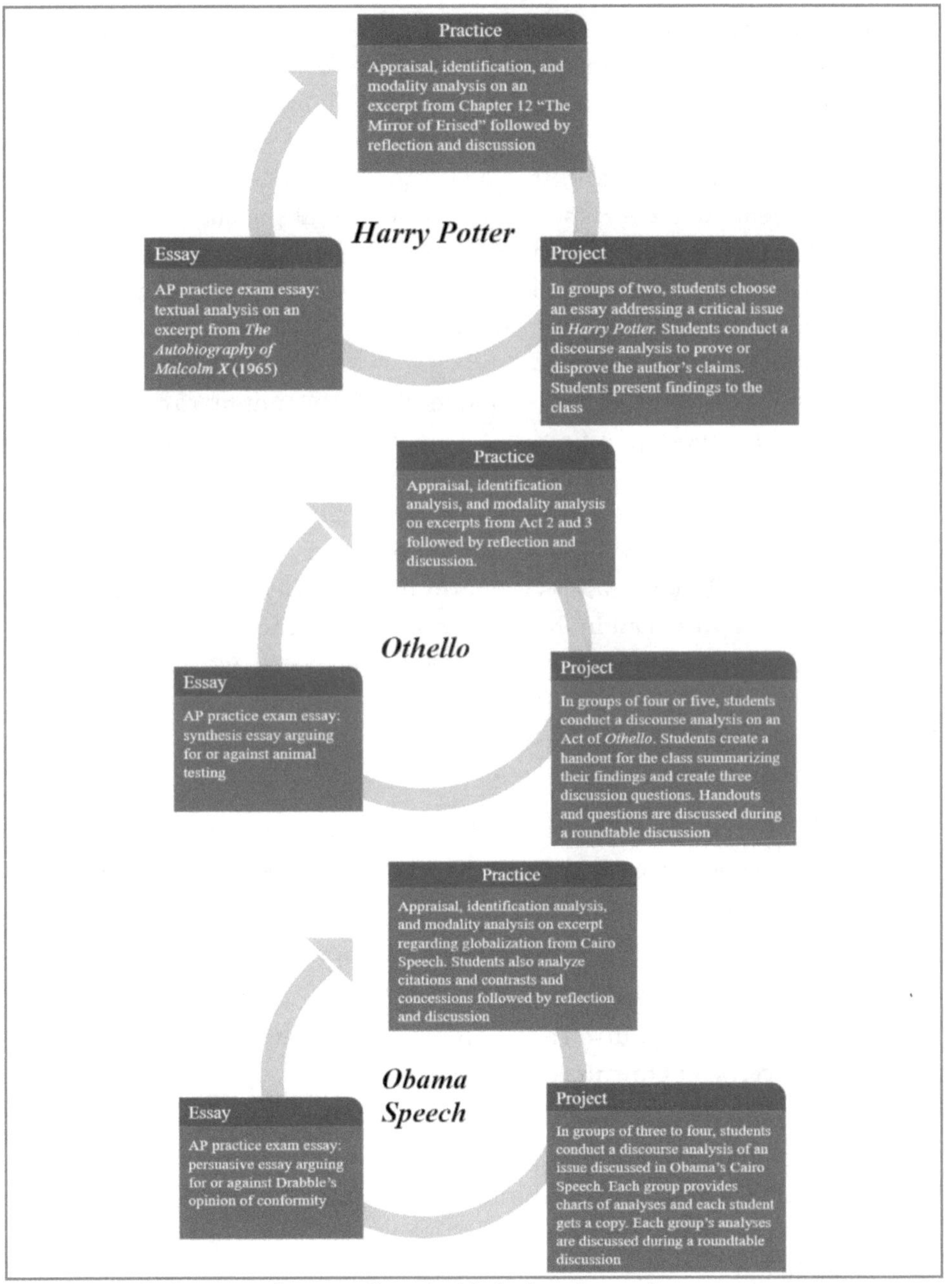

FIGURE 4.6. Assignments, by text, aligned with the learning cycle.

In an effort to engage students in practicing their writing skills before their AP exam as well as to assess their use of discourse analysis, students participate in two additional writing assignments at the end of the semester that are not attached to a particular project. The first of these two essays is a textual analysis prompt on a passage from Shadd Cary (1854), who wrote an editorial supporting the need for an abolitionist newspaper. I use this prompt as a final writing assignment because it provides students with opportunities to make critical comments and use their discourse analysis skills to critique the linguistic elements that make the essay persuasive. The second essay is also a textual analysis prompt on a passage, this one from Mary Oliver's (1995) "Owls"; however, students wrote a response to this prompt at the end of the previous semester. When asking students to rewrite their essay, I ask them specifically to use their new discourse analysis skills in order to see if the linguistic tools help them craft an essay that is more focused on Oliver's language choices as they relate to her feelings about nature.

Students write each essay in class and receive forty minutes to complete each essay. By choosing these specific essays, I am provided with a variety of writing samples of different genres that helped me determine how students applied SFL/CDA and assess their developing critical consciousness for the purposes of this book. In future chapters, I will use evidence from these assignments and student essay responses to build a case as to how a linguistically informed curriculum like the one I just presented in this chapter helps students grow in their ability to critically assess and use language to achieve their social and academic goals.

Reflection Questions for Chapter 4

1. How would you define *ideology* and *hegemony* to students?
2. What are you currently doing in the classroom to support Freire's definition of *dialogue*?
3. How do Freire and Fairclough's beliefs compare to your current classroom goals regarding language education?
4. Do you consider yourself as having *critical language awareness*? Where or how can you grow in your awareness?
5. While I use *Harry Potter*, *Othello*, and Obama's speech at Cairo, can you think of three texts in your repertoire that you could use to create a spiraled curriculum that simultaneously scaffolds critical literacy and the use of linguistic analysis tools? Think of as many as you can. (Go wild here.)

6. Can you think of a curriculum unit in which you take your students through *deconstruction*, *joint construction*, and *independent construction*? How could you take it a step further and create a critical orientation to the text?
7. Which writing assignments might you use to assess students' growth and use of discourse analysis?

5

Community, School, and Participants

Guiding Gist

- This study was done in a suburban school where the majority of students identified as "middle class." The focal participants of this study represent the demographics of my classroom but not necessarily the school.
- The CCSS and IRA/NCTE often have conflicting and contradictory values when it comes to language instruction and reading selections, yet the proposed linguistically informed curriculum can fulfill the standards of both.
- The values of College Board were considered, and preparatory materials provided for AP Language and Composition were utilized in this curriculum in order to prepare students for high-stakes writing assessments.
- A linguistically based curriculum and SFL practices have been successfully implemented in all levels of education (elementary, middle, and high), at varying learning levels, including ESOL, and in schools with different social and economic backgrounds.

In this chapter, I am going to provide some details about the demographics and culture of the school and surrounding community in which I taught, giving you a better idea of who and where I served during this study. I will also disclose the various standards and organizations that inform the construction of my curriculum such as state and district standards (CCSS), College Board requirements, as well as the standards of teacher-led organizations such as ILA and NCTE. (Note: When their joint Standards for the English Language Arts were released in 1996, ILA was known as IRA, the International Reading Association. The organization later changed its name to the International Literacy Association.) This chapter will also invite you into my classroom environment and introduce you to the focal students whose work will be used as samples and discussed throughout the book. I will also briefly discuss my role as a researcher, the data collection methods, and multiple discourse analyses methods and coding systems used to explore student artifacts. In the spirit of SFL, I have split my discussion two sections: context of culture and context of situation.

Context of Culture

As previously stated, context of culture is the larger environment in which language occurs (Halliday, 1999) and enables the "different types of situation to occur" (Halliday & Matthiessen, 1985/2014, p. 9). Therefore, in my discussion of the cultural context of this language study, I will outline the larger community and educational institution in which my curriculum is conducted as well as discuss the standards and testing requirements that influence my teaching practices.

Introduction to the Community and School

Branchview High School[1] is a southeastern suburb that is approximately an hour away from the state's capital. According to 2010 census data, the population of the town in which the school resides is 18,242. Members of the community own local businesses, work in local businesses or the school system, or commute to the city or surrounding towns for their employment. The local businesses are supportive of the high school, donating goods to sports teams, food for celebrations, and money to fundraisers or booster clubs.

When I was writing this book, the student body of the school consisted of 3,712 students, of which thirty-four percent were white and sixty-six percent were racial-ethnic minorities. The average student to teacher ratio was one teacher to twenty students. The female to male ratio was almost 50:50. Five hundred seventy-one students were eligible for free or reduced lunches, approximately sixteen percent, which is a low statistic compared to schools in surrounding counties (United States Department of Education, 2020). In addition, twenty-nine percent of the population was considered economically disadvantaged (Governor's Office of Student Achievement, 2019). While it cannot be denied that some racial tensions exist, the majority of the school is unified by their middle-class social status. In order to better recognize the privileged lifestyle that the students of Branchview enjoy, it helps to look at the student demographics of

1. All names of students and locations are pseudonyms to protect the privacy of participants.

high schools in surrounding areas. The six public schools in closest proximity to Branchview had eighty-three percent, eighty percent, seventy-two percent, seventy-five percent, thirty-nine percent, thirty-four percent, and sixteen percent, respectively, of their students labeled economically disadvantaged, making Branchview the second-most financially well off school in the county (Governor's Office of Student Achievement, 2019). While the student samples presented in this book are from earlier years, there has not been a dramatic shift in the demographics, despite the increase in free and reduced lunch percentages due to COVID-19 nutrition assistance programs.

Standards and Testing Requirements

While the school and surrounding community greatly influenced the work presented in this book, the state standards and testing requirements also play a role in how my curriculum is constructed. Currently, the federal government has encouraged states to adopt the CCSS to hold educators accountable for teaching particular skills and concepts. In order to show the similarities and differences between what the institution values and what practitioners value, I juxtapose the CCSS with the standards constructed by the IRA and NCTE. Making such a comparison is necessary in order to comprehend the multiple, and sometimes contradictory, standards that influence my curriculum.

There are some major discrepancies between some of the IRA/NCTE standards and the CCSS. For example, IRA/NCTE encourages students to use their previous experiences to respond to literature, indicating a value for reader-response theory while also stating that functional reading is important in order to prepare students for the workplace and future studies. The NCTE/IRA does not provide a reading list, but it can be assumed from the verbiage that student-selected works are valued. The CCSS reading list provides numerous subgenres that include genres such as myths, fiction, and plays, as well as contemporary genres such as science fiction and graphic novels, which suggest that these literary genres are approved for teacher use. However, the majority of texts that the CCSS claims would show a "range of reading" (Common Core State Standards Initiative, 2010, p. 58) contain mostly canonical/classical works and white authors. Out of twenty-seven texts, only seven are written by racial-ethnic minority authors and only four women are listed. This is consistent with Applebee's (1991) review of ELA anthologies, which also reveals an embarrassingly low amount of racial-ethnic minority and female authors.

The only writing standards given by the IRA/NCTE state that various strategies should be used when students engage in the writing process and that they should write for their own purposes, leaving room for teachers to determine which methods to use and in which genres students may write. However, the CCSS shows a clear preference in writing genres. Because they are mentioned first, I perceive that persuasive and explanatory writing is valued over narrative writing. A particular standard is that the writer's tone should be objective and formal, keeping students from expressing their passions, beliefs, or values, which, in my opinion, takes the student's voice out of the essay. While student voice is lacking from the CCSS standards, one pleasantly surprising standard under the writing domain is that students should use the internet to produce and publish their work, providing an authentic audience and purpose for writing.

The IRA/NCTE Standards believe that students' language, including conventions, style, and vocabulary, should be determined by the audience and purpose of the communication. Furthermore, students should be able to apply their knowledge of language and conventions such as "spelling, punctuation, media techniques, [and] figurative language" (International Reading Association & National Council of Teachers of English, 1996, p. 3) in their writing. Similarly, the CCSS state that students should understand that "language functions in different contexts" and be able "to make effective choices for meaning or style" (Common Core State Standards Initiative, 2010, p. 54). This is the closest standard that addresses the functional nature of grammar. A positive inclusion to the standards is that teachers should ensure students understand that grammar changes with time and many rules are contested, suggesting that, while grammar is still viewed as a set of rules, those "rules" may sometimes change or be wrong in certain contexts.

The CCSS also has a special section for vocabulary, which shows that diction and word choice is highly valued. Unlike the IRA/NCTE Standards, the CCSS does not require students to respect diverse linguistic patterns or dialects. In fact, it is repeated multiple times that Standard English and an objective point of view are valued in all types of writing and speaking. Furthermore, the IRA/NCTE have a standard that addresses the need to ensure that students whose first language is not English are provided with opportunities to build their competency. No such provision is made for second-language English speakers in the CCSS, suggesting a lack of awareness of the growing linguistic diversity of American classrooms.

It is in the standard of conducting research that the IRA/NCTE Standards and CCSS are most aligned; however, the IRA/NCTE Standards advocates for student choice in research topics while the CCSS does not. Furthermore, IRA/NCTE's standards are meant for all forms of communication, so there are not specific standards that address speaking and listening; on the other hand, the CCSS does address specific speaking and listening skills. For example, students should engage in "civil, democratic discussions" (Common Core State Standards Initiative, 2010, p. 50), which indicates the value of dialogue but does not encourage students to be open to changing their perspective. In fact, it states that students should be able to "qualify or justify their own views" (Common Core State Standards Initiative, 2010, p. 50), suggesting that their definition of *discussion* is really "debate." Furthermore, when listening to speeches, students should be able to recognize fallacies, discrepancies, or distorted evidence.

While Brause and Mayher (2003) pointed out the frustration and futility of standards due to their vagueness, it seems as though the vagueness of the IRA/NCTE Standards are intentional so as to give teachers more autonomy over the classroom. Furthermore, it seems as though the CCSS addresses this complaint by including more details in each standard and providing a list of suggested texts to clarify the desired implementation of the standards.

CCSS and IRA/NCTE Standards in My Classroom

The CCSS and NCTE/IRA Standards directly influence my curriculum and its implementation. Therefore, when I decided to incorporate discourse analysis and linguistically informed methods into my classroom, I had to consider how it could be implemented to cover the required standards and meet the expectations of the CCSS and NCTE/IRA. Table 5.1 shows which standards are addressed and where they are evident in the context of this language curriculum and pedagogical approach.

TABLE 5.1. Implementation of Standards

NCTE/IRA Standard	Implementation
Use of previous experiences; functional reading	Students link previous experiences to dialogue during classroom discussion; students included personal anecdotes in academic writing to support a position or claim; reading of "real-world" texts—Obama's (2009) speech
A variety of print and non-print texts that build students' understanding of the human experience of various cultures	Discussion of Said's *Orientalism*. Watch interview with Said and look at how the East is represented in art
Use various strategies; write for a variety of purposes	Direct instruction, small-group work (two students), large-group work (four or more students), independent work, verbal assessment, written assessment; academic writing (synthesis, persuasive, analytical), personal reflective writing
Conventions, style, and vocabulary should be determined by the audience and purpose of the communication; apply knowledge in writing	All discourse analysis instruction, practice, and analysis

Research based on students' interests; use technological tools	Students choose an article of interest for *Harry Potter* project—use of *Harry Potter* is based on students' interests; internet, PowerPoint/Google Slides/Prezi, Publisher, Word Processor
Focus on communication	Student presentations; classroom round-table dialogue; Socratic seminar
CCSS Standard	**Implementation**
Use textual evidence; summarize; determine themes; analyze character development; question stylistic choices; use context clues; recognize how language adds to meaning; understand elements of structure; understand irony, satire, and understatement; understand that texts have multiple interpretations; recognize intertextuality	All discourse analysis instruction, practice, projects, writing assignments, and analysis
Comprehend a variety of genres; value of canonical texts over contemporary	Various literary genres, including fantasy narrative, canonical drama, and contemporary speech
Persuasive and explanatory writing; organization; support claims with evidence; transitions; sophisticated vocabulary; varied sentence structure; formal and objective tone; Standard English conventions; use technology to produce work	Academic writing (synthesis, persuasive, analytical); personal reflective writing; SFL analysis; internet, PowerPoint, Publisher, Word Processor
Command of Standard English, including spelling, punctuation, and capitalization; knowledge of phrases, clauses, and parts of speech; parallelism; use a dictionary; ability to use a colon, semi-colon, and hyphen; **understand the functionality of language**; special attention to vocabulary: use context clues to determine meaning; thesaurus, and glossary	Discourse analysis requires knowledge of all of the following, and reviews the tenets of Standard English, including spelling, punctuation, capitalization, parts of speech, word choice, etc., as well as questions them
Draw evidence from literary and informational texts to support analysis; evaluate reasoning of texts; incorporate information while maintain fluidity in writing Draw evidence from literary and informational texts to support analysis; evaluate reasoning of texts; gather information from multiple authorities; use print and digital texts; incorporate information while maintain fluidity in writing; avoid plagiarism	Use discourse analysis to provide evidence to support analysis; determining audience and purpose of texts; focus on transitions and lead-ins; avoid plagiarism through direct quotes and citation
Engage in discussions with peers and teacher; use text as evidence when questioning, providing opinion, or defending point of view; respect others' point of view; recognize fallacies, faulty logic, and distorted evidence; use digital media when presenting information, utilizing audio, graphs, visual, and interactive elements to support audience's understanding; follow demands of Standard English	Class discussion and group work; dialogue; SFL analysis and reflection; PowerPoint and Prezi presentations; writing requirements; Socratic seminar

In addition, I also want to take a minute to show, in Table 5.2, how this curriculum fulfills the Language strands of the CCSS mentioned in Chapter 1.

TABLE 5.2. Implementation of CCCSS Language Standards (Common Core State Standards Initiative, 2010)

Language Standard Title/Number	Common Standard	How It Is Addressed in the Curriculum
Conventions of Standard English: CCSS.ELA-LITERACY.L.1	Demonstrate command of the conventions of Standard English grammar and usage when writing or speaking	The use of appraisal, identification, and modality analyses requires students to be fluent in parts of speech in order to code correctly and understand how they convey specific meaning
Conventions of Standard English: CCSS.ELA-LITERACY.L.2	Demonstrate command of the conventions of Standard English capitalization, punctuation, and spelling when writing	Students engage in writing assignments that provide opportunities to practice conventions and encourage students to use varied syntax in order to show relationships between ideas. Contrast and concession and citation exercises provides specific opportunities for instruction on semicolons and formatting
Knowledge of Language: CCSS.ELA-LITERACY.L.3	Apply knowledge of language to understand how language functions in different contexts, to make effective choices for meaning or style, and to comprehend more fully when reading or listening	Discussions and analyses of discourse analysis results allow students to question and assess author purpose with specific language choices. Conducting these analyses with different genres helps students see how choices differ depending on genre and context. Also, through discourse analysis, students recognize that language choices can serve more than one purpose (e.g., an identification noun can serve as a judgment)
Vocabulary Acquisition and Use: CCSS.ELA-LITERACY.L.4	Determine or clarify the meaning of unknown and multiple-meaning words and phrases based on [grade level] reading and content, choosing flexibly from a range of strategies	By analyzing the language around unknown words, students are able to better understand the tone and context of the passage, allowing them to make an educated guess as to the intended meaning of the unknown vocabulary
Vocabulary Acquisition and Use: CCSS.ELA-LITERACY.L.5	Demonstrate understanding of figurative language, word relationships, and nuances in word meanings	Understanding the difference between invoked and explicit affect, judgment, and appreciation words and phrases, students understand how nuance, tone, and context play a role in meaning. Also, understanding modality and how it can scale up or down in intensity helps students pick up on the nuances of meaning
Vocabulary Acquisition and Use: CCSS.ELA-LITERACY.L.6	Acquire and use accurately general academic and domain-specific words and phrases, sufficient for reading, writing, speaking, and listening at the college and career readiness level; demonstrate independence in gathering vocabulary knowledge when considering a word or phrase important to comprehension or expression	SFL and discourse analysis instruction provide a metalanguage to talk about language, presenting a unique opportunity for teachers and students to analyze how it is functioning in texts

Note: English Language Arts Standards (grades 9–10 and 11–12) are presented in full on the Common Core State Standards Initiative website (see http://www.corestandards.org/ELA-Literacy/L/9-10 and http://www.corestandards.org/ELA-Literacy/L/11-12).

I want to reiterate that this curriculum does not present more superfluous work to add to an already overcrowded schedule. Instead, a linguistically informed curriculum can actually support already required standards and fit into existing demands.

I want to reiterate that this curriculum does not present more superfluous work to add to an already overcrowded schedule. Instead, a linguistically informed curriculum can actually support already required standards and fit into existing demands.

Advanced Placement Exams

In AP Language and Composition as well as AP Literature and Composition courses, there is an overwhelming emphasis on expository, analytical, and argumentative writing with a focus on the writing process. The difference between the two courses is that AP Language focuses more on the stylistic elements of works, addressing rhetorical choices and reflecting on how grammar and mechanics help clarify an argument (College Board, 2020a), while AP Literature analyzes literature through more traditional literary analysis (College Board, 2020b). Both courses read a variety of genres and texts from a diverse group of authors. The AP Language and AP Literature exams provide sixty minutes to answer approximately fifty-two to fifty-four multiple choice questions based on reading passages and 120 minutes to respond to three essay questions. The test is considered "high stakes" because the student's score on the exam (1–5) determines if they receive college credit for the course. This equates to big dollars for families.

Understanding the AP exam requirements for AP Language and Composition is necessary as it represents another set of standards that I am expected to cover in my curriculum. One motivation for students to take an AP class is the opportunity to get college credit for the course. Therefore, students and parents, as well as county and school administrators and College Board, are concerned with preparing students to perform well on this exam. In addition, one's value as an AP teacher in the school's AP program is also partly determined by students' scores on the AP exam, which encourages teachers to consider the test as we develop our curriculum.

Therefore, I include regular timed writing and silent reading activities that are created for the sole purpose of having a positive effect on high-stakes test results (see Robinson et al., 1990) and not necessarily governed by students' individual needs or interests (see Airasain & Madaus, 1983; Rupp & Lesaux, 2006; Segel, 1937). Most comprehension tests present students with a short passage followed by multiple-choice questions, like the AP exam, and these tests are not representative of students' experiences in the classroom (Airaisan & Madaus, 1983; Dolch, 1933; Valencia et al., 1989); therefore, I also include similar experiences in the classroom, including timed multiple-choice practice sessions that are representative of what students will experience on the test in order to prepare them for the format they will encounter on exam day.

While I give students multiple choice and reading comprehension practice questions on a weekly basis, much of student writing is also determined by what they will experience on the exam. Students often practice their persuasive, synthesis, and analytical writing skills using previous AP exam prompts so as to get a feel for College Board's writing expectations. According to Rothery and Stenglin (2000), written responses to such prompts often "do not challenge culturally conventional readings of literature" and examiners (or test graders) "expect and reward a culturally conventional reading" (p. 225). This is supported by research from Rothery (1994) as well as Christie and Derewianka (2008), who found no evidence in their studies that students were encouraged to write in critical genres in their years of secondary schooling. With this in mind, I am conscious of developing my students' critical awareness and ability to write from a critical stance in an environment that does not always reward a critical response, putting me in a precarious position that requires me to balance my classroom goals against the expectations of College Board so as to not leave my students at a disadvantage during testing.

Context of Situation

The context of situation, like the context of culture, also influences the implementation of this curriculum and the examples presented in later chapters of this book. To review, *context of situation* is situated within the context of culture and is composed of "what is going on, who is taking part, and what speech acts are designed to achieve" (Halliday & Matthiessen, 1985/2014, p. 365). In order to evaluate the context of situation, this section discusses my classroom demographics, goals, pedagogical context of the approach, including text selections and assignments, and profiles of my focal students.

Classroom Overview

Over the years, I have taught all high school grade levels and preps. However, the examples and results presented in this book are from three sections of AP Language and Composition, since that was what I was teaching when I started collecting data for the book. Within these three sections, I had a total of sixty students and all participated in the curriculum associated with the language study. However, only students who gave permission were transcribed from recordings, and I did not collect work from students who did not get a parent signature. (Everything is on the up and up, folks.) Out of these sixty students, there were forty-one females and nineteen males, meaning males were outnumbered in each class two to one, which does not represent the 50:50 male-to-female ratio of the school. The racial demographics of my students were forty percent racial-ethnic minority, with nine African American students, eleven students who identified as Asian American, four Latinx students, and thirty-six white students. Furthermore, eleven students, or eighteen percent, met the requirements for free or reduced lunches, which is slightly lower than the school's current average. Out of the sixty students, forty-three percent tested gifted and the other fifty-seven percent were previously enrolled in Honors Language Arts before entering AP Language and Composition. All students excelled on state-mandated exams, either meeting or exceeding expectations. It is safe to say that the students discussed in this book represented the norms of their high school, generally identified with the middle class, and were accustomed to the dominant language of academic discourse.

Many times, when I reveal these details about my classroom, readers think that the methods I introduce in the classroom can *only* serve this demographic and then quit listening or reading. Please do not do this. While my data come from this particular demographic, I can tell you that linguistically based curricula and SFL practices have been successfully implemented in all levels of education (elementary, middle, and high), at varying learning levels, including ESOL, and in schools with different social and economic backgrounds (see, e.g., Derewianka & Jones, 2016; Gebhard et al., 2019; Gebhard & Graham, 2018; Maune & Klassen, 2014; McCreight, 2016; Symons et al., 2017). Since the collection of these data, teachers have modified this curriculum for their own students with successful results. I will go into more detail about this in later chapters.

Profile of Participants

In order to answer the research questions presented in Chapter 1, I focus on the written and verbal examples of seven students. These students also participated in a protocol analysis, a one-on-one think-aloud activity to help me understand students' real-time thinking when performing discourse analyses. I chose the following students because they represent an accurate sampling of my classroom demographics and also embody students' various experiences as they engaged in the above-discussed curriculum.

Clara

Clara, a bright African American female with clever and humorous comments during class discussions, had parents who emigrated from Nigeria. While she was not in the gifted program, she was an extremely capable student with a high GPA and would attend one of the major state universities the following year. Clara was one of the eleven students in my AP class eligible for free and reduced lunches. Clara's senior year was challenging for her on a personal level. Her parents decided to get a divorce, and her favorite aunt was dying of cancer. So much change in her life really made Clara question the importance of her grades and her academic life, something that had always been important to her.

Grace

Grace, an outgoing, white redhead, entered AP Language and Composition with feelings of trepidation. Although she was in the gifted program, she was afraid that the class would be difficult for her, and, in the end, lower her 4.0 GPA. While she ended up graduating with a 3.94, she later told me that she found the class to be extremely gratifying and was glad she challenged herself. Grace was popular and well liked, involved in multiple leadership activities, including the varsity tennis team, and not only won the Miss Branchview Pageant but was also awarded Miss Congeniality by her peers. An overachiever by her own definition, Grace expected a lot out of herself and her future.

Isabelle

With a military father stationed in Afghanistan, Isabelle, a raven-haired white female, stated that she was basically raised by a single mother when her father was deployed. For this reason, Isabelle and her mother were very close, and she respected her mother's success as a small business owner. Like Clara, Isabelle was also eligible for free and reduced lunches. While Isabelle struggled throughout the semester, she constantly rose to the challenge and performed to the best of her ability with every assignment, maintaining a B average throughout the year.

Parvesh

Parvesh's parents emigrated from India when he was in elementary school so that he would have a better life and education. His father eventually opened his own business, and Parvesh and his family received their American citizenship while he was in my class. Parvesh came into AP Language and Composition from the gifted program. He was accepted early to a major state university due to his high GPA, student involvement, and multiple AP credits. A young man with a lot of school spirit, Parvesh was involved in the school leadership program and was well liked by his peers.

Sandi

Sandi, a white female, was in my honors language arts class the year before, even though she was in the gifted program. A petite blonde, Sandi sat in the back of the classroom, yet she was not shy during class discussion and did not avoid interaction with fellow students or myself, and so wasn't the stereotypical "I'm-sitting-in-the-back-of-the-room-so-you-won't-talk-to-me" student. Instead, Sandi was always eager to prove her intellect and engage in dialogue.

Tyler

Tyler could befriend *anyone;* I honestly think he said "Hi" to everyone he passed in the hall and knew them by name. He was the friendliest student I think I have ever met, and he earned the amity of people that many other teenagers ostracized. A blue-eyed, blonde-haired white male, Tyler was very influenced by his Christian faith and upbringing, and he was our class expert on the Bible, as he could cite verses and relate them to class discussion at the drop of a hat.

Winnie

One of the fiercest intellects I have encountered in a student to date, Winnie, a girl of Indian descent with long black hair, was eligible for free and reduced lunches and never ceased to amaze me with her insight and academic ability. An "old soul," Winnie's quiet but extremely perceptive observations of the world and interpretations of literature often built on other students' revelations while also encouraging classmates to respond. I think one reason why I admired her was because she seemed to be a natural "dialogist."

The above profiles describe a diverse group of students from different backgrounds, interests, and academic abilities. They also represent varying reactions to performing analyses and engaging in SFL and CDA practices. They had differing degrees of critical awareness as well, making them an ideal sample selection for my attempt to provide an overview of student experiences when engaging in this language curriculum.

Reflection Questions for Chapter 5

1. What are the *context of culture* and the *context of situation* of your current teaching situation or potential teaching situation?
2. What are the institutional standards in which you work? Which are required by your state/county, and which do you find personally valuable?

3. Who are the stakeholders you must consider as you build your curriculum?
4. How do the answers from questions 1 to 3 impact your development of a language curriculum?

Becoming Comfortable with Analyses and Metalanguage: Growth in Confidence and Critical Awareness

6

Guiding Gist

- As students engaged in the *spiraled curriculum* and the *learning cycle*, *modality analyses* showed evidence of increased confidence and comfort with *discourse analysis* tools as they learned more complex concepts and read more complicated texts.
- As new discourse analysis skills were introduced, such as *contrast and concession and citation analyses*, *hedging* slightly increased as students were positioned back in their ZPD.

A major question that is asked when determining the impact of this instructional method is "How does one measure the impact of a linguistically informed language study on students' confidence and critical awareness?" Using the methods discussed in previous chapters, the following pages reveal my results of analyses on students' modality during their oral protocol analyses. By conducting a hedging analysis, I gained insight into students' confidence in their coding, interpretations, and critical observations in order to show the curriculum's impact.

However, before looking at the data, it is important to know the context in which these analyses were conducted. First, multiple protocol analyses were performed with each focal student regarding each text during each stage of the language study. For example, focal students conducted their protocol analysis interview on the *Harry Potter* passage during the *Harry Potter* stage of the curriculum. Each protocol analysis interview was conducted privately, one on one, in my classroom to maximize student comfort. As previously stated, the teacher–student relationship might have caused an increase in hedging, but, if that was the case, it was consistent with each focal student, as they all performed their protocol analyses in the same environment. I would also like to point out that I have knowledge of students' normal use of modality/hedging, based on my insider perspective and daily interactions with them. This allowed me to recognize deviations from their normal speech patterns, which might be more difficult for an outsider to identify. Also, as stated earlier, it is important to remember that the language choices uttered in these responses were spontaneous, making their interpretation different than those we might make in an academic paper.

One final thing before we dive in: the goal of using discourse analysis in my curriculum is less about being nit-picky and getting students to code correctly and more about getting students to think about how they can use their coding to reveal an author or character's attitude to bring meaning and deeper understanding to the text. The ultimate goal is using discourse analysis tools to provide students with the metalanguage to analyze texts. For this reason, I focus less on critiquing *how* my students code language and more on *what they learn* from how they choose to code it. I might get some criticism for this, but the purpose of using discourse analysis in this curriculum is to assist students in achieving specific academic and social goals—specifically, understanding the purpose of specific language choices. In all, I am more interested in what students infer from their coding and how they use it to make meaning and grow in language awareness than assessing whether or not their coding is one hundred percent accurate according to linguists and scholars. They are kids, after all, not specialists. We will not be ripping them apart for "doing it wrong." On this issue, as Kuiil from *The Mandalorian* says, "I have spoken."

The goal of using discourse analysis in my curriculum is less about being nit-picky and getting students to code correctly and more about getting students to think about how they can use their coding to reveal an author or character's attitude to bring meaning and deeper understanding to the text.

Protocol Analysis Passages and Sample Interview

First, I want to provide a visualization of these one-on-one interviews and the texts students were analyzing. Therefore, I have included the excerpts from each text in the curriculum cycle—*Harry Potter*, *Othello*, and Obama's speech—that the focal students used discourse analysis tools to analyze (Tables 6.1–6.3).

TABLE 6.1. Excerpt of *Harry Potter and the Sorcerer's Stone* Passage

Harry's partner was Seamus Finnigan (which was a relief, because Neville had been trying to catch his eye). Ron, however, was to be working with Hermione Granger. It was hard to tell whether Ron or Hermione was angrier about this. She hadn't spoken to either of them since the day Harry's broomstick had arrived.

. . .

"*Wingardium Leviosa!*" he shouted, waving his long arms like a windmill.

"You're saying it wrong," Harry heard Hermione snap. "It's Wing-*gar*-dium Levi-*o*-sa, make the 'gar' nice and long."

"You do it, then, if you're so clever," Ron snarled.

. . .

Ron was in a very bad mood by the end of the class.

"It's no wonder no one can stand her," he said to Harry as they pushed their way into the crowded corridor. "She's a nightmare, honestly."

Someone knocked into Harry as they hurried past him. It was Hermione. Harry caught a glimpse of her face—and was startled to see that she was in tears.

"I think she heard you."

"So?" said Ron, but he looked a bit uncomfortable. "She must've noticed she's got no friends."

Hermione didn't turn up for the next class and wasn't seen all afternoon. On their way down to the Great Hall for the Hallowe'en feast, Harry and Ron overheard Parvati Patil telling her friend Lavender that Hermione was crying in the girls' bathroom and wanted to be left alone. Ron looked still more awkward at this, but a moment later they had entered the Great Hall, where the Hallowe'en decorations put Hermione out of their minds.

Excerpt source: *Harry Potter and the Sorcerer's Stone* (Rowling, 1997, pp. 171–172).

TABLE 6.2. *Olthello* Passage

<table>
<tr>
<td>
CASSIO
Dear general, I never gave you cause.
OTHELLO
I do believe it, and I ask your pardon.
Will you, I pray, demand that demi-devil
Why he hath thus ensnared my soul and body?
IAGO
Demand me nothing: what you know, you know:
From this time forth I never will speak word.
LODOVICO
What, not to pray?
GRATIANO
Torments will open your lips.
OTHELLO
Well, thou dost best.
LODOVICO
Sir, you shall understand what hath befall'n,
Which, as I think, you know not. Here is a letter
Found in the pocket of the slain Roderigo;
And here another: the one of them imports
The death of Cassio to be undertook by Roderigo.
OTHELLO
O villain!
CASSIO
Most heathenish and most gross!
LODOVICO
Now here's another discontented paper,
Found in his pocket too; and this, it seems,
Roderigo meant to have sent this damned villain;
But that belike Iago in the interim
Came in and satisfied him.
OTHELLO
O the pernicious caitiff!
How came you, Cassio, by that handkerchief
That was my wife's?
CASSIO
I found it in my chamber:
And he himself confess'd but even now
That there he dropp'd it for a special purpose.
Which wrought to his desire.
</td>
<td>
OTHELLO
O fool! fool! fool!
CASSIO
There is besides in Roderigo's letter,
How he upbraids Iago, that he made him
Brave me upon the watch; whereon it came
That I was cast: and even but now he spake,
After long seeming dead, Iago hurt him,
Iago set him on.
LODOVICO
You must forsake this room, and go with us:
Your power and your command is taken off,
And Cassio rules in Cyprus. For this slave,
If there be any cunning cruelty
That can torment him much and hold him long,
It shall be his. You shall close prisoner rest,
Till that the nature of your fault be known
To the Venetian state. Come, bring him away.
OTHELLO
Soft you; a word or two before you go.
I have done the state some service, and they know't.
No more of that. I pray you, in your letters,
When you shall these unlucky deeds relate,
Speak of me as I am; nothing extenuate,
Nor set down aught in malice: then must you speak
Of one that loved not wisely but too well;
Of one not easily jealous, but being wrought
Perplex'd in the extreme; of one whose hand,
Like the base Indian, threw a pearl away
Richer than all his tribe; of one whose subdued eyes,
Albeit unused to the melting mood,
Drop tears as fast as the Arabian trees
Their medicinal gum. Set you down this;
And say besides, that in Aleppo once,
Where a malignant and a turban'd Turk
Beat a Venetian and traduced the state,
I took by the throat the circumcised dog,
And smote him, thus. (*Stabs himself.*)
</td>
</tr>
</table>

Excerpt source: Shakespeare (ca. 1604/2002, 5.2.258–355).

TABLE 6.3. Obama Passage

We will, however, relentlessly confront violent extremists who pose a grave threat to our security—because we reject the same thing that people of all faiths reject: the killing of innocent men, women, and children. And it is my first duty as president to protect the American people. The situation in Afghanistan demonstrates America's goals and our need to work together. Over seven years ago, the United States pursued al-Qaeda and the Taliban with broad international support. We did not go by choice; we went because of necessity. I'm aware that there's still some who would question or even justify the events of 9/11. But let us be clear: al-Qaeda killed nearly 3,000 people on that day. The victims were innocent men, women, and children from America and many other nations who had done nothing to harm anybody. And yet alQaeda chose to ruthlessly murder these people, claimed credit for the attack, and even now states their determination to kill on a massive scale. They have affiliates in many countries and are trying to expand their reach. These are not opinions to be debated; these are facts to be dealt with. Now, make no mistake: we do not want to keep our troops in Afghanistan. We see no military—we seek no military bases there. It is agonizing for America to lose our young men and women. It is costly and politically difficult to continue this conflict.

Excerpt source: Obama (2009, paras. 36–38).

Each of these excerpts is what I like to call "meaty," meaning there is a lot to dig into and analyze, allowing students multiple opportunities to engage with the text. Next, I want to provide you with an example of an interview with one focal student, Clara, so that you can witness the organic and student-led nature of conversation. This protocol analysis interview (see Table 6.4) was done during the *Harry Potter* phase, and Clara's use of modal words is coded for future discussion.

TABLE 6.4. Clara's *Harry Potter* Protocol Analysis

Coding:

- high ("must," "ought to," "need to," "has to," "is to") = *italics*
- medium ("will," "would," "shall," "should") = <u>underlined</u>
- low ("may," "might," "can," "could") = **bold**

AMS: Okay, um, thanks for participating. I appreciate it. I want to remind you that your name is not going to be used and will be replaced with a pseudonym that we've chosen. What I'd like you to do is choose a section of this passage on which you would like to do an SFL analysis. As you work, I'd like you to talk out loud what you are thinking. Um, I'll ask you to do an appraisal, identification, and modality analysis. If I ask you any questions during your analysis, don't assume that you have done something wrong. I am simply probing for a deeper explanation to guide my own understanding as to how you use this analysis tool. Um, if at any time you feel uncomfortable, just say so and we will stop the recording. Is that okay with you?
C: Yes.
AMS: Do you have any questions?
C: No.
AMS: Okay. You can have all your notes out if you like. You don't have to do it without your notes.
C: So, first off, I am going to do identification. And, at first, you notice that "she" *is* used multiple, for times, which you, um, I think denotes the fact that, in this paragraph, Ron was trying to show how she *is* being dehumanized, and the fact that Ron, um, *is* showing her as more annoying. And "she" *is*, um, used one, two, three, four, five—five times within that short passage, and it shows how, um, Ron basically *is* saying that, through using "she," it*'s* not like she *is* not a person, she*'s*, she*'s* being dehumanized in the fact that, like, he *is* upset with her because she was trying to be a know-it-all and trying to tell him how to do the spell correctly, and, in the end, she did it right, but he was upset because he was wrong and she was right, but he feels that she *is* always condescending on him. So, and then, um, her name "Hermione" *is* used once, and, um, I think that also signified, along with the "she," that she *is* not denoted in a good connotation in this sense, and the "nightmare" shows a depreciation of her personality and how she annoys the boys instead of being supported by the boys and the characters, and she *is* kind of an outcast. Um, "her" kind of goes along with "she," in the fact that she *is* not, like, significant, and "someone" does not automatically identify who it was. It*'s* kind of showing how she *is* not important. Um...
AMS: So, in that passage, would you just do Hermione or would you do Ron and Harry too?
C: Um, I just did Hermione. I guess you **could** do Ron and Harry too, because, by doing Ron and Harry, you<u>'ll</u> see that Harry is seen at least three times with his name, which shows that Hermione *is* being singly outcast, and even Ron's name shows up, um, twice, which *is* more than Hermione, which shows that, like, he*'s*, they're separated from her. She *is* outcast from them. And it **might** be a sexism thing that *is* found within the novel as well. Um, um... you **could** do modality on "she must have noticed that she's got no friends" and "no friends" *is* absolute, like, when he said, "no one could stand her"; I mean, she *has* no one, literally no one in the school likes her. And "must have" um...
AMS: Where is that on the polarity scale?
C: It *is* definite. It *is* absolute. It shows how, like, she *has* to... it*'s* not an option for her. It *is* apparent to her that nobody likes her, which again sets her apart from everyone else. And then, um, appraisal analysis...
AMS: If you are going to code your appraisal, can you just write your code out in the margin?
C: Yes. Okay.
AMS: Now, when you do appraisal, do you go through and do all the affects, and then go through and do all the judgments, and then go through and do all the appreciations? Or, do you do them all at once, as you go?
C: I usually do them all at once, because I<u>'ll</u> be, like, "Oh, that *is* suddenly an affect because it shows how she *has* a feeling toward someone."

AMS: Okay. Now show me how you do that.
C: Okay, um, well, in the first sentence "Ron was in a very," "very" *is* an appreciation word, because it show the degree to which he was in a bad mood. "Bad mood," I guess, **could** be an affect word, because it *is* showing the feelings he *is* having toward, like, I guess, everything at the moment.
AMS: It is how he feels.
C: Yeah, how he feels. And then, judgment... none for that sentence. And then, okay, you **could** do appraisal on this one too, and, um, "nightmare" would be a judgment, because it *is* showing criticism toward Hermione and how she *is*. And "no one" would be an appreciation, because it *is* showing the value of how no one can stand her. And the affect words would be, um, I think "pushed" *is* kind of an affect word, because, even though it seems like they are going through the corridor and it *is* just crowded, it *is* kind of denoting how Ron *is* angry at the moment. She **could** have used any other word in that place, but she *is* "pushed" to signify maybe the anger underneath to show the tone of this passage. Um, well, I mean, this really doesn't really go along with any of the analysis, but it goes along with one of the articles that talked about feminism and how they show irrational emotion about things, but it *is*n't really irrational. It *is* showing how Hermione *is* having a somewhat rational response to people making fun of her, because it *is* usually... when someone makes fun of you, it generally hurts your feelings, so her response *is* rational, so that kind of disclaims the author's idea that females are seen as irrational throughout the novel.
AMS: So you are saying that it is normal, if someone called you a "nightmare," she would be upset.
C: Yeah. Or, at least, I would be. And, um, it would show how she *has* a calm reaction to that.
AMS: So are you coding this as affect, judgment, or appreciation?
C: Um, "She was in tears"... I guess you **could** do it as affect, because it *is* showing her feelings.
AMS: Um-hum.
C: How they're feeling toward her made her feelings come out and how she feels negative toward this. Um, um... oh yeah, it goes along, too, with the boys sectioning her out from everybody, because, I think, in one of the articles, we talked about the girls separated from the boys, or whatever, and how the boys always show, um, Hermione being as irrational, or whatever, and their being justified, but it actually shows how Ron was irrational, in the sense, because all Hermione was trying to do was help him, yet he got upset in the end, and he, um, he said mean things; he acted irrationally, and he said mean things to her, and it made her cry. So it kind of shows how, um, the "flip"... how the boys were, um, somewhat being, like, judgmental and rude to Hermione and how it undertones how the boys are being irrational in this sense. So I think that, again, um, it denotes how Ron, Hermione, and Harry **can** all act irrationally sometimes. Okay.
AMS: Do you see anything else?
C: Um...
AMS: Now, the stuff that you saw, was this stuff that you picked up the first time you read it or only after you did the analysis?
C: Um, well, I remember, like, I remember feeling bad for Hermione and thinking that it *was*n't fair for them to outcast her and that she *was*n't really trying to be obnoxious. She *was* just trying to help. But I don't really catch how, like, it showed the feministic view and how it showed how Rowling was sort of characterizing the characters in this way until the SFL.
AMS: And which one did you think most helped you identify that? The identification, appraisal, or the modality?
C: Well, I think the identification helped a lot in this passage because, um, if you used, like, if you look at the pronoun used and the proper noun use in their names, you **can** automatically see the attitude toward Hermione in this. You **can** see that she *is* not looked upon favorably in this passage.
AMS: Good. Thanks.

Table 6.5 shows part of the transcript and is coded for a hedging analysis.

TABLE 6.5. Hedging Analysis of Clara's *Harry Potter* Protocol Analysis

Coding:

- subjectivity markers ("I guess," "I don't know") = *italics*
- tentativeness ("kind of," "probably," "almost") = <u>underlined</u>
- pragmatic idioms ("maybe") = **bold**

AMS: Okay, um, thanks for participating. I appreciate it. I want to remind you that your name is not going to be used and will be replaced with a pseudonym that we've chosen. What I'd like you to do is choose a section of this passage on which you would like to do an SFL analysis. As you work, I'd like you to talk out loud what you are thinking. Um, I'll ask you to do an appraisal, identification, and modality analysis. If I ask you any questions during your analysis, don't assume that you have done something wrong. I am simply probing for a deeper explanation to guide my own understanding as to how you use this analysis tool. Um, if at any time you feel uncomfortable, just say so and we will stop the recording. Is that okay with you?
C: Yes.
AMS: Do you have any questions?
C: No.
AMS: Okay. You can have all your notes out if you like. You don't have to do it without your notes.
C: So, first off, I am going to do identification. And, at first, you notice that "she" is used multiple for times, which you, um, I think denotes the fact that, in this paragraph, Ron was trying to show how she is being dehumanized, and the fact that Ron, um, is showing her as more annoying. And "she" is, um, used one, two, three, four, five—five times within that short passage, and it shows how, um, Ron basically is saying that, through using "she," it's not, like, she is not a person, she's, she's being dehumanized in the fact that, like, he is upset with her because she was trying to be a know-it-all and trying to tell him how to do the spell correctly, and, in the end, she did it right, but he was upset because he was wrong and she was right, but he feels that she is always condescending on him. So, and then, um, her name "Hermione" is used once, and, um, I think that also signified, along with the "she," that she is not denoted in a good connotation in this sense, and the "nightmare" shows a depreciation of her personality and how she annoys the boys instead of being supported by the boys and the characters, and she is <u>kind of</u> an outcast. Um, "her" <u>kind of</u> goes along with "she," in the fact that she is not, like, significant, and "someone" does not automatically identify who it was. It's <u>kind of</u> showing how she is not important. Um. . .
AMS: So, in that passage, would you just do Hermione or would you do Ron and Harry too?
C: Um, I just did Hermione. *I guess* you could do Ron and Harry too, because, by doing Ron and Harry, you'll see that Harry is seen at least three times with his name, which shows that Hermione is being singly outcast, and even Ron's name shows up, um, twice, which is more than Hermione, which shows that, like, he's, they're separated from her. She is outcast from them. And it might be a sexism thing that is found within the novel as well. Um, um. . . then you could do modality on "she must have noticed that she's got no friends" and "no friends" is absolute, like, when he said, "no one could stand her"; I mean, she has no one, literally no one in the school likes her. And "must have" um. . .
AMS: Where is that on the polarity scale?
C: It is definite. It is absolute. It shows how, like, she has to. . . it's not an option for her. It is apparent to her that nobody likes her, which again sets her apart from everyone else. And then, um, appraisal analysis. . .
AMS: If you are going to code your appraisal, can you just write your code out in the margin?
C: Yes. Okay.
AMS: Now, when you do appraisal, do you go through and do all the affects, and then go through and do all the judgments, and then go through and do all the appreciations? Or do you do them all at once, as you go?

C: I usually do them all at once, because I'll be, like, "Oh, that is suddenly an affect, because it shows how she has a feeling toward someone."
AMS: Okay. Now show me how you do that.
C: Okay, um, well, in the first sentence "Ron was in a very," "very" is an appreciation word, because it shows the degree to which he was in a bad mood. "Bad mood," *I guess*, could be an affect word, because it is showing the feelings he is having toward, like, *I guess*, everything at the moment.
AMS: It is how he feels.
C: Yeah, how he feels. And then, judgment... none for that sentence. And then, okay, you could do appraisal on this one too, and, um, "nightmare" would be a judgment, because it is showing criticism toward Hermione and how she is. And "no one" would be an appreciation, because it is showing the value of how no one can stand her. And the affect words would be, um, I think "pushed" is <u>kind of</u> an affect word, because, even though it seems like they are going through the corridor and it is just crowded, it is <u>kind of</u> denoting how Ron is angry at the moment. She could have used any other word in that place, but she is "pushed" to signify **maybe** the anger underneath to show the tone of this passage. Um, well, I mean, this really doesn't really go along with any of the analysis, but it goes along with one of the articles that talked about feminism and how they show irrational emotion about things, but it isn't really irrational. It is showing how Hermione is having a somewhat rational response to people making fun of her because it is usually... when someone makes fun of you, it generally hurts your feelings, so her response is rational, so that <u>kind of</u> disclaims the author's idea that females were seen as irrational throughout the novel.
AMS: So, you are saying that it is normal, if someone called you a "nightmare," she would be upset.
C: Yeah. Or, at least, I would be. And, um, it would show how she has a calm reaction to that.
AMS: So, are you coding this is affect, judgment, or appreciation?
C: Um, "She was in tears"... *I guess* you could do it as affect, because it is showing her feelings
AMS: Um-hum.
C: How they're feeling toward her made her feelings come out and how she feels negative toward this. Um, um... oh yeah, it goes along too with the boys sectioning her out from everybody, because, I think, in one of the articles, we talked about the girls separated from the boys, or whatever, and how the boys always show, um, Hermione being as irrational, or whatever, and their being justified, but it actually shows how Ron was irrational, in the sense, because all Hermione was trying to do was help him, yet he got upset in the end and he, um, he said mean things; he acted irrationally, and he said mean things to her, and it made her cry. So, it <u>kind of</u> shows how, um, the flip... how the boys were, um, somewhat being, like, judgmental and rude to Hermione and how it undertones how the boys are being irrational in this sense. So I think that, again, um, it denotes how Ron, Hermione, and Harry can all act irrationally sometimes. Okay.
AMS: Do you see anything else?
C: Um...
AMS: Now, the stuff that you saw, was this stuff that you picked up the first time you read it or only after you did the analysis?
C: Um, well, I remember, like, I remember feeling bad for Hermione and thinking that it wasn't fair for them to outcast her and that she wasn't really trying to be obnoxious. She was just trying to help. But I don't really catch how, like, it showed the feministic view and how it showed how Rowling was sort of characterizing the characters in this way until the SFL.
AMS: And which one did you think most helped you identify that? The identification, appraisal, or the modality?
C: Well, I think the identification helped a lot in this passage because, um, if you used, like, if you look at the pronoun used and the proper noun use in their names, you can automatically see the attitude toward Hermione in this. You can see that she is not looked upon favorably in this passage.

AMS: Good. Thanks.

By looking at these examples, I hope that you can better understand the interview and coding process that took place with each text and each focal student in order to garner the results discussed below.

Modality in Students' Protocol Analysis Interviews

As previously stated, Halliday focuses on select verbs and where they fall on a polarity scale of *high*, *medium*, and *low*:

- high—must, ought to, need to, has to, is to
- medium—will, would, shall, should
- low—may, might, can, could.

(Halliday & Matthieseen, 1985/2014, p. 363)

Therefore, when conducting a modality analysis of students' verbal protocol analysis, as they articulated their thought process while performing an analysis, I coded each transcript according to Halliday's scale to determine students' commitment to their observations when conducting and analyzing a discourse analysis (see Figure 6.1).

This modality analysis can help quantify the success of the implemented spiral curriculum and the growth of students in an area that is typically hard to measure, due to its abstract and personal nature: confidence and critical awareness. As students learned complex concepts and dealt with more complicated texts, they showed their growing feelings of confidence through their increased use of high modality words and decreased use of low modality verbs, when such modal operators were appropriate. The percentage of high modality words used increased by 7.75 percent from *Harry Potter* to *Othello* and 6.9 percent from *Othello* to Obama's speech for a total increase of 14.65 percent. On the other hand, the use of low modality words decreased by 10.32 percent from *Harry Potter* to *Othello* and by 2.28 percent from *Othello* to Obama's speech for a total of 12.60 percent (see Figure 6.1). Because high modality words generally show assurance in one's opinion and low modality words indicate a distancing or lack of obligation to one's response (Fairclough, 1992b), it can be surmised that these results show students' increased comfort with SFL and CDA as they were scaffolded from one text to the next.

Tyler was a focal student whose protocol analysis transcripts illustrated this progression. During his *Harry Potter* protocol analysis, 54.76 percent of Tyler's verbs were highly modal, 19.05 percent were medium, and 26.19 percent were low. In his *Othello* protocol analysis, 63.26 percent of the verbs he used were

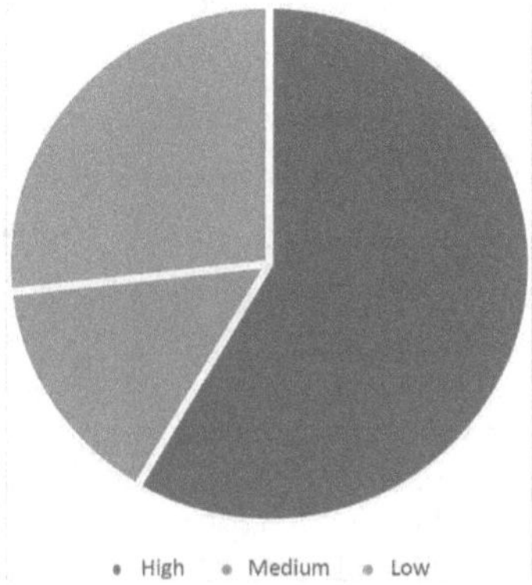

Modality Distribution in *Harry Potter* Protocol Analysis

Modality	Frequency	%
High	382	58.41
Medium	97	14.83
Low	175	26.76
Total	*654*	*100*

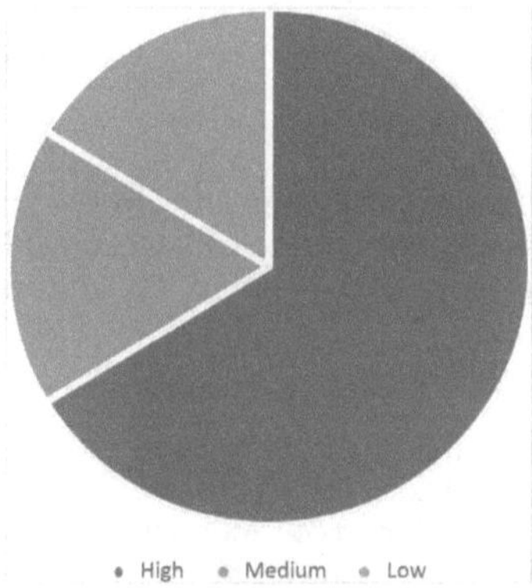

Modality Distribution in *Othello* Protocol Analysis

Modality	Frequency	%
High	569	66.16
Medium	151	17.56
Low	140	16.28
Total	*860*	*100*

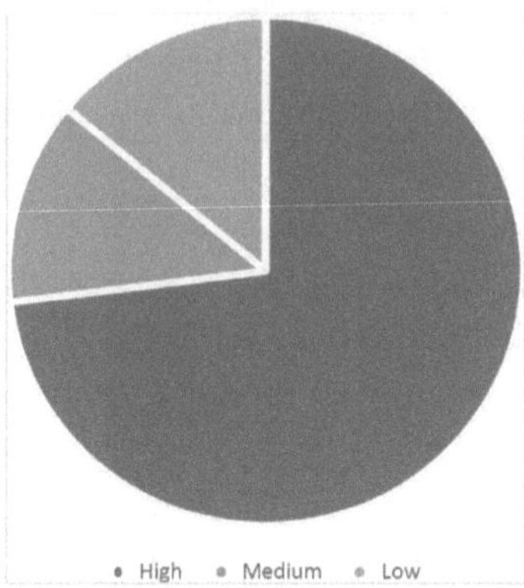

Modality Distribution in Obama Speech Protocol Analyses

Modality	Frequency	%
High	850	73.02
Medium	151	12.97
Low	163	14.01
Total	*1,164*	*100*

FIGURE 6.1. Frequency of *high, medium,* and *low* modal operators per text.

highly modal, 20.19 percent were medium, and 16.34 percent were low. His Obama protocol analysis revealed that 74.26 percent of his verbs were highly modal, 17.82 percent were medium, and 7.9 percent were low. When comparing the transcripts of his analysis of each text (Table 6.6), you can see Tyler's growing confidence with his linguistic and analysis skills and his ability to critically analyze them.

TABLE 6.6. Examples of Tyler's Modality per Text

Text	Quote from Transcript
Harry Potter	"Dying to try"—that is[a] defiantly affect, and it is showing what the characters are wanting to do. You could say that this is a judgment on Neville. So the word "relief" is kind of a judgment on Neville. For some reason, Harry does not want to be a partner with Neville. And you could also say that it was an affect for Harry, because Harry was relieved, and he didn't want to be his partner, it looks like. (Tyler, *Harry Potter* protocol analysis, lines 8–11)
Othello	The next thing I would label would be the "villain." I would actually label it two things. I would label it a judgment. . .[b] it is not his name, it is. . . you could call it an identification, but it is a label that Othello was placing on to Iago. And a negative label at that. "Heathenish and gross"—I get a picture of, you know, way back in the day, when the Bible was being written, that "heathenish," really, when it comes to mind, and just like an outcast, not welcome, not wanted. It is very negative; and "gross" is a very negative connotation. (Tyler, *Othello* protocol analysis, lines 43–48)
Obama	And "innocent," I'm going to say, is an appreciation, because it makes the killing more extreme. You could kill a person that—quote, unquote—"deserves death," who, by law, needs to be punished, but the "innocent" obviously makes the whole situation. . . I'm going to continue actually with this entire phrase because "men, women, and children," as a whole, suggests that they want to decimate everybody and it's all-inclusive. It also shows how it affects everybody. I was going to say "duty" with the "President," but I don't get too much from that to be really honest. "President" I would definitely say is a judgment word. And he is identifying himself as the American people also. I also find it very interesting that he says that his first duty isn't to protect *all*[c] people. (Tyler, Obama protocol analysis, lines 10–17)

[a] Underlined words indicate coded modality words; [b] ellipsis indicates a pause in student dialogue; [c] *italics* indicate that the student emphasized this word.

Table 6.6 shows three examples of Tyler using analysis tools to code text and his attempts to explain his coding, what it means, and the social implication. The reason I chose these sections as examples is because they show Tyler's varied use of modality with his coding as well as his interpretation and explanation. His high modality in the use of the word "is" shows his certainty when coding affect words. Tyler seemed to be confident in finding words that express feelings. However, when he got to the word "relief," his modality changed to low ("could"), because he saw the word functioning in two ways: (1) as a social judgment on Neville, based on his own experiences in working with partners on school projects; and (2) as an affect word expressing Harry's emotions. Table 6.7 features Tyler's *Harry Potter* appraisal analysis.

TABLE 6.7. Student Work: Excerpt from Tyler's *Harry Potter* Appraisal Analysis

<table>
<tr><th>Student Coding</th><th colspan="3">Student Chart of Coding</th></tr>
<tr><td rowspan="4">On Hallowe'en morning they woke to the delicious smell of baking pumpkin wafting through the corridors. Even better, Professor Flitwick . . . put the class into pairs to practice. Harry's partner was Seamus Finnigan (which was a relief, because Neville had been trying to catch his eye). Ron, however, was to be working with Hermione Granger. It was hard to tell whether Ron or Hermione was angrier about this. She hadn't spoken to either of them since the day Harry's broomstick had arrived.</td><td>Appraisal</td><td>Positive</td><td>Negative</td></tr>
<tr><td>Affect</td><td>relief</td><td>hard to tell; angrier; hadn't spoken to either of them</td></tr>
<tr><td>Judgment</td><td>Professor; partner</td><td></td></tr>
<tr><td>Appreciation</td><td>delicious; even better</td><td></td></tr>
</table>

Coding: affect words are in **bold**; judgment words are underlined; appreciation words are in *italics*. This coding is consistent throughout the study.

Excerpt source: Rowling (1997, pp. 170–171).

Here, Tyler recognized that the word "relief" indicated something about the power relationship between Harry and Neville; however, his use of low modality shows his uncertainty in making this observation. Similarly, he noted how one word—"relief"—might possibly be coded as two attitudes, both judgment and affect, but, since he was new to discourse analysis, his low modality might have showed his struggle with coding it as both or determining if the word fit best as affect or judgment.

When coding words during his appraisal analysis of *Othello* (see Table 6.8), you can see, through his use of "would," a medium modality word, that he was more comfortable with coding the word "villain" as two things; however, while he was mostly sure that "villain" was a judgment, he was less certain that it could also be used as an identification, as indicated by the low modal verb "could." It seems as though he is contemplating this new concept, and his low modality indicated he sees multiple possibilities for his response.

TABLE 6.8. Student Work: Excerpt from Tyler's *Othello* Appraisal Analysis

<table>
<tr><th>Student Coding</th><th colspan="3">Student Chart of Coding</th></tr>
<tr><td rowspan="5">Cassio
Dear general, I never gave you cause.
Othello
I do believe it, and I ask your pardon.
Will you, I pray, demand that demi-devil
Why he hath thus ensnared my soul and body?
Iago
Demand me nothing: what you know, you know:
From this time forth I never will speak word.
Lodovico
What, not to pray?
Gratiano
Torments will open your lips.
Othello
Well, thou dost best.
Lodovico
Sir, you shall understand what hath befall'n,
Which, as I think, you know not. Here is a letter
Found in the pocket of the slain Roderigo;
And here another: the one of them imports
The death of Cassio to be undertook by Roderigo.
Othello
O <u>villain</u>!
Cassio
Most heathenish and most gross!
Lodovico
Now here's another discontented paper,
Found in his pocket too; and this, it seems,
Roderigo meant to have sent this damned <u>villain</u>;
But that belike Iago in the interim
Came in and satisfied him.
Othello
O the <u>pernicious caitiff</u>!
How came you, Cassio, by that handkerchief
That was my wife's?
Cassio
I found it in my chamber:
And he himself confess'd but even now
That there he dropp'd it for a special purpose
Which wrought to his desire.</td><td>Appraisal</td><td>Positive</td><td>Negative</td></tr>
<tr><td>Affect</td><td>pardon</td><td>demand; demi-devil; ensnared; torments will open your lips; understand; slain; death; villain (× 2); heathenish</td></tr>
<tr><td>Judgment</td><td></td><td>villain (× 2); pernicious caitiff</td></tr>
<tr><td>Appreciation</td><td>dear</td><td></td></tr>
<tr><td colspan="3"></td></tr>
</table>

Excerpt source: Shakespeare (ca. 1604/2002, 5.2.259–285)

While Tyler was still hesitant to code a word as two things, in this example, he was questioning how the word "villain" fit into two separate analyses: appraisal and identification. This was a more complex thought process than that of coding a word twice using the same coding tool as shown in his *Harry Potter* example. Therefore, while he still used a low modality verb when coding, he used it when contemplating a more complex concept. Similarly, like in *Harry Potter* where he used his previous school experiences to assist in coding the word "relief," he did the same in *Othello* with "heathenish and gross." Tyler used his knowledge of religious discourse, an area in which he felt he had some expertise as he used the high modal word "is," to explain how he interpreted the purpose of that particular language—to connote hell and damnation.

Finally, in his Obama protocol analysis (see Table 6.9), you can see Tyler's confidence in his appraisal analysis through his use of high modal verbs. He only used a low modal verb "could" when providing a hypothetical example as to why the use of the word "innocent" evoked emotion, which is an example of a low modality word being used in a way that did not indicate uncertainty or distancing from his opinion, showing the complex nature of a modality analyses, as low modality is appropriate in such contexts.

TABLE 6.9. Student Work: Excerpt from Tyler's Obama Appraisal Analysis

<table>
<tr><th>Student Coding</th><th colspan="3">Student Chart of Coding</th></tr>
<tr><td rowspan="4">We will, however, relentlessly confront <u>violent</u> extremists who pose a grave threat to our security—because we reject the same thing that people of all faiths reject: the killing of innocent men, women, and children. And it is my first duty as <u>president</u> to protect the <u>American people</u>. The <u>situation</u> <u>in Afghanistan</u> demonstrates America's goals and our need to work together. Over seven years ago, the United States pursued <u>al-Qaeda</u> and the <u>Taliban</u> with broad international support. We did not go by choice; we went because of necessity. I'm aware that there's still some who would question or even justify the events of 9/11. But let us be clear: <u>al-Qaeda</u> killed nearly 3,000 people <u>on that day</u>.</td><td>Appraisal</td><td>Positive</td><td>Negative</td></tr>
<tr><td>Affect</td><td>security; men, women, and children; protect; support; choice; necessity; clear</td><td>confront; violent; extremists; grave; threat; rejection; killing; situation; pursued; alQaeda; Taliban; necessity; aware; question; justify; 9/11; killed; on that day</td></tr>
<tr><td>Judgment</td><td>President; American people</td><td>violent; situation in Afghanistan; alQaeda, Taliban; on that day</td></tr>
<tr><td>Appreciation</td><td>first; innocent; broad international</td><td>relentlessly</td></tr>
</table>

Excerpt source: Obama (2009, paras. 36–37).

Unlike his *Othello* protocol analysis, in which Tyler used low modal verbs when suggesting that the word "villain" could appear in both his appraisal and identification analysis, here, he used medium and high modal verbs, suggesting his confidence in his recognition that a word can play multiple roles in constructing meaning. In addition, his final sentence in this example, "I also find it very interesting that he says that his first duty <u>is</u>n't to protect *all* people," showed absolutely no hesitancy to critically evaluate not what was in the text but what was missing—a major goal of CDA (see Fairclough, 1995). The fact that no low modality words or hedging words appeared in this statement suggested confidence in his ability to not only code language but also to critique its social meaning. In fact, he is so confident that he spontaneously used boosters such as "definitely" and "obviously"—language choices we do not see in his discussion of *Harry Potter* or *Othello*, showing he is fully committed to his interpretation.

Hedging in Students' Protocol Analysis Interviews

Based on Fairclough's (1992b) reasons for hedging, I coded students' protocol analyses using Wilamová's (2005) categories to determine their degree of confidence in performing discourse analysis and analyzing texts using SFL analysis tools. When coding, I found that students did not utilize all categories but frequently hedged their responses using *subjectivity markers* ("I guess," "I don't know"), *tentativeness* ("kind of," "probably," "almost"), and *pragmatic idioms* ("maybe"). Therefore, I limited coding to frequent hedges that fell within those categories. Table 6.10 shows the frequency of such hedges per text.

Table 6.10 indicates that the highest frequency of subjectivity markers occurred in students' protocol analysis of *Othello*, although not by a significant margin. The highest percentage of hedges was tentative markers, showing students' possible desire to be vague in their analyses of all texts. However, there was a substantial increase of tentative hedges in students' Obama protocol analysis compared to those of the other texts. On the other hand, the use of pragmatic idioms was comparable for all texts. Table 6.10 also shows how students used the most hedging devices during their Obama analysis, followed by *Harry Potter*, and the least during their *Othello* analysis. This evidence was counter to my predictions (that hedging would decrease overall as they progress through the spiraled curriculum). More on this later.

During my coding of hedges during the interpretation stage, I coded hedges related to students' certainty of what the word or phrase meant based on their prior knowledge and personal experiences to make sense of the features of/

TABLE 6.10. Frequency of Hedging Devices per Text

Text	*Harry Potter*		*Othello*		Obama Speech	
Hedging Device	Frequency	%	Frequency	%	Frequency	%
Subjectivity markers	44	33.34	46	35.66	38	27.74
Tentativeness	84	63.63	79	61.24	94	68. 61
Pragmatic idioms	4	3.03	4	3.10	5	3.65
Total	*132*	*100%*	*129*	*100%*	*137*	*100%*

patterns in texts by seeing them as a product of larger discourses (Fairclough, 1992b). Based on her previous knowledge of the language used during arguments, Winnie hedged during her interpretation of her *Othello* identification chart saying, "I guess the identification shows more of the accusing that is going on here" (Winnie, *Othello* protocol analysis).

Winnie was uncertain of what the language in the identification chart was saying, not her coding of the language. When coding hedges during the explanation stage, I looked for students' uncertainty of their denaturalization of language and recognition of what that language meant in a social context. For example, when explaining his appraisal chart of Obama's speech, particularly his use of the words "facts" and "opinions," Parvesh stated, "while he is doing this he's talking to his audience . . . he is kind of trying to persuade them that it was a good idea . . . so when he is talking about these 'facts' he has to use all these negative affect words and negative appreciation words to describe the extremists like 'threat,' 'killing,' 'killed,' 'murders,' and that way the audience knows that al-Qaeda is bad" (Parvesh, Obama protocol analysis).

In this example, Parvesh articulated his hunch that Obama is using negative affect and appreciation words when discussing al-Qaeda, and he explained how and *why*. In essence, he tentatively expressed his recognition of the social purpose of the language chosen in this speech: to illicit a specific emotion from the audience to get them to agree with Obama's argument. While I did code for students' problematization of language, students' questioning of how language was perpetuated or challenging of unjust language was rare during students' protocol analysis. I concluded that this was because most problematization occurs during dialogue (Freire, 1970/1986), which is a social event and happened during classroom discussion. Since a protocol analysis is an activity focused on the thoughts of one person, dialogue rarely took place, limiting students' problematization of language.

However, Tyler showed a wonderful example of problematizing language despite a lack of dialogue when he discussed his identification coding of people in Afghanistan. He stated, "You hear that name and it is almost always associated with violence and evil . . . That is how he labels them. So those names really bring up emotion. And I think that we look over that really easily because we are just labeling them a group of people" (Tyler, Obama protocol analysis). While uncertain of his generalization of "always," as indicated by his hedge "almost," Tyler was challenging language that aims to stereotype a group of people. This example shows the complexity of a hedging analysis, because Tyler was conscious that generalizations can be dangerous and lead to stereotypes as they do not always recognize individual experiences. In this case, Tyler's hedge has positive implications: by avoiding absolute statements, Tyler showed his recognition that not all people associate Afghanistan with violence and evil, but that many Americans do based on the media coverage regarding the country.

Hedging in Harry Potter *Protocol Analyses*

Through creating Table 6.11, I was able to review my transcripts for patterns that might provide insight into the meaning of the results. The discussion below focuses on each text and utilizes these data to explain students' insecurity in various stages of their analysis as indicated by their hedges.

As Table 6.11 indicates, students used 132 total hedging devices during their protocol analyses of *Harry Potter.* After looking at the stages in which these devices were used, the increased number of hedges during the description stage made sense in context of the spiraled curriculum. The analysis showed that students desired to distance themselves from their responses as they were still learning how to use discourse analysis tools and were therefore uncertain of their own ability to code words as well as to interpret and explain their coding.

Specifically, students hesitated when claiming that a particular word or phrase should be coded, possibly showing their uncertainty with their new SFL knowledge and therefore distancing themselves from their decision. Hence, in the case of this text, much of the hedging occurred in the description and interpretation stage of the CDA process. Looking at Rothery and Stenglin's (1994) teaching and learning cycle (see also Figure 4.5 in Chapter 4), students were in the *deconstruction* stage, still classifying language choices. For example, as Clara attempted to code words for her appraisal analysis, she used many subjectivity markers:

> "Bad mood," I guess, could be an affect word because it is showing the feelings he is having toward, like, I guess, everything at the moment...."She was in tears"... I guess you could do it as affect, because it is showing her feelings. (Clara, *Harry Potter* protocol analysis)

TABLE 6.11. Hedges per Text for Each CDA Stage

Text	Description	Interpretation	Explanation	Problematization
Harry Potter	48	45	39	1
Othello	36	42	31	0
Obama	37	59	41	1

In this example, Clara showed her ability to identify inscribed appraisals (see Table 6.12 for Clara's *Harry Potter* appraisal analysis)—that is, words that explicitly indicate the attitude of the character or speaker (Macken-Horarik, 2003), such as "bad mood" as well as "she was in tears." However, even though her analysis was correct, Clara's lack of confidence in her coding was indicated through her use of subjectivity markers.

By using such subjectivity markers, Clara might have been attempting to tell me, the teacher, that this is how *she* read the text, and that, in fact, her assessment might be wrong because it was only a "guess." By using the word "guess" in conjunction with the low modality word "could," Clara further indicated that "other possibilities [were] available" (Christie, 2002, p. 111), protecting her ego, if I were to tell her she was incorrect, while also providing her with other answer options, if her initial "guess" was deemed as wrong.

Sandi also showed her initial uneasiness in conducting an appraisal analysis:

> Okay, so the fact that she has a "small voice" instead of . . . shows she's kind of nervous about speaking so that can be, I guess, it can be judgment, because, if she's scared to speak, then she knows she's done something wrong, so it kind of shows that she has morals that she knows she's done wrong. (Sandi, *Harry Potter* protocol analysis)

Through her subjectivity markers and tentativeness, Sandi was intentionally vague in her coding of the phrase "small voice," and for good reason, as the coding of this section was particularly subjective. Table 6.13 presents an excerpt of Sandi's *Harry Potter* appraisal analysis.

TABLE 6.12. Student Work: Excerpt from Clara's *Harry Potter* Appraisal Analysis

<table>
<tr><th rowspan="2">Student Coding</th><th colspan="3">Student Chart of Coding</th></tr>
<tr><th>Appraisal</th><th>Positive</th><th>Negative</th></tr>
<tr><td rowspan="4">Ron was in a *very* **bad mood** by the end of the class.
"It's no wonder **no one can stand her**," he said to Harry as they pushed their way into the crowded corridor, "she's a nightmare, honestly."
Someone knocked into Harry as they hurried past him. It was Hermione. Harry caught a glimpse of her face—and was startled to see that **she was in tears**.
"I think she heard you."
"So?" said Ron, but he looked a bit uncomfortable. "She must've noticed **she's got no friends**."</td><td>*Affect*</td><td></td><td>bad mood; she was in tears; no one can stand her; she's got no friends</td></tr>
<tr><td>*Judgment*</td><td></td><td>nightmare</td></tr>
<tr><td>*Appreciation*</td><td></td><td>very</td></tr>
<tr><td colspan="3"></td></tr>
</table>

Excerpt source: Rowling (1997, pp. 171–172).

TABLE 6.13. Student Work: Excerpt from Sandi's *Harry Potter* Appraisal Analysis

Student Coding	Student Chart of Coding		
Then a small voice came out of the shadows. "Please, Professor McGonagall—they were looking for me." "Miss Granger!" Hermione had managed to get to her feet at last. "I went looking for the troll because I—I thought I could deal with it on my own—you know, because I've read all about them." Ron **dropped his wand.** Hermione Granger, telling a downright lie to a teacher? . . . "Well—in that case. . ." said Professor McGonagall, staring at the three of them, "Miss Granger, you foolish girl, how could you think of tackling a mountain troll on your own?" Hermione **hung her head.** Harry was **speechless.** Hermione was the last person to do anything against the rules, and here she was, pretending she had, to get them out of trouble. It was as if Snape had started handing out sweets.	**Appraisal**	**Positive**	**Negative**
	Affect		speechless; hung her head
	Judgment		small voice; downright lie; foolish; pretending
	Appreciation		

Excerpt source: Rowling (1997, pp. 177–178).

In this section of the passage, Hermione was taking the blame for chasing the troll, effectively getting Ron and Harry off the hook. This is a lie; the troll found Hermione, and Ron and Harry chased it. Yet, in an act of friendship, she takes the blame and receives the chastisement from Professor McGonagall. In my initial coding of this passage, I coded "small" as an appreciation word, because it amplified the sound of her voice, and "small voice" as affect, because I felt as though it showed that Hermione was scared and nervous. However, Sandi's explanation of her coding of "small voice" as judgment (Table 6.13) was acceptable. While I felt that the phrase evoked emotion, Sandi stated that the emotion revealed Hermione's shame and therefore judged her as a moral person. It is this subjectivity associated with SFL that might have caused Sandi's tentative interpretation.

This type of hedging during students' appraisal analysis was consistent, as shown by Grace's question "And 'small,' that almost, um, would be an appreciation word?" (Grace, *Harry Potter* protocol analysis). In another portion that Grace analyzed, "small" was amplifying the size of the head, making it an appreciation word (see Table 6.14 for Grace's appraisal analysis). This further shows the subjectivity of coding, as, in the section Sandi analyzed, "small" also amplifies the size of her voice but the phrase "small voice" illustrates how she was feeling as well, and, according to Sandi, judged her as a moral person.

TABLE 6.14. Student Work: Excerpt from Grace's *Harry Potter* Appraisal Analysis

Student Coding	Student Chart of Coding		
It was a horrible sight. Twelve feet tall, its skin was a dull, granite gray, its great lumpy body like a boulder with its *small* bald head perched on top like a coconut. It had short legs thick as tree trunks with flat, horny feet. The smell coming from it was **incredible.** It was holding a *huge* wooden club, which dragged along the floor because its arms were so long.	**Appraisal**	**Positive**	**Negative**
	Affect		incredible
	Judgment		horrible; twelve feet tall; gray; lumpy; bald; short legs
	Appreciation		small; huge

Excerpt source: Rowling (1997, p. 174).

The fact that Grace turned her interpretation into a question further suggested her lack of confidence in her language analysis ability. However, this uncertainty was not restricted to appraisal analyses.

As Winnie showed, hedging was also apparent when conducting an identification analysis. After creating her identification chart, determining which nouns and pronouns were used for each character in the passage (see Table 6.15 for Winnie's identification chart of the *Harry Potter* passage), Winnie stated, "I guess calling the troll 'something' is also a judgment because it's kind of making it seem inhuman" (Winnie, *Harry Potter* protocol analysis, line 29).

During her interpretation of her identification analysis, Winnie was able to foresee how she would code the word "something" by realizing the social intention of using the word "thing." While this was a critical realization that moved her into the explanation stage of CDA, her hedging words decreased the gravity of the realization. In fact, it seemed that Winnie might feel as though she was reading too deep into her interpretation and therefore distanced herself from her response by defining her interpretation as a "guess" and discrediting the seriousness of her critical recognition through her tentative "kind of."

Since this was the first time that students utilized discourse analysis to address critical issues in a text, little problematization came from their explanations. In

TABLE 6.15. Student Work: Winnie's Identification Analysis of *Harry Potter* Passage

Harry		Ron		Hermione		Troll	
Harry	2	Ron	2	Hermione	1	The troll	2
him	1	he	1			it	10
						pea-brain	1
						something	1

fact, the only other problematization besides Tyler's example came from Grace when I questioned her as to why she originally thought J. K. Rowling was a male:

> GRACE: . . . when I read things, I naturally assume it was written by a male. I'm sometimes surprised when I find that it was written by a female.
> AMBER: Why?
> GRACE: Just because. . . I don't know. Maybe it is because, in my family, my dad, you know, goes to work, and my mom, I mean, they have equivalent roles, but I'm assuming that, especially in the business world I'm looking into, it is typically the guy CEO, and I just assume that they are the ones writing and having these opinions, and they are the ones—I don't know why. It's not that I think—I'm not—I don't naturally think women, which is weird because I am female but—I don't know.
> AMBER: If you had to guess why that was, what would you guess?
> GRACE: Just because how I've been raised. It's not that my parents have always been "women can't do this." They are not like that at all, but I've always seen, in my world, that the men. . . but women aren't not successful, but the men are the ones that have their name on things, which is why I just assume, and that women always, to me, have that stereotypical soft spoken and don't necessarily put out their opinions to get judged by men because they feel like men typically take up more fields. Like, most fields are made up by men, and so I know that I am a loud and outspoken person, and I speak my view and opinions—but I do also, even in my leadership roles, I think that, if I am going to be judged on what I say, it is going to be judged by men, not so much the females in the group, because females are more empathetic, a little bit. (Grace, *Harry Potter* protocol analysis)

Here, Grace began to identify a harmful ideology that has infiltrated her idea of what is considered normal or "common sense." Not only that, she recognized how her family perpetuated this ideology and the effect it had on the way she viewed male and female roles in the world. She also problematized her own actions: her hesitancy to speak freely in front of males because of her fear of judgment. This example showed Grace's struggle with identifying how she hegemonically contributed to the desires of the patriarchy through her hesitancy to speak in front of males. This is an example of problematization because, although she made no suggestion for change, she did question the source of her beliefs. However, her hedging of "I don't know" and "maybe" showed the difficulty of questioning one's own way of thinking and beliefs. We cannot fault her for this—developing critical awareness is HARD work.

Hedging in Othello *Protocol Analyses*

While students' hedging was most apparent during their consideration of SFL coding when discussing *Harry Potter*, their hedging while discussing their analysis of *Othello* did not decrease by any significant amount (129 for *Othello* compared to 132 for *Harry Potter*; see Table 6.10). In fact, similar to *Harry Potter*, students hedged the most during the description and identification stages. However, when I reviewed the transcriptions to find a possible explanation for the similarities, I found that the difficulty of Elizabethan English played a role in students' uncertainty when coding and interpreting words. Clara demonstrated this fact when she said, "I'm guessing that 'caitiff' is a bad word to call somebody" (Clara, *Othello* protocol analysis, line 38). Clara's subjectivity marker revealed that she was using context clues, the text around the word in question, to determine its meaning. See Table 6.16 for Clara's appraisal analysis chart.

TABLE 6.16. Student Work: Clara's *Othello* Appraisal Analysis Chart

Appraisal	Positive	Negative
Affect		ensnared, torments
Judgment	general, Sir	demi-devil, villain (× 2); caitiff
Appreciation		body, soul, pernicious, damned, most (× 2)

While she admitted that she did not know what the term meant (according to Merriam-Webster, n.d., a *caitiff* is "a base, cowardly, or despicable person"), she makes an educated "guess." Tyler showed comparable struggles:

> TYLER: Speaking of the words that we don't know . . . I don't even know what this means but I get a horrible feeling when I read that.
> AMBER: So you don't have to know what it means?
> TYLER: Yeah. Even the sound, and it has an exclamation point at the end, which makes it more powerful, and it matches that "villain," that accusation. (Tyler, *Othello* protocol analysis)

Tyler's hedge, "I don't even know," protected him as he interpreted the text, because, even if his response were wrong, his previous admission safeguarded his ego. Table 6.17 presents Tyler's appraisal analysis chart of *Othello*.

TABLE 6.17. Student Work: Tyler's *Othello* Appraisal Analysis Chart

Appraisal	Positive	Negative
Affect	pardon	demi-devil, ensnared, demand, know (× 2), torments, slain, death, villain, heathenish, gross, discontented, confess, desire
Judgment		villain (× 2); pernicious caitiff
Appreciation	dear	

In this passage, Tyler was also speaking of the word "caitiff," the word with which Clara also struggled. However, while Clara used context clues, Tyler used punctuation to determine the word's meaning, recognizing that exclamation points are used in dialogue that is meant to be angry or passionate, and recognizing that similar punctuation was used when the insult "villain" was spat, therefore drawing a parallel between the words *caitiff* and *villain*, even though he was uncertain of his interpretation.

Similarly, Sandi also struggled with the language of the play:

> SANDI: "Cruelty" is an affect because, if you're cruel to someone, it's going to appeal to their emotions, and "torments" is the same. What did he mean when he said this? "You shall close prisoner rest"?
> AMBER: It means that he's going to be held in jail until his trial.
> SANDI: "Faults" can be a judgment, because it is showing he is the one who must take up for it. So, it kind of shows that he is immoral because they did something wrong. "The Venetian state"... is that like their government, kind of?
> AMBER: Yes.
> SANDI: So, should I make that appreciation, or should I make it judgment?
> AMBER: Well, is it amplifying anything?
> SANDI: No. So, it's just judgment. This "soft"—does it mean, like, "be quiet"?
> AMBER: Yes, kind of like "quiet" or "wait a minute."
> SANDI: So, I'll code this as affect, because he is kind of asking for something... (Sandi, *Othello* protocol analysis)

Much can be gleaned from this short interaction. First, one can notice Sandi's confidence when coding words with which she was familiar, such as "cruelty" and "torments" (see Table 6.18 for Sandi's appraisal analysis of *Othello*).

TABLE 6.18. Student Work: Sandi's *Othello* Appraisal Analysis Chart

Appraisal	Positive	Negative
Affect		taken off, cruelty, torment, soft you, I pray you, speak of me as I am, malice, mood, tears, malignant
Judgment	power, command, Cassio rules, Venetian state	slave, fault, deeds
Appreciation		unlucky, melting

Her use of the high modal verb "is" indicated her certainty that these words should be coded as affect. However, when we get to the word "shall" and the Elizabethan syntax of the sentence, "You shall close prisoner rest," Sandi asked for assistance in determining what it meant, unable to code or interpret. See Table 6.19 for Sandi's modality analysis of *Othello*.

After I answered her question, Sandi skipped the analysis and coding of the sentence altogether. This could indicate one of two things: (1) she was so uncertain of the language that she did not attempt to code it at all—the ultimate hedging device being evasion—or (2) she did not find anything to code in the sentence. I tend to lean toward option 1, because the word "shall" could have been coded in a modality analysis and the word "prisoner" is a judgment.

While Sandi skipped over the word "shall" completely, Clara grappled with the verb:

> "Shall understand what hath befallen" . . . "shall," I think, is a medium modality because it's not it's saying, like . . . wait . . . no, I think it's high because . . . "you shall understand" . . . I feel like it's saying "you will understand eventually" . . . so <u>maybe</u> it's medium, like, "you may not understand right away but you will eventually," so I'll keep this medium. (Clara, *Othello* protocol analysis)

TABLE 6.19. Student Work: Sandi's *Othello* Modality Analysis

Grammatical Resource	High Modality	Medium Modality	Low Modality
Modal verbs	must forsake, go with us, torment, come, bring him away, know't, speak	hold him	Soft you, I pray you
Modal adverbs		till	
Modal adjectives	taken off, malignant		Perplex'd, unused
Modal nouns	power and command, slave, cruelty, deeds		nothing, one
Modal phrases and clauses	Cassio rules, it shall be his		must you speak

Here, Clara showed her knowledge of "shall" being a prediction verb, similar to that of "will," which would classify as a medium modal verb. Table 6.20 presents Clara's modality analysis for *Othello*.

TABLE 6.20. Student Work: Clara's *Othello* Modality Analysis

Grammatical Resource	High Modality	Medium Modality	Low Modality
Modal verbs	do, will	shall	ask
Modal adverbs	never (× 2); most (× 2)		
Modal adjectives			
Modal nouns			
Modal phrases and clauses	Demand me nothing		Will you, I pray

However, her wavering back and forth showed her struggle with coming to this conclusion, and her pragmatic idiom, "maybe," makes her conclusion just a suggestion. If the verb had been "will" and not "shall," such hedging might not have occurred, therefore showing how verbs that were not directly discussed during direct instruction but are common in Shakespeare's plays caused students to be uncertain in their analyses.

Next, Sandi showed her lack of familiarity, and the lack of knowledge of most students, about Italian politics. Being able to tentatively interpret that the Venetian state had something to do with the government, due to her previous experience using the word "state" in American government discourse, she was able to eventually code the phrase as a judgment (see Table 6.18 for Sandi's appraisal analysis of *Othello*). When asking about the word "soft," another Elizabethan term, Sandi also shows her discomfort with coding and interpreting her analysis, giving a tentative explanation that it "kind of" indicated that Othello was no longer in a position of power to demand actions from his subordinates.

The Elizabethan language also hindered students' ability to explain and problematize their analysis of the text. However, explanation was not impossible, as shown by Winnie. She explained, during her modality analysis, "I'm putting the word 'ask' as a low modality word, like, not demanding or anything. He's <u>kind of</u> trying to be a bit more humble about it, so it's less intense" (Winnie, *Othello* protocol analysis) (see Table 6.21 for Winnie's modality analysis of *Othello*).

TABLE 6.21. Student Work: Winnie's *Othello* Modality Analysis

Grammatical Resource	High Modality	Medium Modality	Low Modality
Modal verbs	believe, demon (× 2), ensnared	think	ask
Modal adverbs	never, most (× 2)		
Modal adjectives	best, slain		
Modal nouns	nothing, torments, death	demi-devil Sir general	
Modal phrases and clauses	I never will speak word, Most heathenish and most gross	O villain!	

Here, Winnie showed confidence when describing or coding the verb "ask" and with equal confidence identified it as "not demanding or anything." As she moved toward a critical orientation to the text through independent construction (Rothery & Stenglin, 1994), she hesitantly tried to explain the social effect of selecting the verb "ask" to that of another verb. Her tentative marker "kind of" shielded her from a negative reaction to her explanation of how we use the verb "ask" when we are not in positions of power, showing her uncertain but growing ability to denaturalize language, even though she did not verbally problematize it in her protocol analysis.

Hedging in Obama Protocol Analyses

When analyzing the chart, I was surprised to see an increase in the frequency of hedges, because I expected hedging to decrease as students became more comfortable with SFL and CDA. In order to explain this deviation from my expectations, I returned to the transcripts. In order to determine the analysis method with which students were least comfortable, I coded each hedge according to the type of analysis method used (see Table 6.22). I found that students hedged a lot when attempting to code, interpret, and explain contrast and concessions as well as citations—the two new analysis methods introduced for examining this nonfiction text.

TABLE 6.22. Hedges Coded by Analysis Method

	Appraisal Analysis	Modality Analysis	Identification Analysis	Contrast and Concession Analysis	Citation Analysis
Frequency	31	19	26	27	34
Percentage	22.63%	13.87%	18.98%	19.70%	24.82%

Therefore, I surmised that the introduction of new discourse analysis skills could have been the cause for the increase in hedging, as they made up 44.52 percent of all the Obama speech hedges.

When analyzing *contrasts and concessions*—a technique meant to make speakers seem open minded and knowledgeable as they appear to agree with one point, and then immediately counter it with a contrasting idea—Sandi represented students' uncertainty identifying, interpreting, and explaining this new technique. Table 6.23 presents Sandi's contrast and concession analysis of the Obama speech.

TABLE 6.23. Student Work: Sandi's Obama Contrast and Concession Analysis

Concession	Contrast	Grammatical Resource Used to Show Relationship
We did not go by choice	We went because of necessity	parallelism
I'm aware that there's still some who would question or even justify the events of 9/11	al-Qaeda killed nearly 3,000 people on that day	But let us be clear
The victims were innocent men, women, and children...	al-Qaeda chose to ruthlessly murder these people	And yet
These are not opinions	These are facts	parallelism

When explaining her chart, she stated:

> I think he is making his effect stronger by using these contrasts, especially because he's showing how correct he is. And he is <u>kind of</u> putting a reality to what we see in the news, like, like speaking directly to them about the reality of what's going on. So that <u>kind of</u> makes his words more effective and his position more powerful over them as president. Because he is stating these facts. (Sandi, Obama protocol analysis)

Sandi was trying to explain the rhetorical purpose and social effect that including specific contrasts had on the audience; however, while she made this attempt, she relapsed in her use of tentative hedges, showing her uncertainty in her explanation.

The same type of hedging occurred when students tried to identify and discuss citations. For example, Isabelle attempted to clarify how she defined *citation* (see Table 6.24 for Isabelle's citation chart).

TABLE 6.24. Student Work: Isabelle's Obama Citation Chart

Citation	Purpose	Status of Source	Effect
It is costly and politically difficult to continue this conflict.	support	logic	makes it a priority
The victims were men, women, and children from America and other nations who had done nothing to harm anybody.	support	logic	shows American as the victim
alQaeda killed nearly 3,000 people on that day	support	statistic	puts a number to the cause

She explained:

> For a citation, I think of <u>kind of</u> like numbers, like when he says many other nations that is just like a clump of nations who lost people. And I think it's a citation because that in fact did happen. I mean, it's really broad, but, I mean, a lot of victims were lost in America and other nations. (Isabelle, Obama protocol analysis)

This example shows Isabelle's uncertainty of how she defined a citation, therefore making her uncertain in her coding.

On the other hand, Parvesh was able to identify citations but lacked confidence when explaining the meaning when he says, "so it makes it so it sounds a lot worse so they can <u>kind of</u> feel for the US and see why alQaeda is such a threat" (Parvesh, Obama protocol analysis). Parvesh showed confidence in his interpretation of what the citation said but hedges in his explanation of its social meaning (see Table 6.25 for Parvesh's citation analysis).

TABLE 6.25. Student Work: Parvesh's Obama Citation Chart

Citation	Purpose	Status of Source	Effect
Over seven years ago, the United States pursued alQaeda and the Taliban with broad international support.	support	date	shows that we never gave up and that we had support all that time
alQaeda killed nearly 3,000 people on that day	support	advisory-cabinet?	explain how bad alQaeda is by the amount of people they killed
They have affiliates in many countries and are trying to expand their reach	support	advisors?	puts a number to the cause

Based on this further examination, I concluded that, if the two new analysis tools—contrast/concession and citations—had not been introduced, then my hypothesis of seeing hedging steadily decrease would have been correct. Huzzah! Victory! Furthermore, this hedging was connected with students grappling with new analytic methods, which relates back to Vygotsky's ZPD. Once students became more proficient in appraisal, identification, and modality analyses, I introduced new analysis methods. In this way, students were dealing with new terms and looking for new elements/patterns of language, and, therefore, they increased in hedging as they dealt with more difficult work. It is my hope that, by looking at these student examples, you can see the benefit of not just teaching discourse analysis tools to students during this language study, but that, by utilizing them yourself, you can gauge the progress of your students' growth and comfort levels with using discourse analysis. And grow they will.

Reflection Questions for Chapter 6

1. In your classroom, when do you witness students hedging? Which hedges introduced in this chapter are most utilized? By whom? Under what circumstances? Why do you think this is?
2. What is the value in using discourse analysis to determine a student's growth? In this chapter, I used modality and hedging analyses to measure confidence and critical growth. What else could these methods measure?

A Changing World View: Language Analysis and Developing Critical Consciousness

7

Guiding Gist

- Students can analyze an original text using discourse analysis tools to prove or reject the claims of scholars.
- Students' discussion of discourse analyses can lead to critical dialogical events that encourage students to recognize that there can be multiple possibilities when interpreting the purpose of language choices.
- Through dialogue, students are able to use their peers' lived experience to interpret text and the results of their discourse analyses.
- Students can rely on their discourse analyses and coding of text to support their critical observations about power relationships and the institutions in which they are a part.

While conducting a modality analysis on students' protocol analyses and assessing the frequency of hedges played a role in determining students' *comfort* with their growing critical consciousness, it is not enough to fully explain the many forms in which a linguistically informed curriculum aids in supporting critical development. With that in mind, this section shares more student work and dialogue showing students using their linguistic and discourse analysis knowledge to recognize, explain, or discuss various critical issues within the spiraled texts. While looking at the focal events that I include in this chapter, it is my hope that you can visualize opportunities in your classroom to increase critical discussion around language use in texts and perceive how a linguistically informed curriculum can help provide those opportunities. By looking at how it happened in my classroom with my students, it may help you recognize when and how it can happen organically and when students need a little nudge to go deeper.

As mentioned previously, I coded student work and dialogue based on the following critical themes:

- recognition of *othering* or *dehumanization*
- critical issues, such as stereotyping, gender issues, power relations, and racism
- subversive nature of unjust language
- questioning social norms or personal beliefs

After coding, I chose focal events that I felt exemplified students' development from description to problematization, showing how discourse analysis tools aided in developing students' critical awareness and questioning of language.

When reading the experiences relayed in this chapter, it is important to remember that they were not the only instances of critical development but, instead, best capture how the above-noted themes were realized and addressed by students. In the same breath, it is equally important to recognize that not all class discussions, presentations, or student work achieved critical goals. I say this in an attempt to guard against romanticizing the experiences discussed below, reminding you that the examples presented are excerpts from larger discussions and that not every experience resulted in the problematization or critical analysis of language. However, the following examples do show how the joint construction of knowledge can lead toward a critical understanding of texts.

Focal Event 1: Winnie and Andrew's *Harry Potter* Presentation

To review, for students' *Harry Potter* project, they were asked to choose an article that discussed a critical issue in the selected novel and to perform a language analysis of excerpts from *Harry Potter* to assess whether Rowling's language supported or disproved the author's claims. Details for the *Harry Potter* project can be found in Table 4.4 in Chapter 4.

I continue to share this focal event (Simmons, 2016c) because it included students' awareness of the othering, the dehumanization of house-elves, and the unequal power relations between wizards and other magical creatures. It also shows students discussing their own language experiences in order to problematize the purpose behind Kreacher's use of language, affectively denaturalizing it and questioning its purpose.

Winnie and her partner, Andrew, chose the article "Hermione and the House-Elves: The Literary and Historical Contexts of J. K. Rowling's Antislavery Campaign" (Carey, 2003), which addresses the parallels between the plight of house-elves and slavery. In order to understand the article, students needed a working understanding of critical race theory. Winnie expressed her understanding of the theory when she defined *critical race theory* for the class. She stated, "Critical race theory is pretty much trying to describe a relationship between race and power, and we found plenty of examples of that in the book" (Winnie, *Harry Potter* presentation). While her summary of the theory was basic and even minimal, it was accurate and specifically focused on the elements of the theory that were relevant and applicable to their language analysis. Figure 7.1 features slides from Winnie and Andrew's presentation that summarize the author's claims and their analysis and summary of results.

One of Carey's (2003) arguments that Winnie and Andrew found interesting was the observation that the speech of the house-elves mimicked Hollywood's inaccurate portrayal of the African American dialect. As Winnie stated in her presentation:

> WINNIE: And our second claim was that the speech of the house-elves was odd and derived from pronoun and word order mistakes similar to the 1930s and 1940s' Hollywood misrepresented conceptions of African American dialect. We didn't entirely agree with this one either, because we found some word mistakes, but we didn't find any pronoun errors, like any Yoda-ish speaking there. We found the pronoun mistakes but not the word order mistakes. And we did an identification analysis on a passage where Kreacher, Sirius's house-elf, was talking and it says, "Mistress would never forgive Kreacher if the tapestry was thrown out, seven centuries it's been in the family, Kreacher must save it, Kreacher will not let master and the blood traitors and the brats destroy it." And we see the point that the author was making about pronouns because there aren't any pronouns used at all. Kreacher refers to everybody by a title, not even a name. He has a name for himself, and that's it. Um, so, in a way, by using "master" and "mistress," he is giving them a kind of respect, but he is also distancing him from them because he would not call them by name like he calls himself by name. And he also doesn't call Harry and Ron and Hermione by their names, but you can see that one has the opposite purpose—to distance himself because he doesn't like them. (Winnie, *Harry Potter* presentation)

The quote that Winnie and Andrew analyzed was from *Harry Potter and the Order of the Phoenix* (Rowling, 2003, p. 110). Table 7.1 shows their coding and identification chart as they presented it to the class.

After performing their identification analysis, Winnie and Andrew were able to illustrate to the class how Rowling's language supported the claim that the lack of the house-elves' pronoun use made them seem childlike and ignorant,

Hermione and the House-Elves: The Literary and Historical Contexts of J.K. Rowling's Antislavery Campaign

Synopsis of Author's Claims

- J.K. Rowling uses the "plight [of the house-elves] as a commentary on the society and economy of the magical world she creates" (Carey 1), in order to encourage her young readers to be politically active.
- The speech of the house-elves is "odd, charactrized by pronoun and word-order mistakes, and is reminiscent of 1930's and 40s Hollywood misconceptions of Aftrican American dialects" (Carey 103)
- The house-elves servitude is a psychological enslavement as well as a physical one. Many house-elves have "lost the ability to conceive of themselves as free" (Carey 104).
- Whereas Harry's sympathy with the house-elves is personal, Hermione views the situation as one that necessitates public awareness and action. Her approach is more political than personal.
- Wizards have placed themselves at the top of the social hierarchy in the magical world as a result of their enslavement of other sentient beings.

Claim 1:

J.K. Rowling uses the "plight [of the house-elves] as a commentaray on the society and economy of the magical world she creates" (Carey 1), in order to encourage her young readers to be politically active.

"You know, maybe it wouldn't be a bad idea to show people *exactly* how horrible it is to clean *all the time*—we could do a sponsored scrub of the Gryffindor common room, all proceeds to S.P.E.W., it would raise awareness as well as funds—"
~Hermione, pg. 159

Appraisal Analysis:

- *Exactly*- describes the degree at which Hermione wishes for people to understand the common duties of house-elves.
- Horrible- describes her thought of cleaning all the time
- *All the time*- describes the stress in such a task for long periods of time
- Sponsored- approved of by high authorities

Affect	Judgment	Appreciation
	horrible	exactly
	sponsored	all the time

Claim 2:

The speech of the house-elves is "odd, characterized by pronoun and word-order mistakes, and is reminiscent of 1930's and 40s Hollywood misconceptions of African American dialects" (Carey 103).

"Mistress would never forgive Kreacher if the tapestry was thrown out, seven centuries it's been in the family, Kreacher must save it, Kreacher will not let Master and the blood traitors and the brats destroy it"
~Kreacher pg. 110

Identification Analysis:

- Kreacher always refers to himself and others by name or title, but never through pronouns. The lack of pronouns used supports Carey's claim.

Kreacher	3
Master	1
Mistress	1
Blood Traitors	1
Brats	1

Claim 3:

The house-elves servitude is a psychological enslavement as well as a physical one. Many house-elves have "lost the ability to conceive of themselves as free" (Carey 104).

"She still does not care for clothes, Harry Potter. Nor do the other house-elves, none of them will clean Gryffindor Tower anymore, not with the hats and socks hiding everywhere, they find them insulting."
~Dobby, pg. 385

Modality Analysis:

All of the underlined words have a negative polarity. "Nor", "none", and "anymore" show how most of the other house-elves resent the clothes hidden in gryffindor Tower, while "insulting" reinforces this attempt to free them.

Claim 4:

Whereas Harry's sympathy with the house elves is personal, Hermione views the situation as one that necessitates public awareness and action. Her approach is more political than personal.

"Dobby wishes he could help Harry Potter, for Harry Potter set Dobby free and Dobby is *much, much* happier now...."
~Dobby, pg. 386

Appraisal Analysis:

- Wishes he could help- shows Dobby's good intentions as well as his powerlessness to carry the out
- Free- positive connotation, implies relief/happiness
- *Much, much*- amplifier that reinforces Dobby's happiness
- Happier- describes Dobby's emotion towards Harry

Affect	Judgment	Appreciation
free	wishes he could help	much, much
happier		

Claim 5:

Wizards have placed themselves at the top of the social hierarchy in the magical world as a result of their enslavement of other sentient beings.

"The last three [a centaur, a goblin, and a house-elf] were all looking up *adoringly* at the witch and wizard."
~Description of the fountain at the Ministry of Magic, pg. 127

Appraisal Analysis:

Last- shows level of importance compared to wizards and witches
Looking up- describes the subordinate position of these beings
Adoringly- describes the emotion these statues are showing as well as implies that humans are superior

Affect	Judgment	Appreciation
Adoringly	last	
	Looking up	
	Adoringly	

Analysis

When we read children's literature, we rarely think of what ideals are being conveyed through the characters and wording. J.K. Rowling's *Harry Potter* series increasingly uses Hermione as a medium for her anti-slavery message to her readers as the young student develops an eager determination to free house-elves. This is a radical, yet moral ideal in the wizard world, and met with hard criticism and a lack of support. This concept is traditionally used in children's literature. Yet Hermione is seen to persevere and take political approach to this ideal. This is Rowling's call-to-action for her readers to be aware of their political surroundings and not be afraid to stand up for what they believe is right. Rowlin's subtle political approach adds a unique turn to the otherwise traditional message found in her series.

FIGURE 7.1. Winnie and Andrew's PowerPoint Presentation (cited sources: Carey, 2003; Rowling, 2003).

TABLE 7.1. Student Work: Winnie and Andrew's Full *Harry Potter* Identification Analysis

Student Coding	Student Chart of Coding			
	Witches and Wizards		**House-Elf**	
	Name	**#**	**Name**	**#**
Mistress would never forgive Kreacher if the tapestry was thrown out, seven centuries it's been in the family, Kreacher must save it, Kreacher will not let master and the blood traitors and the brats destroy it.	Mistress master blood traitors brats	1 1 1 1	Kreacher	3

Excerpt source: Rowling (2003, p. 110).

but refuted the claim that inverted syntax increased this image by pointing out the lack of "Yoda-ish" phrasing. However, Winnie and Andrew not only described (through their coding/chart) and interpreted the text by explaining what the coding exposed ("and we see the point that the author was making about pronouns because there aren't any pronouns used at all. Kreacher refers to everybody by a title, not even a name. He has a name for himself, and that's it"), they also attempted to explain the social meaning behind the interpretation ("so, in a way, using 'master' and 'mistress,' he is giving them a kind of respect, but he is also distancing him from them because he would not call them by name like he calls himself by name. And he also doesn't call Harry and Ron and Hermione by their names, but you can see that one has the opposite purpose—to distance himself because he doesn't like them").

In their explanation, Winnie and Andrew concluded that not using a person's name distances you from that person and that Kreacher shows how this can be done out of respect or abhorrence. They also showed how the only proper name used is Kreacher's and that he uses it only to refer to himself. Winnie and Andrew thought that this is because Kreacher is othered due to his race and that this is shown by his lack of a title other than his own name. However, they did not investigate or problematize the reason *why* any further.

It is moments like this one where dialogue is crucial. When Winnie and Andrew finished their presentation and invited students to make comments or ask questions, the following interaction occurred (Simmons, 2016c, p. 199):

> ALAN:[1] Well, I kind of have a comment on the speaking in third person. For me, and for many Asian people, in our language, we speak in the third person. Like, I will say my name and tell them what I was going to do.

1. In excerpts of class dialogue, names of students who participated in the curriculum but were not focal students will appear. Names of focal students will be italicized for clarification, and my name will be underlined to ensure that the reader does not confuse a teacher comment/question with that of a student.

AMBER: So you would say, "Alan is going to the store?"

ALAN: Yeah. But that sounds weird in English. (*Laughs.*) But that's normal for us. We don't really use words like "I" and "me" and stuff.

WINNIE: It kind of makes you wonder if the elves have another language that they're switching from to speak in English.

AMBER: Ooh. (*Imagine me wide eyed and impressed.*)

ANDREW: I think that, if you're not using the first person "I" and "me" and stuff, like, that it is kind of, like, pointing out their lack of individualism. Since, like, they're not free, by speaking in the third person, it's indicating that they don't think of what *they* want.

AMBER: So your claim is that the lack of "me" and "I" kind of takes the focus off themselves, like they are not introspective to their wants and needs? They are more concerned with what's outside of them?

ANDREW: Yeah.

TYLER: I could also see it both ways. I can see it as a detachment from themselves, but I can also see it as, you know, "I, Tyler, want this." So, in a sense, you're putting your name to it, which *is* individualism because, you know, it's like *your name*. It's not just "I" because everyone can be "I."

WINNIE: And I can kind of see it as being the only thing they do have power over—is their own name. (*Harry Potter* discussion)

So many wonderful critical and dialogical things are going on in this passage that it is hard to know where to start. First, the discussion built off Winnie and Andrew's results from their coding and interpretation of their identification analysis, showing that, without this tool, this specific discussion on the social purpose of language may not have occurred. Second, Alan brought in his own experiences with his first language, Korean, to provide a possible explanation for Kreacher's language use. This knowledge was then validated as important when Winnie utilized Alan's "funds of knowledge" (Moll et al., 1992) to question Carey's (2003) assumption that the purpose of Kreacher's dialect was to make the house-elves seem childlike and ignorant when she says, "It kind of makes you wonder if the elves have another language that they're switching from to speak in English." By making this a possibility, Winnie questioned the social norm that a lack of pronoun use means one is ignorant of how language is used. In fact, Winnie's problematization of this assumption based off of Alan's experience actually made them question who was really ignorant in this power relationship. If, in fact, house-elves have a home language they are converting to English, wouldn't that make them more knowledgeable of language than the wizards since they could speak two languages? Looking at Kreacher as the more educated race flipped the status quo.

However, Andrew seemed to believe that Kreacher's lack of the use of the pronouns *I* and *me* is a psychological effect of slavery. In essence, when I asked him later to clarify, he said that he believed that Kreacher had been trained to only think of others and never himself, making him unable of personal introspection. Piggybacking off this comment, Tyler recognized Andrew's observation and added another psychological explanation: "Putting your name to it which *is* individualism because, you know, it's like *your name*. It's not just 'I' because everyone can be 'I'." Tyler proposed that Kreacher's use of his name was intentional in order to express his individuality. According to Jackson (1990), pronouns function as a method of economy, cutting down the repetition of names. However, pronouns are often used to indicate possession. Therefore, being called by a pronoun instead of by one's name can suggest one's place in the social hierarchy—that of a lesser being. Taking this into consideration, Tyler's observation of Kreacher's rejection of using a pronoun to refer to himself might indeed be an act of resistance to his subjugation by the wizarding class.

Making this observation critical, Winnie concluded the conversation by relating it to the original power relationship, stating that Kreacher's use of his name is his attempt to regain some power, therefore humanizing himself when others meant to dehumanize him. This interaction shows how students built knowledge together by listening to one another's experiences and thoughts. Not once did a student discredit another's contribution, and each time a student joined the conversation, it opened up more possibilities as to the social purpose of Kreacher's language. Furthermore, this critical discussion stemmed from students' critique of a language analysis, and they used their analysis to support their observations.

Later, in a written reflection about the article she read, Winnie stated:

> The identification analysis in my presentation shows the dehumanization of house-elves by referring to them with pronouns such as "it" or "creature." Hermione sees this dehumanization as yet another mistreatment of a sentient people and tries to stage a "sponsored scrub of the Gryffindor common room" in order to "show people exactly how horrible it is to clean all the time" (Rowling, 2003, p. 159). Political demonstrations such as this inspire young readers to get involved in advocating for the change of issues that they find unfair or intolerable. (Winnie, *Harry Potter* reflection)

Here, Winnie uses her discourse analysis results to explain how Hermione's problematization leads readers to make similar critical realizations about the role they play in social inequality in their cultures, leading to the desire to be a part of social change.

As we conclude with this first focal event, I feel like it is important to point out that the definitive answer to why Kreacher speaks in the third person isn't important to the greater goal of this assignment. There is no right answer as neither Kreacher nor Rowling inform us of their intention. It is the questioning and acceptance of multiple possibilities and the discussion of the meaning of each of those interpretations that makes this dialogical event critical and so utterly brilliant.

Focal Event 2: Clara's Group's Presentation of Their *Othello* Analysis

In groups of four (see Table 4.5 in Chapter 4 for project details), students were asked to perform an appraisal, identification, and modality analysis of one act in *Othello*, create a handout that summarized the results, present the results to the class, and create three questions in order to involve the class in discussion.

I selected this event for three reasons:

1. the group's recognition that Othello is othered due to his racial difference
2. their focus on the varied power relationships between characters that depend on race and social/economic status
3. the development of critical questions regarding class and race from their language analysis

The class dialogue generated from these questions shows students' problematization of language and their questioning of Shakespeare's purpose behind using such language.

Clara's group performed their analysis on Act 1 (see Table 7.2 for their handout). From their analyses, the group was able to focus on the power relationships between the characters, finding that their identification analysis revealed who is respected more than others. For example, their handout stated that:

> Roderigo uses "we" about five times in the act to highlight the importance and his dependence upon the relationship that he and Iago share [and] Brabantio is often referred to as "sir" or "signior"; therefore, this shows that he has high rank in society, and he serves as a well-respected man.

Similarly, they stated that "Othello is referred to as 'the Moor' seven times in the first scene alone, which emphasizes the importance of his race, and how this characterization of color sets him apart from the rest of the characters in the play" and "within the first act, Desdemona is often referred to as 'she' or 'daughter.' The lack of the use of her name shows that there was a patriarchal society in the play."

TABLE 7.2. Student Work: Clara's Group's Handout[a]

***Othello* Analysis for Act 1**
Identification Analysis:
• Iago: In Act 1, Iago refers to himself as "I" forty-nine different times, which shows he is authoritative in his speech, and also that, whenever he speaks, it usually pertains to himself or what he wants others to do for him. • Roderigo: Roderigo also focuses on himself and what he wants, much like Iago, which is represented by his use of "I" twelve times in Act 1. Also, Roderigo uses "we" about five times in the act to highlight the importance of his dependence upon the relationship that he and Iago share. • Brabantio: Brabantio is often referred to as "sir" or "signior" (sixteen times within the act); therefore, this shows that he has a high rank in society, and he serves as a well-respected man. In Act 1, he uses the pronoun "you" sixteen times when referring to Roderigo and Iago, which shows that he lacks respect for the two characters. • Othello: Othello is given numerous names within the act. He is referred to as a "Barbary horse," "black ram," "gondolier," "thief," and "an abuser of the world," which all characterize him in a derogatory and secluded manner. Othello is referred to as "the Moor" seven times in the first scene alone, which emphasizes the importance of his race, and how this characterization of color sets him apart from the rest of the characters in the play. The use of "I" by Othello represents his authoritative presence. • Desdemona: Within the first act, Desdemona is often referred to as "she" or "daughter." The lack of the use of her name shows that there was a patriarchal society set in the play. The lack of use of Desdemona's name makes her seem less important or an afterthought when compared to the male characters. • Duke: The Duke is often referred to as "the duke" or "he," which shows that the characters respect his power and authority.
Appraisal Analysis:
• Iago, throughout Act 1, shows a negative persona toward the situations that he faces. In the beginning of the act and also toward the end, Iago holds a commanding voice over Roderigo, telling him, "Proclaim him in the streets; incense her kinsmen . . . plague him with flies." He also uses his experience and age to bully Roderigo into doing his bidding, which shows that Iago's character as power hungry. He is someone who preys on those who are weaker than him to get things done. Iago is also viewed in a negative light because of the judgments that he makes against Othello, calling him a "Moor," "Barbary horse," "gondolier," "black ram," and "devil." These show the bigotry that Iago has toward his general, due to the way he characterizes Othello as an animal and constantly points out his race. • Roderigo uses judgment words such as "sir" and "signior" to emphasize his respect for Brabantio, and also so that he (Roderigo) can win the affection of Brabantio, so that he can marry Desdemona. Roderigo, also, uses positive judgment, affect, and appreciation words when trying to reinforce Iago. • Brabantio uses negative judgment words against Othello such as "thief" and "abuser" because he believes that Othello has stolen his daughter away from him. Appreciation words such as "bad" and "foul" are also used by Brabantio to describe his distaste for Othello. • Othello uses positive judgment and affect words such as "beloved" and "love" when speaking of Desdemona, but he also shows his dominance in the relationship by ordering her to "come." When speaking to Brabantio, Othello also uses kind judgments such as "signior," which shows his kindness and wisdom to treat his superiors with respect even when it is not shown to him.

continued on next page

TABLE 7.2. Continued.

Modality Analysis:
• Within the beginning of Act 1, Iago has high modality, using phrases such as "I am what I am" and adverbs like "surely," yet, when addressing Othello, Iago's modality drops at some points. He uses the phrases "I pray" and "I think" when talking to Othello, which shows a shift in power between the scenes. When Othello is absent, Iago holds power, but, when Othello is present, Othello holds most power. • Roderigo uses low modality, such as "I rather would" and "I think I can," which shows how he plays subordinate to Iago. • Brabantio uses medium to high modality depending on who he is addressing. He uses the adjectives "worser" and "wretched" when addressing Othello, which shows his blatant hate for what Othello has done to Desdemona. • Othello uses high modality, which emphasizes his sureness in himself. He uses modal nouns such as "I'll" and modal verbs "shall" to stress the definite authority that he has. • Cassio and the Duke also played a role in the modality within this act. Both of these characters showed low modality. The Duke showed low modality, using phrases such as "may help," because he was trying to play the peacemaker between Brabantio and Othello. Cassio held low modality because, during his dialogue, he was speaking to Othello, who is a higher rank than he, therefore his low modality was out of respect for Othello.
Questions for Socratic:
1. Roderigo is in a higher class than Iago yet it is Iago who holds the power and authority in the relationship. What do you think Shakespeare was trying to say about class in regards to Iago and Roderigo? 2. Why do you believe that Shakespeare references Othello as "the Moor" while not differentiating anyone else's races? 3. In Act 1, Scene 2, Othello shows good judgment in not attacking Brabantio when he verbally attacks Othello for "enchanting" Desdemona. How does Othello's wisdom change throughout the play?

[a]Adapted from Simmons (2018, p. 83).

Students also used their appraisal analysis and modality analysis to support their interpretation. The group stated that Iago's judgments toward Othello ("Moor," "Barbary horse," "devil," "thief") "show the bigotry that Iago has toward his general due to the way he characterizes Othello as an animal and constantly points out his race." Students' modality analysis also shows their advanced understanding of the nature of power relationships. Clara's group found that "Iago's modality drops at some points. He uses the phrases 'I pray' and 'I think' when talking to Othello, which shows a shift in power between the scenes. When Othello is absent, Iago holds the power, but when Othello is present, Othello holds most power." In this way, students recognized the nuances in modality shifts and how they exposed deliberate relationships between characters (Humphrey et al., 2011). In addition, focusing on attitudinal values helped them *analyze* characters rather than just summarize the plot or list character traits (Christie & Derewianka, 2008). Students also showed their recognition that power relationships are not permanent but that they shift and change depending on who is involved and the context of the social situation (Fairclough, 2003; Foucault, 1975/1995). These comments show students' ability to interpret their language analysis coding and also explain the social implications of such choices to the class. However, the group's discussion questions to the class regarding these selections allowed for the denaturalization and questioning of such language choices.

After interpreting and explaining their data in their small groups, students created discussion questions to present to the class in order to problematize their analysis results. Clara's first question was "Roderigo is in a higher class than Iago, yet it is Iago who holds the power and authority in the relationship. What do you think Shakespeare was trying to say about class in regards to Iago and Roderigo?" Such a *great* question, right? Clara's group found that their modality and identification analyses revealed that Iago has power over Roderigo despite the fact that Roderigo is from a higher social class. Because this goes against the social norm, that the educated and wealthy have power over the less-educated and poor, Clara's group posed this question, attempting to make sense of what the language revealed about this relationship even though it was at odds with what they considered "normal." Below is an excerpt from the conversation that derived from this question:

> BECCA: I think it might be saying that people in the higher classes might not be as smart as some of them in the lower classes.
>
> LAURA: I think that he's saying that Roderigo is more, like, more book smart, and Iago is, like, more street smart, and he had, um, more common sense than Roderigo.
>
> MANDY: Um, I think that, like, even though Roderigo is upper class, you think he'd be the smarter one, and Iago is tricking him. But then with Iago being lower class, he's mischievous, and he's almost, dirty almost, and the villain, which is normally associated with the lower class. They seem dirtier, I guess.
>
> RHADIKA: I guess it's, like, just because you have more money doesn't mean you can't be deceived. This is kind of weird, but it kind of reminds me of *Aladdin*. How, like, Aladdin is lower class, and he has to lie to get food, and he has to be tricky in what he does. And it's almost like Iago being lower class; he's tricky to benefit himself.
>
> AMBER: Do you think it's kind of stereotypical? Do you think that he is supporting negative stereotypes, especially those of the lower class by making him deceitful and the villain and the trickster and taking all these negative traits and giving them to somebody who wasn't born into wealth? Is that supporting a harmful stereotype?
>
> BECCA: Yes.
>
> LAURA: I think that he's kind of. . . the goal was to kind of separate the classes because it was also such a major focus back then during Shakespeare's time. It's

like the separation of the caste system and upper is better than the lower class, and it's like him filling out the stereotypes of how the lower class is trickier than the upper, even though they're just the same. They just do it differently. (*Othello* discussion)

In the above excerpt, students first identified that negative stereotypes of the lower class exist when Mandy said, "But then with Iago being lower class, he's mischievous and he's almost, dirty almost, and the villain, which is normally associated with the lower class. They seem dirtier, I guess." Second, Rhadika tried to make sense of this stereotype using intertextuality, relating it to her previous experience with this stereotype, the movie *Aladdin*. Based on students' comments, I gave a name to their observations, "negative stereotype," encouraging students to question the purpose of such a stereotype. Students then attempted to investigate why Shakespeare perpetuated harmful stereotypes of the lower class, coming to the conclusion that Shakespeare was perpetuating the ideology of his community—that the lower class was constantly trying to "trick" the upper class out of their wealth, a stereotype still held today. Laura challenged the stereotype saying, "even though they're just the same. They just do it differently." Here, I almost spit out my coffee. Laura recognized that the upper class is just as "tricky," a nicer way of saying "subversive" and "self-serving." Clever girl.

While this conversation counts as critical dialogue, questioning how and why harmful language was perpetuated, it could have escalated to an assessment of our own world. I'm at fault here for why it didn't. As the teacher, I should have encouraged this line of questioning, coaxing students to analyze how and why such language was perpetuated in our modern society, not just Shakespeare's, and the steps we could take to change it. In hindsight, I am so disappointed I did not act on this line of questioning.

While Clara's group questioned power relationships in relation to class, their second question directly questioned the purpose of Shakespeare having characters call Othello "the Moor." The second question read: "Why do you believe that Shakespeare references Othello as 'the Moor,' while not differentiating anyone else's race?" This question directly relates to the othering of Othello due to his racial difference, and the following discussion transpired:

BLAIRE: Isn't everybody else white?

AMBER: Yeah.

BLAIRE: So, maybe he referred to him as the Moor based on his color because that stuck out the most to everybody else. I don't know, maybe he just thought that

referring to him as Othello didn't make him ... not special enough, but didn't show the significance of his position. Because, back then, African Americans weren't in high authority positions. So, I guess, by calling him the Moor over and over again, it demeans him, but, at the same time, something about him stuck out more than anything else and that's why he's the leader. I don't know. I'm struggling with that.
JENNY: Well, most of the time it's Iago who is calling him the Moor, so it's only showing his resentment toward Othello. That's it, I think.
SUSANNE: Yeah, like what she said. The reason why Iago is calling him the Moor is because he is jealous of him because he has a reason to call him that with a bad connotation because he wants him to mess up.
MICHELLE: I also think that this might be some foreshadowing because he's kind of using it degrading, and then, at the end, he ends up killing Desdemona, so maybe that's the reason. (*Othello* discussion)

In this portion of the conversation, students recognized that the purpose of calling Othello "the Moor" was to separate or "other" him because of his race; however, some students seem to be trying to justify the use of the term. For example, Blaire suggested that Shakespeare uses the name "Moor" to point out that, even though Othello is Black, he is in a position of power so some positive feature had to stick out for him to be named general. However, one can see her struggle with this explanation when she says, "I don't know. I'm struggling with that." Her admission that she was having difficulty understanding the purpose was brave and dialogic, opening the door for others to help her understand. This is an example as to how hedging ("I don't know") can be used to open dialogue. Jenny, Susanne, and Michelle did just that, providing other possibilities as to why Othello is othered. I, too, attempted to expand this questioning:

AMBER: How many times does he call him the Moor?
SARA: About seven
CLARA: Yeah, seven.
AMBER: So what does that say that they call him a Black man more than they call him by his name? Instead of calling me "Ms. Simmons," what if you were to call me "teacher?" Which they do; they call him general. Or "white lady?"
SARA: It would show a lack of respect.
AMBER: What is the purpose? What is the function of calling me that?
SARA: To degrade him.
BLAIRE: To make you feel like we have more power over you.
AMBER: How does that do that?

Jessica: Because it's not special. Like calling you "white lady" isn't your position like teacher. Like, calling you "teacher," which shows how you have authority over us and tell us what to do. But "white lady," I don't know, kind of makes me feel like slaves. Like not having names.

Sara: It's like, if we were to call you "white lady," it's like we're using your race against you personally, like your race is a flaw, and we're getting into bad connotation, like, "Oh the white lady's coming." So I don't know, but here, when he refers to him as "Moor" and "black ram" or anything that he's calling him, he's just highlighting... it's excluding him and using his own race against him as if being Black was something that he should basically be ashamed of.

Clara: I think it takes away your identity, because calling you the "white lady," it's like a general statement that could refer to any white person. It's a female, so taking away who you are as a person. Whereas, like, "Ms. Simmons is my language arts teacher who I go to second period every day"... The "white lady," it doesn't really carry any respect or character that your name does. (*Othello* discussion)

Going back to their original analysis and using it as support for our discussion, I attempted to recontextualize the discussion by applying a racial marker to myself, even though I fully recognize that "white lady" carries a different social meaning and connotation due to white privilege. However, in the moment, I was struggling to find a modern example or experience students felt comfortable using to compare to *Othello*. I often use myself in hypothetical comparisons, and, once I did this, students were better able to understand the effect and purpose of using such language based on their own experiences with naming. Clara articulated the importance of proper names and the social implications of taking one's name away (see Jackson, 1990).

This discussion (Simmons, 2018, pp. 83–84) not only problematized the purpose and implications of Shakespeare's racist language but also brought to mind students' own experiences with race relations:

Blaire: I think that if we were to call you "white lady," it would just be saying that you were one in a population and that there would be so many others.

Amber: What if I was the only white lady?

Clara: That would make you stand out. If you're called that, it would characterize you as that person.

Blaire: Which is what calling Othello "the Moor" creates for him. It creates the image that he is the only one, so he does stand out more, which I think brings out some of his character...

Miguel: I think this whole thing about the Moor and calling somebody by their name ... I think is more of attacking the race and making them a representative of their entire race. And so, by calling Othello "the Moor," it is like making Othello represent all Black people.

AMBER: And how do you think that makes him feel? I mean, can you imagine speaking for an entire race of people? Has anyone ever felt like they've been in a position like that before? Like being the only girl in the group of boys and feeling like everything that you said was a representation of what girls think? Or Hispanic people, or African Americans, or whatever the situation? . . .

MIGUEL: Yeah. When I was in preschool, I was the only Hispanic kid in my class.

AMBER: Was there a sense of pressure that came with that?

MIGUEL: Yeah, there was a sense of it, but it's something that you get accustomed to.

MICHELLE: Yeah, I would say that it's kind of like labeling him one thing. It's probably not just a Moor. It's like calling all Hispanic people "Mexican." You do that to somebody who was not Mexican . . . I mean it, not offending any Mexicans, it's just that there are other countries in South America that people originate from.

MIGUEL: Has anyone ever heard someone call the Spanish language Mexican?

MICHELLE: Yes! I've heard people call Chinese Asian too.

MIGUEL: Yeah, I mean there are different dialects of Spanish depending on where you're from, like, in certain areas of Mexico, the Spanish there is different.

MICHELLE: Yeah, it's like European English and then American English.

BLAIRE: Yeah, but going back to Othello feeling like he's talking for everybody, I feel like the more Iago called him "the Moor," the more pressure it put on him. Because he knew he'd find a flaw, and, you know, you have one if someone keeps calling it out over and over. It was to break down Othello, and, by emphasizing his flaws, I think it's speeding up the process, instead of calling him by his name, which doesn't really do anything. (*Othello* discussion)

Miguel and Michelle are not alone in having felt like the sole representative of a race or culture due to their racial or ethnic minority status in a classroom environment. What I find most moving about this interaction is not only Miguel and Michelle's comfort in sharing their feelings with the class but the class's reaction to their sharing. Not once did a student try to downplay their experiences with a false comparison to their own experiences (e.g., "I understand how you feel because, one time, I was the only white person at [fill in the blank]"). Instead, Blaire, a white female who probably never had such an experience, related Miguel and Michelle's experiences with race back to *Othello*, using their experiences to better understand the text and the ramifications of language that others someone because of their race (Simmons, 2018). Aronowitz (1998) would agree that this was a situation in which students were able to use one another's varying experiences to understand themselves, the world, and the text.

Othello Mini Event: Tyler's Group's Presentation

This particular act of *Othello* allowed a deep dive into gender inequalities as well. A group from another class analyzed the same act but chose to focus on how Desdemona was portrayed throughout the act. They observed that "Desdemona is called 'daughter' fourteen times and referenced as a pronoun fifty-two times. In addition, Desdemona is called 'jewel,' 'wife,' 'lawful prize,' and 'food,' along with titles of respect such as 'lady' and 'mistress.' What stands out to us is that Desdemona is an 'object,' a possession of the men around her to be talked about and owned." From this identification analysis, of Desdemona, the group posed the question: "Based on the identification analysis, how is Desdemona dehumanized?"

When discussing Desdemona's status as an object and women's roles in Shakespearian society, the group looked at Desdemona's use of modality, pointing out that "Desdemona uses low modal verbs, especially when speaking to her father. We think that this shows that she, as a woman, has little power over the situation and can only get what she wants through making suggestions such as 'I would not' or 'I may profess.'" Through these observations, it is evident that students' identification analysis and modality analysis of Desdemona led them to recognize her lack of power in society, allowing them to better understand the power relationships between her and Brabantio.

Focal Event 3: Dialogue Generated from Obama Projects

The Obama projects (see Table 4.6 in Chapter 4 for project details) asked students to conduct a discourse analysis of a portion of the speech, provide copies of the analysis charts for the class, and interpret and explain their findings. I selected this event because it shows students identifying how the West "others" the East through Obama's language choices; it discusses cultural differences, and it shows students questioning their own beliefs and practices, even suggesting changes that could make our education system more "globalized."

Focusing on their identification analysis (see Table 7.3 for Sandi's group identification analysis), in her reflection, Sandi revealed that "the identification analysis does somewhat show the 'us' versus 'them' situation. Obama uses 'we' referring to him and America thirty-six times, while he refers to the East and the West as a whole only nine times. Even though he is trying to bring the two regions together, his word selection separates them more."

TABLE 7.3. Student Work: Sandi's Group Obama Identification Analysis

Participant 1: West		Participant 2: East		Collective	
Name	**#**	**Name**	**#**	**Name**	**#**
America	1	Israel	9	Us	2
Our	1	Its	1	Everyone	1
We	3	Palestine	7	Children of Abraham	1
Christians	1	Their	3		
		Gaza	1		
		West Bank	1		
		Arab States	4		
		Muslims	2		
		Jews	1		

She supports this comment with the results of her appraisal analysis (see Table 7.4 for Sandi's group's appraisal analysis), saying that the negative judgment and affect words used in conjunction with the East further separate them from the West.

TABLE 7.4. Student Work: Sandi's Group's Obama Appraisal Analysis Chart[a]

Appraisal	Positive	Negative
Affect	strong bonds, unbreakable, aspiration, peace, security, dignity, opportunity, achieve peace, ensure, live, work, develop, serve, progress, enable, responsibility, pursue, sustain, recognize, action, development, pursue peace, peacefully, mothers, holy land, ensure	source of tension, destruction, endured pain, humiliations, stalemate, painful, tragic, persecuted, enslave, tortures, shot, gassed to death, killed, denying, violates, obligation, devastates, self-defeating, tears, blood, fear, conflict, distract, problems, lack of opportunity
Judgment	well known cultural and historical ties recognition cannot be denied Jewish Muslims Christians their state	anti-Semitism, Arab–Israeli conflict, baseless, distraction, ignorant, hateful, threatening, vile stereotypes, intolerable, undeniable point fingers
Appreciation	continuing, critical, important	major Holocaust Third Reich refugee camps stalemate distract pursue

[a]Adapted from Simmons (2016).

Latching on to the East versus West concept, the discussion moved to questioning not the East's unwillingness to globalize but our own. The excerpted discussion below was based on a question that was brought to my attention when I was reading an Egyptian Muslim colleague's opinion about the speech (see also Table 4.6 in Chapter 4). The question read:

> One could say that *globalization* is the "widening, deepening, and speeding up of world-wide interconnectedness in all aspects of contemporary social life, from the cultural to the criminal, the financial to the spiritual" (Crossley & Watson, 2003, p. 53). A colleague of mine once said, "To be blunt, while education and media in the Muslim world has been dramatically Westernized over the last twenty years, I have to ask how Western education/media has been changed to reflect Muslim or 'Eastern' values in the last twenty years for us to accept this interpretation of 'mutual' global exchange?" As a student in a Westernized culture, do you think your education has been "globalized" to reflect Muslim or "Eastern" values?

Students shared their responses to this question as follows:

> LAKISHA: No. Generally, overall, no. For me, personally, I have learned, especially [in] my AP classes like World History, a whole lot more, but I feel like we are still taught this stereotype. It's just, like, they want you to get a taste of this other part of the world, but they only feed you, like, a stereotype. Like, we know, like, the clothes that they wear but that's, like, it. And they don't really go very deep into their culture. I've never been asked to really understand... but I think that, as a whole system, there is no cultural exchange...
>
> MISTY: I think that, if we had more teachers from the East or who are Muslim, it would be, like, more relevant in the classroom because they know about it. A lot of our teachers are not from that culture. I mean they know about it, but it's not a part of them; it's not personal, and I don't think that they know enough about it to teach it to us from a personal aspect. So, I think that if we had more teachers from the East, there would be more globalization in a classroom.
>
> AFZAL: I definitely understand what she's saying, but I guess, going along with my sect of Islam, our leader has started programs over here in the US, and they correlate to different cultures in the US, mostly on the Western side of the US, and he started studies over there, and he has initiated a program in London also in which you go over there and learn about it, and then you come back to the US and teach it. So, of course, right now, it's not that much, but I think that, over the years, it can progress, and not just with Muslims. I mean, you could go all over the world. Asia or other places in the East, and those teachers could come over here and teach also. But it just takes initiative to try to globalize the West.

AMBER: And who is putting forth that initiation? That effort?

AFZAL: Exactly.

AMBER: Is it us? Are we asking people to come over and saying, "Come over, we want to learn about you. We want to learn new things so that we can incorporate your values into our culture?" Or is it saying that the "minority" culture is saying, "Hey, you need to know about us." Which way is it going?

AFZAL: It has to be mutual.

WINNIE: I feel like, up to this point in our education, we have not really been exposed to a lot of that, because, right now, we are taking a lot of the basic classes, and we do not get to choose them. But, as we start going to college, and we go into further graduate programs, we can take a course on Islamic history or take a course on any other cultural experience and learn more about it from there. But I feel like, up to this point in our education, we are not exposed to it as much as we should be. It's just that we're trying to get in all the basics.

AMBER: But should it be a basic?

WINNIE: It should because, regardless of what we do with our lives, we will be dealing with people from different cultures and different races and that is something fundamental that we need to know.

RHADIKA: I just want to go back to what Lakisha said about stereotypes and how we talked about Said's *Orientalism*, like, how every time we would see one of the stereotypes, we would automatically relate it back to *Aladdin*, and it's really showing how little we know about their culture, and this is stuff that we really should've had in World History. And we only get World History in seventh and tenth grade, and it's hard to remember stuff from that distance. It's hard to remember stuff when you're little in seventh grade. I don't even remember if I learned anything about world history in elementary school. I mean, I just kind of. . . it seems, like, if we had started learning younger, we might have had more interest to learn it, like how what Winnie said—in college, we will have a chance to take deeper-level classes, but, if you don't have a basic knowledge of it, why would you want to take it? You don't know anything about it, so it's kind of. . . (Obama discussion)

In order to understand the context of this discussion (see also Simmons, 2016c, p. 202), it is important to know that Afzal and Winnie identify as Muslim while Lakisha, an African American female, Misty, a white female, and Rhadika, an Indian American female, did not. What was striking about this conversation was Lakisha, Misty, and Rhadika's ability to problematize their culture's educational system. First, Lakisha recognized the problem, mentioning that all they learn is the stereotypical characteristics of a culture. Agreeing with Lakisha that this is a problem, Misty suggested a way to increase the globalization of our school by hiring more teachers who are Muslim or from the East, effectively providing students with an authentic connection to Eastern values and traditions. Commenting on Misty's suggestion, Afzal shared that his sect of Islam was already trying to incorporate Muslim educators into Western schools.

However, when I questioned who was initiating the globalization, the students realized that such initiatives did not mean that the West was receptive to such educational opportunities. Further critiquing our system, Winnie stated that students do not have an opportunity to explore other cultures until college, meaning not every student will have a chance to expand their knowledge on world cultures because college is not necessarily available to all students. Winnie concluded that cultural studies should be a part of "the basics" because every student will eventually be required to interact with someone from another culture and, the more they know about the culture, the more authentic and successful the interaction.

Referencing a previous conversation regarding "Orientalism" and our stereotyped view of the East as portrayed in the Disney film *Aladdin*, Rhadika realized how little she really knew about the East. What she did know came from a Western source, and that knowledge came sporadically. In essence, her idea of the East was naturalized through "coercion and consent" (Fairclough, 1989, p. 33)—she admittedly accepted the *Aladdin* stereotype. Furthermore, it seemed as though Rhadika was advocating for a continuous cultural education, not just a unit here and there every three years. She also observed the effects of such little globalization in the education system. She recognized that, if the public education system did not value globalization or the values of other cultures, it becomes a part of the student's ideology. Without any education on other cultures or any indication from powerful institutions that other cultures are valuable, why would any student choose to educate themselves? The result is a cyclical pattern of anti-globalization. This recognition of how ideology is sustained and perpetuated can help students transcend ideology (Fairclough, 1992b).

To summarize these events, students' discussion of discourse analysis coding and analysis of texts provided a means for them to assess how language was positioning participants and to critically examine the purpose behind such language choices. When discussing each text, students relied on the results of their analyses to support their claims while also using personal experiences to challenge the status quo (CCSS.ELA-LITERACY.RL.1). For example, students' analysis of the house-elves' language led to a discussion that problematized our assumption that the house-elves have less control of language than the wizards. Using Alan's personal experience with translating Korean into English, students considered the possibility of house-elves being more linguistically capable than wizards, which, in turn, opened up a discussion as to why the house-elves chose to speak in the third person. Students concluded that it might be a form of resistance to their dehumanization or as an affirmation of self.

When analyzing *Othello*, students were able to rely on their discourse analysis coding to support their interpretation of power relationships between characters as well as differences in how characters were viewed based on their social class. Furthermore, with the Obama speech, language analysis led students to challenge not only language practices, but the perceived values of their education system. Not only were they willing to assess an institution of which they were a part, but they also made suggestions for change.

Reflection Questions for Chapter 7

1. How can the demographics of your school or classroom affect critical dialogue and critical language analysis? What challenges might you face? Or, how might your demographics support productive discussions about language use?
2. Think about my colleague's comment: "To be blunt, while education and media in the Muslim world has been dramatically Westernized over the last twenty years, I have to ask how Western education/media has been changed to reflect Muslim or 'Eastern' values in the last twenty years for us to accept this interpretation of 'mutual' global exchange?" Based on your educational experience, how would you answer this question?

8

Application of Language Knowledge: Developing Language Skills in Academic Writing

Guiding Gist

- After SFL instruction and engaging in CDA, students were more able, or willing, to select critical examples and focus on critical themes from stimulus materials, using modality analyses, identification analyses, or appraisal analyses to assess an author's purposeful use of language.
- Not only did students analyze texts using discourse analysis tools, but also, when responding to persuasive writing prompts, students utilized the same tools (appropriate modality, contrast and concession, citations, and appraisal words) as a persuasive device in their own writing.
- In their writing, students utilized SFL metalanguage to identify and articulate the linguistic elements used by an author in order to provide evidence from the text to support their main argument.
- This linguistically informed language curriculum supported the values of College Board and the CCSS by helping students identify and effectively write about the purposes of the language features used by an author.
- Evidence from essays written before and after instruction show evidence that a linguistically informed curriculum helps students write responses that are more focused on analyzing an author's purpose instead of simply providing a summary of the text's meaning.

While students' CLA and usage of discourse analysis tools developed during teacher-guided classroom activities, students' writing was also impacted by their growing knowledge of language and grammar as a system of choices. While tracking this progress helped determine the usefulness of discourse analysis and a linguistically informed curriculum in terms of student success on writing assessments, I also wanted to see if students found value in what they had learned. One way to determine this was to analyze students' independent construction to see if students used their new awareness and skills in their own written responses to formal writing prompts when they were not prompted to do so by the teacher. In this section, I share students' responses to AP exam-style essay questions to show how their writing and analysis of texts improved and reveal their value of the language study through their use of newly developed language analysis methods.

Application of SFL/CDA in Academic Writing

To review, I ask students to engage in writing assignments that ask them to respond to an AP Language and Composition writing prompt. The following essays prompts are listed in the order in which they are presented in the curriculum. The full curriculum calendar can be found in Chapter 4.

Essay Prompts

- Malcom X textual analysis essay: The prompt reads, "carefully read the following autobiographical narrative by Malcolm X excerpted from *The Autobiography of Malcolm X* (1965). In a well-constructed essay, identify the author's purpose and intended effect and analyze the rhetorical strategies and techniques he employs to achieve this" (Murphy & Rankin, 2002, p. 212; see also X & Haley, 1965).
- Animal testing synthesis essay: The prompt for this synthesis essay dealt with the controversial issue of animal testing and asked students to "Read the following sources carefully. Then, in an essay that synthesizes at least three of the sources, take a position that supports, challenges, or qualifies the claim that animals should not be used in research" (Ehrenhaft, 2010, p. 232).
- Drabble free-response essay: For this particular essay, the prompt read, "In 2001, *The American Scholar* published an excerpt from a talk given by English author Margaret Drabble. In her talk, Drabble claimed that 'Our desire to conform is greater than our respect for objective facts.' Using appropriate evidence from your reading, observation, and/or experience, write a carefully reasoned essay defending, challenging, or qualifying Drabble's assertion about conformity" (College Board, 2008, p. 24).

- Shadd Cary textual analysis essay: The prompt states, "Read the passage carefully, considering the circumstances in which it was written. Then, in a carefully written essay, analyze the techniques Mary Ann Shadd Cary uses to establish the necessity of her newspaper" (College Board, 2008, p. 23).
- "Owls" textual analysis essay: Mary Oliver's (1995) "Owls" question asked students to "Carefully read the following passage from 'Owls' by Mary Oliver. Then write an essay in which you analyze how Oliver's style conveys the complexity of her response to nature" (College Board, 2001, p. 3).

To provide an overview, in the Malcolm X essay sample responses, focal students concentrated on how Malcolm's purpose of writing his biography was to express his emotional reaction to being discriminated against in order to promote change. Students focused on prejudiced language and portrayed stereotypes, issues that we concentrated on when discussing inequality in the wizarding world of *Harry Potter*.

While students did not use discourse analysis tools in their responses to the animal testing essay prompt, it is apparent that they did recognize the usefulness of modality and appraisal words through their own language use, which was not as apparent in their Malcolm X essays. Similar to how Iago uses high modality to persuade Othello that Desdemona was having an affair with Cassio, students used high modality and strong affect, judgment, and appreciation words to manipulate readers to agree with their point of view.

Similar to the Malcolm X response, students focused on critical themes when responding to the Drabble quote. It is possible that the critical dialogue surrounding our discourse analysis of Obama's speech moved students to select critical examples, showing a greater willingness to discuss critical issues as the comment itself "our desire to conform is greater than our respect for objective facts" does not particularly encourage students to make critical observations, unlike the Malcolm X essay that focused on race and discrimination. In this essay, if students wanted to make a critical comment about society, they had to be inspired to do so on their own, as the prompt did not lead them to such conclusions. Finally, only after their analysis of all three texts in the curriculum cycle did students use specific discourse analysis tools to show how Shadd Cary manipulates her audience and exudes power through her use of the plural pronoun "we." Similar to how Obama speaks for America using "we," Shadd

Cary does the same for the *Freeman* community. The next few sections of this chapter will provide details and examples of how this came to pass.

Malcolm X Essay Analysis

The first essay students wrote after their direct discourse analysis instruction and *Harry Potter* language study was a prompt responding to an excerpt from Malcolm X's autobiography (X & Haley, 1965). The Malcolm X prompt was chosen in conjunction with the *Harry Potter* unit because its passage, although autobiographical, was most similar to *Harry Potter* due to its narrative style.

Tyler wasted no time in using his new metalanguage to analyze the passage. In a body paragraph, he writes:

> Malcolm X also loads this section with heavy words, full of connotation and emotion. An analysis on modality shows highly charged words that carry power, show force, and go deep into the reader. An identification analysis shows stereotypes and negative feelings toward Black people, and an appraisal analysis leads one to feel as if they are walking in the very shoes of Malcolm X himself, as they carry deep feeling, deep meaning, and draw the reader to empathize with Malcolm X. . . . Through discourse analysis and identification of a few rhetorical strategies, any reader is able to see what changed his world and ours.

This was a solid first try at using his new analysis tools to analyze a passage in a forty-minute writing window. However, there is still some vagueness to the response that leaves much to be desired. If he had cited evidence from those analyses to support his claims instead of just saying the analyses proved it, then he would have had a very strong argument indeed. Later in this chapter, I will show how, at the end of the language curriculum, students are able to do just that.

While Tyler boldly strode into the brave new world of linguistics, I was disappointed that most students did not analyze the language of the passage using their new discourse analysis tools. I then realized that I was looking at what I believed was *missing* from students' writing, and not at what was there—a tragic flaw of many a heroic teacher.

When I looked for what student essays had in common, besides the fact that none used a discourse analysis tool, I found that students did make an assessment as to the critical nature of the passage, fighting against racial prejudice and stereotypes, and made some sort of comment on how the language reiterated the critical purpose of the passage. Many students made critical observations similar to that of Grace, one of our focal students:

> Malcolm X effectively uses his autobiography to inform people of the discrimination experienced by African Americans. Additionally, his purpose is to prompt readers and all of society to question their formed stereotypes. . . . In paragraph three, Malcolm X uses a rhetorical question to hint to readers that they too need to be questioning their way of thinking as he did.

Grace recognized Malcolm's critical questioning of the world around him and his use of rhetorical questions to articulate that questioning. To me, this reflects Grace's own budding critical consciousness. She recognized the critical nature of the topic and assessed what language devices Malcolm X uses to get his audience to question the world around him, an analysis Grace might not have been able to make if we had not just engaged in our own critical questioning of race, gender, and class discrimination in *Harry Potter*.

Animal Testing Synthesis Essay

This essay asks students to read multiple sources and make an argument supporting or refuting animal testing using appropriate sources for support. While students did not use discourse analysis tools to assess the validity or merit of the sources, they did use high modality and appraisal words to manipulate their reader as modeled by persuasive speakers they read. Take Sandi's thesis statement for example:

> Some sources may argue that animal testing is disrespectful to animals—a form of racism to a species different from their own. However, these sources are extremely biased in their opinions. They may consider morals and the suffering of animals; however, they disregard the suffering of their own human race. (Simmons, 2018, p. 87)

From this example, I see how Sandi's language study manifested itself in her own writing choices. Unlike the Malcolm X response, Sandi knew she was to write persuasively, and she recognized that strong affect, judgment, and appreciation words would be appropriate along with high modality words to convince her audience of her certainty on the matter.

First, Sandi set up her thesis like a contrast and concession. She credited her opposition by pointing out their strong feelings feels about animal testing by using the negative judgment word "disrespectful" and the negative appraisal word "racism." Then, she swiftly changed positions, suggesting that, while their feelings were strong, through her use of strong diction, her opinion on the matter—that animal testing is necessary to save human lives—was stronger and more morally correct by pointing out the flaws in their argument using equally negative diction and both low and high modality. She does this first by making the judgment that they are "biased" and amplifying that fact with the appreciation word "extremely." Then she used the affect word "opinions" to suggest that their feelings were irrational. Sandi selected the low modality phrase "may consider" to decrease the strength of their conviction and "morals" and, in the same sentence, condemned them by using the highly modal verb "disregard," to highlight their lack of concern for the human race. By looking at Sandi's writing, our deconstruction of language as a class through direct instruction, as well as the joint construction she experienced through class discussion and group projects, helped her to successfully control and analyze language when she was asked to independently construct a text.

Not once in this thesis did Sandi state her own feelings about the topic. Instead, she chose to state her position by refuting her opposition. In order to do this successfully, she utilized her knowledge about modality and appraisal, knowing when to use high and low modality and using negative appraisal words.

While Sandi showed her skill in her thesis statement, Parvesh utilized his knowledge of modality and contrast and concession to craft a strong conclusion to his animal testing essay. He wrote:

> Animal testing will always be present in science. The question is if it is morally acceptable. Sources A and D provide countless examples of the benefit of animal research to prevent human diseases, but is it enough? It is. In the bigger picture, it is more important for humans to thrive than rats. It is natural selection at work. Scientists will never think to purposely create experiments that are intentionally cruel to animals, but they will always consider it morally acceptable to use animals to get the best knowledge to provide the best care for humans.

Here, we can see Parvesh using his new knowledge of citations and contrast and concession to construct a strong and memorable conclusion. He correctly points out the purpose of two of the provided sources—to provide examples of animal testing that led to the eradication of human diseases—and creatively points out that these sources are enough to prove his argument with the use of a question and highly modal simple sentence. He ends his paper with a contrast and concession: "Scientists will never think to purposely create experiments that are intentionally cruel to animals, but they will always consider it morally acceptable to use animals to get the best knowledge to provide the best care for humans." Using the concessive conjunction "but" and high modal verb "will" and absolute words such as "never" and "always" in both his contrast and his concession, Parvesh successfully persuades his audience that animal testing is not intended to be intentionally cruel but is instead meant as a means to save humans lives.

These results support Rothery and Stenglin's (2000) research that suggested that the appraisal system can aid students in writing more effective analyses of texts and support CCSS standards (e.g., CCSS. ELA-LITERACY.W.1). In this case, instead of analyzing another author's use of appraisal words, students themselves utilized them as a persuasive devise.

Drabble Essay

This prompt asks students to support, refute, or qualify Drabble's statement that "our desire to conform is greater than our respect for objective facts" (College Board, 2008, p. 24). In this essay, students were expected to use their life experiences and previous academic knowledge (historical events, literature, etc.) to support their position. In essence, the prompt provides students with the most freedom in how they choose to respond. They could, essentially, write about anything they felt related to the quote as long as it supports a position. It is this fact that led me to realize that my students were growing in their ability to critically view the world, as, out of all the options they could possibly write about, many chose to focus on critical themes discussed during our language study. Parvesh's response is a prime example of this conscious choice.

Parvesh chose to write about how our desire to conform despite the facts led to some of the most heinous hate crimes in world history. His first example was Nazi Germany. He talked about soldiers "just following orders" and concluded that "they were afraid to be different; they felt comfortable in the norm and would not stop if their leader, Hitler, told them not to." His second example was the Civil Rights Movement in America. Parvesh wrote, "Many of the whites were racist because they were taught that way by friends and family." In his final example, Parvesh used his own experiences in high school. He wrote:

> If you are not the norm, you are an outsider. If you are an outsider, you are weird. This logic is usually how many children think, me included. I feel safe if I dress and act and live like the majority of my school because I am not different. It is easy for me to conform to the ideas that are most prevalent because then I am easily accepted. Leaving it would mean one is exposed and different from others.

Parvesh's last sentence in his conclusion summarized his critical realization: "Being the norm may not be right, but it is easy to do."

In this essay, Parvesh wrote about our fear of being "othered" by not adopting the norms, or dominant ideology, of our society. He also chose to write about the negative consequences of not questioning the dominant ideology. First, he referenced the Holocaust and how accepting the norm led to unspeakable atrocities. Second, he wrote about how this harmful ideology was perpetuated in our society, using the Civil Rights Movement as an example. He pointed out how children are taught to be racist, not born racist. Parvesh then critiqued his high school culture, focusing on students' fear of being labeled "weird" if they did not fit the norm and how that fear led kids to adopt the norm, even if it is harmful to themselves or others. Finally, Parvesh looked inward—the most difficult and brave step in developing a critical consciousness. Parvesh recognized how he perpetuated the norms of his culture, which was essentially a hegemonic act as it furthered his fear of being different and did not work against it (Fairclough, 1995). The influence of our dialogue was also evident in his language choices. Parvesh used terms like "norms" and "outsider," terminology used when discussing othering in all three of the texts we studied.

Furthermore, the organization of Parvesh's essay followed the order of my implemented spiral curriculum in regard to scaffolding critical literacy (see Figure 8.1).

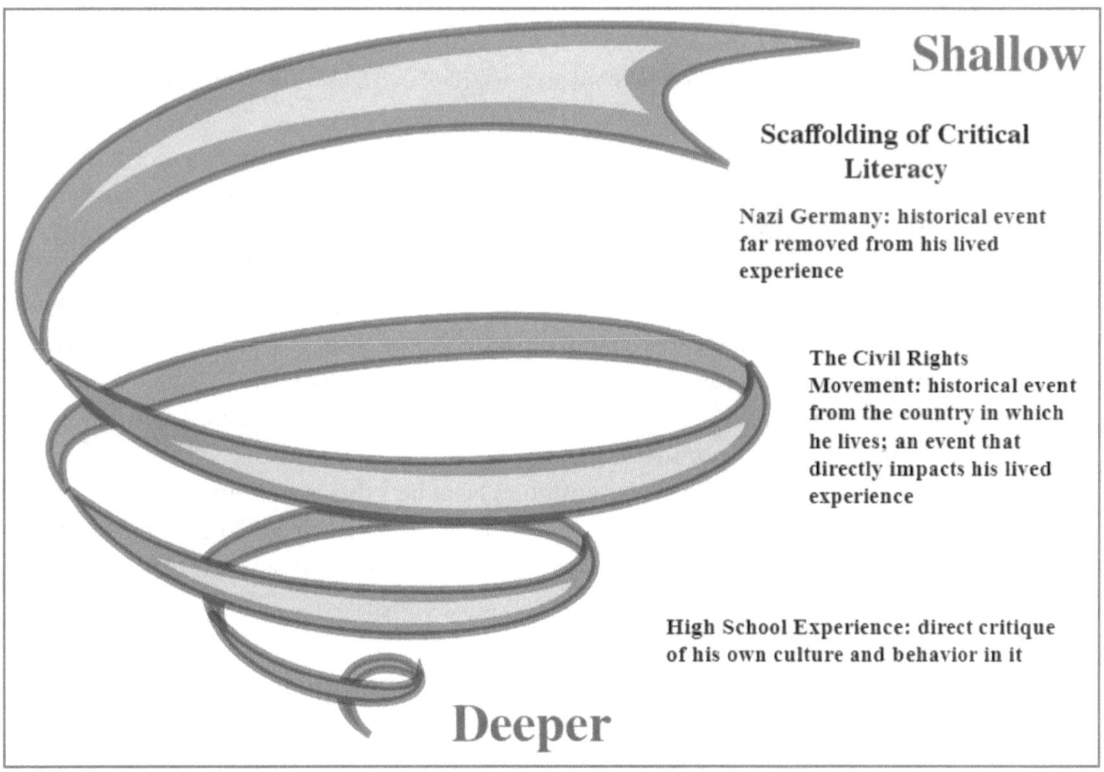

FIGURE 8.1. Parvesh's essay in the framework of the spiraled curriculum.

In his essay, Parvesh begins by assessing an element of history far removed from his own experience and actions. He then moved to a critical issue that occurred in the history of the country in which he lived. His last example addressed his place in the world and his perpetuation of a harmful cultural norm. He began with a critical critique of a society far removed from his own: Nazi Germany. He then moved to something closer to his own culture but from a different time period, one in which he did not live: the Civil Rights Movement. He concluded with a direct critique of his own culture and behavior in it: high school. This observation suggests that the spiraling of critical literacy in this curriculum guides students to the eventual questioning of their own actions and how they view the world.

Isabelle also showed critical development when responding to this prompt. In a body paragraph, she wrote:

> If the world was dependent on conformity, there would be one culture, one type of literature, one religion, one music genre, and one mind. The creation of religions in different cultures across the earth is the most influential and important aspect of people's lives. From one country to the next, there are people who pride themselves on their culture and live devoted to their religion. Religion is a part of their identity. There are also rebellions when trying to cause changes in religion, and even relocation. When people are forced to conform, they often rebel.

This paragraph begins with the recognition that diversity is what makes the world interesting. She then pointed out differing religions as a way that the world is culturally diversified and recognized that the existence of multiple religions allows for individual identity. She vaguely cited moments in history when people were forced to abandon their religious identity and how it led to rebellions or relocation. This paragraph suggests Isabelle's recognition that multiple cultural identities and religions are an asset to our global community and that trying to make everyone conform is not only fruitless but leads to a boring and vapid population.

The body paragraph also supports Isabelle's thesis statement that "there will always be a desire to conform somewhat; however, the world's diversity creates more advancement in technology, health and science, and culture." Isabelle's thesis statement, which is a contrast and concession, celebrates diversity and sees it not as something that should just be tolerated but as something that is necessary for human advancement.

Shadd Cary Essay

It wasn't until after our work with all the texts that students began utilizing their discourse analysis tools in the discussion of their AP exam analyses. It just might have taken students this long to feel comfortable utilizing analysis tools in their independent construction and analysis of texts. Each text did share similarities in genre with the prompt students were asked to respond to, in order to support student scaffolding (*Harry Potter* was a narrative, as was Malcolm X's autobiography; *Othello* was a drama/narrative whose characters used persuasive language and techniques, as did the sources provided in the animal testing prompt; the Drabble essay asked students to argue a particular point, which was the main goal of Obama's speech). However, Obama's speech—in essence, a persuasive speech—was the text most recently read by students and was most similar in genre to the Shadd Cary passage, which was a persuasive essay arguing the need for a newspaper addressing the concerns of African American freedmen and fugitive communities. This may mean that students were more influenced by their work with Obama's speech than the two previous texts when writing this response. It may also account for students' increased use of linguistic tools with this particular writing analysis, as Obama tended to use similar techniques as Shadd Cary.

Recognizing that Shadd Cary chose plural pronouns for a rhetorical purpose, many students chose to conduct an identification analysis to use as support when discussing the effect of this linguistic choice. For example, Winnie wrote the following paragraph:

> Mary Ann Shadd Cary writes this article from a first person plural perspective. The use of this strategy allows the African American readers of *Provincial Freedom* to feel as though they are a part of a united group with the potential to have a powerful voice in their society due to their numbers and united front. Using words like "we" and "us" includes herself among her readers and prevents her from seeming as though she were above them in any way.

Through her discussion of identification, Winnie made the critical recognition that the first-person plural pronoun gives power, community, and voice to a population that has been historically disenfranchised and silenced.

Similarly, when Grace conducted an identification analysis, she was able to not only identify but also discuss the effect of specific pronoun choices:

> After conducting an identification analysis on this passage, it was discovered that Cary uses many plural pronouns. She uses "we" twenty-three times, "our" fourteen times, "us" ten times, and "ourselves" two times. She uses these pronouns to ellict [*sic*] a "we are all in this together" effect. She simply shows the power of her group, and how determined they are to make a change. According to her, they cannot be stopped. (Simmons, 2018, p. 86)

With discourse analysis, I like to tell the kids that "the proof is in the pudding." By giving Grace a way to organize and code what she was intuitively sensing, she was able to provide the empirical evidence needed to support her claim that Shadd Cary used specific pronoun choices to create unity.

Unlike Grace and Winnie, instead of doing an identification analysis, Clara found value in assessing Shadd Cary's modality:

> She uses absolute words such as "must" repeatedly to show how dire and important it is to speak out. By saying, "we must have a mouthpiece," it shows the utter importance of being heard. She also uses words such as "never" and "denied" to describe the importance of the paper. Cary tells others that they were never given this opportunity from Canadian or American newspapers, in lines 29–33; therefore, they must take advantage of the resources they are now given. The reader is also constantly noticing words such as "need," "want," and "always" during the passage. Cary uses these words to give a stronger, more passionate feeling to her newspaper. The use of these high modality words show her confidence in what she is saying. Her emotions play a large role in persuading her readers to agree with her.

Based on her study of language and the purposes for certain modality choices, Clara concluded that the purpose of Shadd Cary's modality was to express her passion and "show her confidence in what she is saying." It is evident from each of these examples that students found the metalanguage of SFL helpful in identifying and articulating the linguistic elements utilized by Shadd Cary to support her argument for an African American newspaper.

Furthermore, when relating these results to Vygotsky's (1978) theory of learning, I can see that, due to students' individual learning needs, some students needed more time to receive teacher guidance, collaborate with peers, and practice independent construction before they felt comfortable incorporating SFL and CDA into their repertoire of analysis skills. Most of my students were continually developing and applying learned skills to their independent construction, and, as you implement this learning cycle, you might witness something similar.

Analysis of Student Writing before and after a Linguistically Informed Instruction

In this section, I make a comparison between the focal students' responses to an AP exam textual analysis question before the language unit and after it. The prompt asks students to "Carefully read the following passage from 'Owls' by Mary Oliver. Then write an essay in which you analyze how Oliver's style conveys the complexity of her response to nature" (College Board, 2001, p. 3). From our class, students understood "style" to be *how* an author presents their material, including the medium, purpose, and tone, as well as the rhetorical devices, syntax, and diction used. In essence, *style* is the unique choices an author makes in each of these categories to make their work meaningful and memorable.

Isabelle's "Owls" Essays before and after SFL Instruction

Based on her working definition of this term, her knowledge of what is valued in such AP exam responses, and her understanding of the passage, Isabelle wrote the following essay:

> **Isabelle's Essay before SFL Instruction**
>
> Oliver owns a style of writing not easily understood at first glance. She captivates the readers' minds by creating subjectivity within nature. The diction expresses the terror and indulgent sexual tension Oliver experiences. The immobilizing beauty of the roses creates a vivid imagery.
>
> In reading the piece, Oliver includes intimate words to pass on her manifesting discomfort she feels for the mystery nature holds. In the describing of the horned owl as "razor-tipped" and having "heavy, crisp, breathing snapping of its hooked beak," she views the owl as representative of evil. The owl is sadistic in its eating habits, by indulging in his [preys'] brains, leaving the rest of the carcass as waste. Through the terror the owl embodies, "terror is naturally and abundantly part of life, part of even the most becalmed, intelligent, sunny life—as, for example, my own," there is an acceptance with the various emotions people experience throughout life; terror is just one of them. The roses impose an arousing connotation for the author. She describes the roses having "red and pink and white tents of softness and nectar," giving the roses a vivid fulfillment of desire Oliver seeks. "I'm stuck, I'm taken, I'm conquered, I'm washed into it"—a parallelism that

communicates the awing grasp the roses have on her. Her insatiable yearning of the beautiful appearance of the roses deforms her reality into a state "full of dreaming and idleness." She plays with the idea of being so perplexed by beauty in saying "let the mind be teased by the stretches of imagination, by such balance," the word "teased" personifies a flirtation between her and nature.

Though appalled by the behavior of the horned owl, she is infatuated with the appearance of the roses due to their deceiving front. The colors "red, pink, and white," all own a symbolic trait that range from highest to lowest intensity. Red can be associated with lust or infatuation; a sexualized color. In *The Scarlet Letter*, when the letter represents the sin of a love affair built on a shallow foundation of infatuation. The pink is a soft tone that can symbolize young love. The white is related to purity and cleanliness. [In] the ballet *Swan Lake*, the good swan is white and untouchable by the evils of the world. The swan's innocence is the essence of idle beauty. The parallelism: "I drop to the sand, I can't move, I am restless no more; I am replete, supine, finished, filled to the last edges with an immobilizing happiness" serves the purpose of the infatuation the author has with the roses before her eyes. Her helplessness against the natural beauty is overwhelming to the reader. The reader, like the author, is overpowered against the force of nature; mother nature herself. The roses are similar to Venus, the goddess of sex and love in the *Aeneid*. Venus seduces her own son by transforming herself into a beautiful huntress; upon discovering her false appearance, her son is terrified in learning of his mother's perverted trickery and love. The deception proves to be dangerous and horrifying.

In final analysis, Oliver goes deeper [than] just a vicious owl and lovely roses. She uses the owl and roses as pawns for the chess game called life. Her word usage exposes her terror and insatiable appetite for the mystery behind nature's true existence. Oliver's trance and curiosity of the roses create imagery.

Written in class under the time constraint of forty minutes, the above essay is written exactly as it appeared in the student's original and has many strengths. As I have discussed before (see also Simmons, 2023), Isabelle recognized the complexity of the passage, therefore realizing that it parallels Oliver's complex feeling about nature. She also recognized many elements of style used by Oliver, including imagery, parallelism, and provocative diction. For example, she understood that the diction used to create an image of the horned owl was to re-create the fear she feels about nature for the reader. Similarly, Isabelle correctly identified Oliver's use of parallel structure to reiterate the paralyzing effect the beauty of the roses has on Oliver. While these examples show how Isabelle used elements of Oliver's style to explain her feelings about nature, there is much in this essay that deviates from the prompt.

Isabelle attempted to explain how color connotation symbolizes Oliver's feelings, trying to show how the owls represent fear of nature and the roses represent love. Knowing that AP exam graders value the inclusion of previous knowledge in students' responses, Isabelle included references to *The Scarlet Letter*, *Swan Lake*, and *The Aeneid* to showcase her retained literary knowledge. While this might seem like a shrewd maneuver, it does nothing to explain how Oliver's style represents her complex feeling toward nature, making the references only supportive of her reasoning behind her connotation with the colors red and white. In fact, when I did an appraisal analysis of Isabelle's paper, it showed that 40 percent of her affect, judgment, and appreciation words had nothing to do with the owls or roses, showing that she strayed from the topic. In addition, she only mentioned three literary elements: imagery, diction, and parallelism. Finally, Isabelle concluded with the cliché of "life as a chess game" and again mentioned imagery, yet the reader is uncertain as to where in her essay she explained the purpose of the imagery, as she only mentioned the term in the introduction and conclusion. Y'all, I don't know about you, but I *hate* it when students resort to clichés. . . so unoriginal.

Isabelle clearly recognized how the diction describing the owl and the roses represented feelings of terror and love, yet her paper seems unfocused and rambling, un-centered on Oliver's style, despite her discussion of diction/imagery and parallelism. In fact, it is almost simplistic, in its analysis of how Oliver uses language, and more complex in its analysis of the text's meaning. That's awesome, but it is not what the prompt asked her to do. From this essay, I guess that Isabelle tried to impress the graders by including everything she possibly could (literary allusions, literary devices, and language analysis), and, in the process, did not answer the prompt as clearly and concisely as she could have. It is my suspicion that, if she had discourse analysis tools available to her, she would have been able to more fully analyze Oliver's language use using her knowledge of linguistics, building an argument for the benefit of a linguistically based language curriculum.

At the end of the year, after students' went through the curriculum presented in this book, I asked students to write a response to the same prompt using their new skills. Students were given the same parameters—40 minutes in class—to respond. Here following is Isabelle's response to the same prompt after SFL instruction.

Isabelle's Essay after SFL Instruction

Mary Oliver is not simply praising roses or demoralizing owls in the piece "Owls"; she is exposing the fear that consumes her being. The owls are the more obvious terrible creatures, yet the seemingly harmless roses also exude terror. Based on an SFL usage of identification, similarities in word usage parallel the terror that Oliver feels.

Through analyzing Oliver's pronouns and nouns for the owl and the roses, it is blattent [*sic*] how she feels about them. For example, she gives three specific types of owls and flowers. The owls have names such as the snowy owl, screech owl, and the great horned owl. The flowers, she uses names like lupines, poppies, and rose. This is significant because she is creating a contrast or degree in the fear that she feels for each type. The great horned owl and roses are the most terrorizing. She makes them a threat. She makes us feel threatened the way she feels threatened. Also, her constant use of "it" in describing both creatures—Oliver seems all but comfortable in uttering their names. The purpose in using "it" protects her from experiencing the discomfort they give off.

By speaking in the first person, her experience makes it that much more intimate of a relationship she has between the apparent and subtle terrors in nature. She uses high modality for her own feelings. The usage of "must," "know," "can't," and "can" all destroy any doubt Oliver is comfortable talking about the owl. She is, without a doubt, frightened. This high modality also carries with the roses. The modality analysis categorizes these two creatures, the owl and the roses, in two different states of mind: terror and sublime happiness. However, at the end of the last paragraph, Oliver asks the question: "And is this not also terrible?" Her endless terror of the owl also exists with the flowers; her modality shows how she is afraid of how they awe her, which is yet another way nature is so complex.

In Isabelle's opening paragraph, she articulated her more mature understanding that Oliver's complex emotions about nature stem from its ability to possess and paralyze her, whether through fear or beauty. In this essay, Isabelle's comment about how she used discourse analysis to prove this serves as a more complete thesis statement than her previous essay: "The immobilizing beauty of the roses creates a vivid imagery."

In her first body paragraph, Isabelle explained how her identification analysis revealed how the great horned owl and the roses were mentioned more often and with the pronoun "it." She also suggested that Oliver's use of the pronoun "it" was to distance herself from these two elements of nature because she feared them. In this paragraph, Isabelle's close look at how the objects were identified successfully revealed how Oliver felt about them, focusing her essay on Oliver's elements of style and language use in relation to her feelings toward nature.

In addition, while, at first glance, it looks like her first essay used more of the original text for support of her analysis, many of the quotes did little to support Isabelle's analysis of Oliver's style; for example, "Her insatiable yearning of the beautiful appearance of the roses deforms her reality into a state 'full of dreaming and idleness.'" However, while her second essay used fewer quotes for support, the words she chose to include in her essay represented how Oliver's style expressed her feelings, showing how SFL afforded Isabelle with the resources to analyze how language accomplished Oliver's goal. They were used with more focus and intention.

While Isabelle added previous knowledge about *The Scarlet Letter* and *Swan Lake* in her first essay in an attempt to impress the graders, it did not do much to show how Oliver uses style to convey her feelings. In her second essay, the discourse analysis tool served as her incorporation of previous knowledge, accomplishing the same goal of catering to graders' desires but keeping her response focused on Oliver's language use.

Performing an appraisal analysis on this essay shows that 100 percent of Isabelle's affect, judgment, and appreciation words related to language or Oliver's portrayal of the roses or owl (Table 8.1).

In addition, instead of only focusing on imagery, parallelism, and diction, Isabelle showed her knowledge about language by using metalanguage *and* discussing it—a feature that was lacking in the previous essay. She mentioned SFL, pronouns and nouns, first person point of view, and modality (Table 8.2).

She also explained the results of her discourse analysis and explained the implications of her results, effectively informing the reader which indicators in Oliver's language led her to conclude that Oliver was both scared and awed by nature's power.

TABLE 8.1. Appraisal Analysis of Isabelle's Second "Owls" Essay

Coding: • affect = **bold** • judgment = <u>underlined</u> • appreciation = *italics*
Mary Oliver is not *simply* **praising** roses or **demoralizing** owls in the piece "Owls"; she is exposing the **fear** that **consumes** her being. The owls are the *more* obvious **terrible** creatures, yet the *seemingly* **harmless** roses also exude **terror**. Based on an SFL usage of identification, similarities in word usage parallel the **terror** that Oliver feels. Through analyzing Oliver's pronouns and nouns for the owl and the roses, it is blattent [*sic*] how she feels about them. For example, she gives three *specific* types of owls and flowers. The owls have names such as the snowy owl, screech owl, and the great horned owl. The flowers, she uses names like lupines, poppies, and rose. This is significant because she is creating a contrast or degree in the **fear** that she feels for *each* type. The *great* horned owl and roses are the *most* **terrorizing**. She makes them a **<u>threat</u>**. She makes us feel **threatened** the way she feels **threatened**. Also, her constant use of "it" in describing both creatures—Oliver seems *all* but **comfortable** in uttering their names. The purpose in using "it" **protects** her from experiencing the **discomfort** they give off. By speaking in the first person, her experience makes it that *much more* **intimate** of a relationship she has between the apparent and subtle terrors in nature. She uses high modality for her own feelings. The usage of "must," "know," "can't," and "can" all **destroy** *any* doubt Oliver is **comfortable** talking about the owl. She is, without a doubt, **frightened**. This high modality also carries with the roses. The modality analysis categorizes these two creatures, the owl and the roses, in two different states of mind: **terror** and **sublime happiness**. However, at the end of the last paragraph, Oliver asks the question: "And is this not also **terrible**?" Her **endless terror** of the owl also exists with the flowers; her modality shows how she is **afraid** of how they **awe** her, which is yet another way nature is *so* **complex**.

TABLE 8.2. Use of Metalanguage in Isabelle's Second "Owls" Essay

Coding: • use of metalanguage = **bold**
Mary Oliver is not simply praising roses or demoralizing owls in the piece "Owls"; she is exposing the fear that consumes her being. The owls are the more obvious terrible creatures, yet the seemingly harmless roses also exude terror. Based on an **SFL usage** of **identification**, similarities in word usage parallel the terror that Oliver feels. Through analyzing Oliver's **pronouns and nouns** for the owl and the roses, it is blattent [*sic*] how she feels about them. For example, she gives three specific types of owls and flowers. The owls have names such as the snowy owl, screech owl, and the great horned owl. The flowers, she uses names like lupines, poppies, and rose. This is significant because she is creating a contrast or degree in the fear that she feels for each type. The great horned owl and roses are the most terrorizing. She makes them a threat. She makes us feel threatened the way she feels threatened. Also, her constant use of "it" in describing both creatures—Oliver seems all but comfortable in uttering their names. The purpose in using "it" protects her from experiencing the discomfort they give off. By speaking in the **first person**, her experience makes it that much more intimate of a relationship she has between the apparent and subtle terrors in nature. She uses **high modality** for her own feelings. The usage of "must," "know," "can't," and "can" all destroy any doubt Oliver is comfortable talking about the owl. She is, without a doubt, frightened. This **high modality** also carries with the roses. The **modality analysis** categorizes these two creatures, the owl and the roses, in two different states of mind: terror and sublime happiness. However, at the end of the last paragraph, Oliver asks the question: "And is this not also terrible?" Her endless terror of the owl also exists with the flowers; her **modality** shows how she is afraid of how they awe her, which is yet another way nature is so complex.

Clara's "Owls" Essays before and after SFL Instruction

Clara was another student whose written analysis of the "Owls" passage improved significantly as a result of discourse analysis instruction.

Clara's "Owls" Essay before SFL Instruction

Nature brings out simple yet stunning emotions. Nature portrays everything pure, yet everything tainted, making them seem as one. Mary Oliver's essay "Owls" questions how it is possible to have such fear and admiration for a thing as simplistic as nature. By her use of imagery, diction, parallelism, and personification, Oliver shows a muddled feeling toward nature.

The style of Mary Oliver's writing gives off the mood and the voice of the writer. The rhetorical devices used give a sense of being awestruck. For instance, when Oliver states "a sweetness so palpable and excessive that, before it, I'm struck, I'm taken. . ." (para. 2). The imagery in the passage displays her emotions for fear and beauty of nature. "I know this bird. If it could, it would eat the whole world." (para. 1) "I have found myself thinking of summer fields, fields full of flowers—poppies and lupines." (para. 2) The parallelism used when speaking of the owls versus speaking of the flowers shows the similarities between what seems like opposites. Mary Oliver is terrified of the great horned owl, she is breath taken by the flowers that she sees. Both have a representation of fear. One from a tainted feeling and one from lust. Yet both feelings are out of her control. The personification used in "Owls" is a tool to illustrate nature to human life and apply Oliver's question of how is it possible?

Oliver questions throughout the passage: Why are things the way they are? What makes something beautiful? What makes one see both sides? What is the nature of ourselves? Can beauty be dangerous? How is it possible? Oliver shows a certain energy for nature by her use of rhetorical devices. Mary Oliver focuses on the meaning of life itself not only seeing the black and white of this world, but also the grey.

Similar to Isabelle, in her first essay, Clara was able to identify that Oliver has "muddled feelings" about nature, articulating Oliver's confusion about how she feels about nature. Clara decided that she was going to show how Oliver uses imagery, diction, parallelism, and personification to reflect those confusing feelings. Let's see how well she did that, shall we?

First, Clara put a discussion of all of these elements into one large body paragraph. When students do this, it is a blinking red light that they probably are going to struggle with the analysis part of the writing assessment, and lo and behold, she did. She was able to identify devices used in Oliver's essay, but her explanation as to why she uses them and exactly how they successfully reveal her feelings was lacking. She selected chunks of the essay to quote, but gave no context to the selected quote, instead stringing them together with no linking thought or explanation. In her conclusion, she tried to employ a sophisticated form following function technique by using rhetorical questions to mimic Oliver's questioning of nature. However, she said the questions show Oliver's "energy" but did not elaborate on how they do that. She made a broad, sweeping statement but did not follow it with details or sufficient proof. Clara's first attempt at this essay shows a student who can identify literary devices in a text and even the tone and purpose of passage, but struggles to bring those two elements together to explain and analyze why and how the devices reveal the tone or support the purpose. Let's look at her essay after SFL instruction:

Clara's "Owls" Essay after SFL Instruction

In the passage "Owls," Mary Oliver discusses the complexity of nature. First, she characterizes variations of owls ranging from the great horned to the snowy white owl, and then she goes on to characterize a sea of roses. Though there is [an] obvious feeling of malice and fear toward to great horned owl, Oliver also highlights how the utter completeness she gains from the roses also cause her the same deep horror.

Through diction as well as syntax used within "Owls," Mary Oliver introduces to the reader the pondering of nature and its encompassing beauty as well as terror. Through the word choice that Oliver used to portray both the owls and the roses shows her continuous questioning of nature. When describing the screech owl and snowy owl, Oliver uses judgment words such as "wanderer," which depicts a harmless, innocent image. She follows in these judgments by using appreciation words such a "luminous" and "delicate," which adds to the serene image. She then goes on to characterize the great horned owl as "hunters of our world" and "death-bringers." These two judgments foil the characterization given to the screech owl and snowy owl. She calls the great horned "merciless" and "insatiable." It is through these two opposing descriptions of these three different owls that the reader begins to understand Oliver's bewilderment. These two contrasting characterizations lend to the question: How could both beauty and evil exists from one source?

Oliver is wondering how two completely unsimilar [*sic*] things or animals can be from one source.

Another example of diction that Oliver uses to portray her inquisitiveness about nature is through her modality. When discussing the great horned owl she uses high modal phrases such as "I know," "I have," and "I must," which all add to her assurance of the characteristics of the great horned owl. In contrast, Oliver uses lower modality when asking her rhetorical questions in lines 53–56. She begins to question the attributes of nature rather than using absolute verbiage like she did in the previous passage. This question showing shows the complexity and unknown of nature.

In addition to the diction used, Oliver also uses syntax to help convey her image or view of nature. When discussing the roses (48–52), Oliver uses parallelism to convey her ultimate bliss from the roses. She uses the contraction "I'm" or "I am" repeatedly to denote her state. Yet, she then contrasts her sentences by using rhetorical questions. Through these questions, she truly questions nature and its characteristics.

Within "Owls," Mary Oliver uses a variation of word choice and sentence structure to convey her pondering of nature. She is perplexed by the idea of good and evil in natural organisms coming from the same source. Through her diction and syntax, her confusion is conveyed.

In her second essay, written after discourse analysis instruction, we see a similar theme presenting itself: focus. Instead of listing four language devices to discuss, Clara chose two: diction and syntax. In her analysis of these two elements, she focused on judgments and modality. While the first paper cited excerpts of the passage in their entirety, Clara used specific judgment words from the passage to discuss how these words show Oliver's feelings toward the owls, roses, and nature in general. By doing this, she was able to point out the contrast between how Oliver judges the owls and roses and point out the contradictions and confusion surrounding her feelings. Clara used her modality analysis to do something similar: show the contrast between the effect of nature on Oliver (the use of high modality) and her understanding of those feelings (low modality). She argued that this "shows the complexity and unknown of nature."

The last body paragraph focused on parallelism, something that was also done in the first essay when she wrote, "The parallelism used when speaking of the owls versus speaking of the flowers shows the similarities between what seems like opposites." However, in the second essay, it seems like an identification analysis helped Clara focus on what part of the structure was actually repeated: "I'm" and "I am." Making this recognition, Clara was able to make the claim that "She uses the contraction 'I'm' or 'I am' repeatedly to denote her state. Yet, she then contrasts her sentences by using rhetorical questions."

She is on to something here but does not quite get there. If she were to pair her identification analysis with her modality analysis, she would have been able to come up with the analysis that the absolute "I am" in conjunction with the questions and the wavering between the two shows her confusion with regard to her feelings about nature. Even though she didn't take this explanation far enough, in my opinion, the proof and analysis of parallelism is still stronger than the first essay.

Sandi's "Owls" Essays before and after SFL Instruction

Sandi's before and after essays also show comparable changes and growth.

Sandi's "Owls" Paper before SFL Instruction

Throughout the essay "Owls" by Mary Oliver, there is an overwhelming sense of [good] versus bad being portrayed by the elements found in nature. There is also a hint of man versus nature being wicked. As an obvious though to the reader, Oliver's essay describes the torture and unimaginable acts of "the great horned owl" (1); however, one is surprised to know Oliver uses the same unimaginable sufferings to describe the beautiful luscious roses. The author finds anguish in her feelings that nature can be both strikingly picturesque and vicious at the same time.

"When the great horned owl is in the trees" (1), Oliver compares the owl as if it were almost a man-eating machine. This owl, with "its razor tipped toes" (2) would grab innocent animals, such as rabbits and blue jays, and eat only their heads with the "heavy, crisp, breathy snapping of its hooked beak" (4–5). In a way, the preyed-on can be compared to the headless horseman from *The Legend of Sleepy Hollow*. They are a warning to the reader to be afraid of the great horned owl. This fear Oliver has creates emotions of paranoia not only for herself, but for the reader. As Oliver writes, "if one of those should touch me, it would be the center of my life and I must fall" (12–13), one can envision the horror and inhumane things an owl is capable of doing. This, coupled with feelings about the rose, stirs emotions the reader is able to identify with but may be unable to describe.

> As described in lines 38 to 42, Oliver has "stood listening to the owl's arguing song drifting through the tree," she finds herself "thinking of summer fields." These summer fields "are red and pink and white tents of softness and nectar" (45–46). Because of the immensely and overwhelming beauty of these roses, a sense of fear has taken over Oliver; the same fear of whether or not nature is being beautiful or nature is a death trap.
>
> This feeling of confusion and fear is normal in people. Our experiences, both favorable and not, shape who we are and how we perceive things. Have you ever felt that you should be mad about a certain thing but you are joyful and grateful or vice versa? This is how Oliver feels about nature. Conflict arises when Oliver is torn between her sentiments that nature can be both cruel and beautiful at the same time. She feels that nature is "sheer rollicking glory of the death-bringer" (28–29) and at the same time she is "struck to the heart and saturated with a simple happiness" (60–61). Yes, this feeling may seem frightening or cruel, but it in itself is a part of life. However, we must not be afraid when these feelings arise in ourselves. Rather, we can draw from our previous life experiences. This way, when horror strikes, we can see beyond it and find beauty.

In Sandi's "before" paper, we see a lot of similar traits that we see in Isabelle's "before" paper. For example, Sandi seemed more consumed with explaining what the essay means than analyzing how Oliver uses language to convey that meaning. This is apparent in her thesis statement: "The author finds anguish in her feelings that nature can be both strikingly picturesque and vicious at the same time." Notice that she did not mention any language devices that Oliver uses to convey this and no metalanguage was used in the essay. Like Isabelle, Sandi tried to incorporate previous knowledge with Washington Irving's "The Legend of Sleepy Hollow" and the reference to the headless horseman; however, the comparison was a stretch and again did not focus on Oliver's language. Something different about Sandi's "before" paper is that she seemed more focused on the reader's experience than Oliver's. We see this when she said "we" and "the reader." She even asked us a rhetorical question in an attempt to explain Oliver's emotional experience: "Have you ever felt that you should be mad about a certain thing but you are joyful and grateful or vice versa?" She said that this is how Oliver feels but does not explain how that is so. As we see with Isabelle and Clara, Sandi's paper does not quite answer the prompt.

In her later paper, Sandi conducted an identification analysis and a modality analysis to find evidence "to determine the polar opposite emotions Oliver displays toward the main subjects of her piece, the owls and the roses."

Sandi's "Owls" Paper after SFL Instruction

By doing discourse analysis on Mary Oliver's "Owls," the audience is able to determine the polar opposite emotions Oliver displays toward the main subjects of her piece, the owls and the roses. An analysis reveals why these complex emotions make nature so beautiful yet so complex.

An identification analysis is able to provide information of the characterization of the owl. When speaking about the owl, Oliver mentions him by many different names. She begins with "the great horned owl," because that is the name of its kind. However, as her description of the owl continues, she uses other names like "pure wild hunters of the world" and "death-bringer." These names carry a terrifying connotation, yet, in the next section of her piece, she describes fields of flowers that are "palpable" and sweet. She refers to different types of flowers like "poppies" and "lupines" or even roses of all colors. The contrast between how she identifies the two objects of focus and how many times Oliver emphasizes the exquisite terror and "immobilizing happiness" contributes to the complexity of her feeling about nature.

As well as identification analysis, modality can also be used in order to determine the author's feeling about nature. All of Mary Oliver's language uses high modality. However, her word choice changes as soon as the subject does. When describing the owl, she uses negative high modal adjectives like "merciless" and "sheer rollicking glory" to describe his scream. Oliver uses a phrase that really sticks out in the modality analysis when she says he has "an insatiable craving for the taste of brains." In contrast, the flowers are written about with positive high modality. Nouns like "immobilizing happiness" and verbs like "I'm struck, I'm taken, I'm conquered . . ." all let the reader know how completely wonderful this field of flowers is to her. The modality analysis categorizes these two elements of nature, the owl and the flowers, into two different states of mind: terror and sublime happiness.

However, at the end of the last paragraph, Oliver asks the question, "And is this also not terrible?" Her endless terror of the owl also exists the flowers control over her, which is yet just another way nature is so complex.

By focusing on the naming of the owls and the roses, Sandi was able to provide evidence to support her analysis that these apparent contrasts reveal the "complexity of her feeling about nature." In her modality analysis, she focused on Oliver's use of high modal adjectives and nouns to express the strength of her fear and happiness. She also pointed out the absolute certainty created with the use of high modal verbs like "I'm struck, I'm taken, I'm conquered" to express the totality of her feelings. She juxtaposes this certainty against her question at the end of the essay, "And is this also not terrible?" Here, Sandi got closer to the heart of what Clara was circling in her modality analysis: that the contrast and flip-flopping between the high modal verbs and questions show Oliver's confusion and the complexity of her feelings about nature.

These before and after comparisons seem to validate Macken-Horarik's (2006) and Schleppegrell's (2011) findings that metalanguage awareness does indeed help students identify language features in a text and help them effectively write about how they are being used and implemented by an author, which is a skill highly valued by AP exam graders and the CCSS.

This section reveals how instruction on discourse analysis and CLA manifested itself in students' writing. While students did not necessarily use discourse analysis when writing every essay, our critical discussions that stemmed from our language study played a role in determining the topics students chose. Furthermore, as evident in Sandi's animal testing essay, her understanding of how writers manipulate audiences' emotions through language was evident in her mimicking the same persuasive elements. In addition, Parvesh's Drabble essay mirrored the critical scaffolding intended by the spiral curriculum. Analyses of students' Shadd Cary essays and a comparison of students' "Owls" essays suggest that, when students did use discourse analysis methods, their responses were more focused on how authors' language use supported their purpose of writing and less on plot summary, improving students' ability to answer the prompt.

Reflection Questions for Chapter 8

1. Which writing assessments in your state, county, or classroom are considered "high stakes"? How do you currently prepare students for those writing assessments?
2. While I am sure you differentiate the difference between plot summary and analysis in academic writing, what tools do you currently provide students to help them analyze and not just summarize texts?
3. How can a linguistically informed approach and knowledge of discourse analysis methods help students tackle those writing assessments and serve as a resource in analyzing texts and prompts?

9 Bringing It All Together: Where Do We Go from Here?

Guiding Gist

- Instruction on how to use discourse analysis tools to code and analyze language encourages students to see language as a set of choices, not rules.
- A linguistically informed approach helps students analyze not only the purposes behind the language an author used, but also what was left out.
- Discourse analysis instruction supports the critical questioning of texts and provides students with the linguistic evidence to prove and metalanguage to explain their claims.
- Students' ability and comfort with discourse analysis differs depending on their familiarity of the social context and where a text is positioned in the spiraled curriculum.
- Classroom dialogue and student writing samples show that students' ability to discuss the social meaning of language and effectively use linguistic tools to strengthen their own arguments can deepen over a relatively short period of time.
- Evidence suggests that this instruction transcends the classroom, as students used these tools in their college classes and in assessing daily language experiences.
- A linguistically informed approach to language instruction fulfills many of the CCSS standards: language, reading, writing, and overall literacy.

To review, the purpose of this book was to attempt to answer the following research questions:

- How can SFL provide a metalanguage for teachers and students to discuss the linguistic choices authors are making? How can this metalanguage enhance educators' and students' ability to articulate the social meaning behind authors' language choices?

- How can this instruction be scaffolded for student success?
- How do students respond to a linguistic analysis of various genres of text such as student-valued, canonical, and nonfiction texts? Are there differences in students' engagement with each genre? If so, what accounts for those differences?
- How does introducing a linguistically informed approach into the classroom allow a teacher to guide students toward language awareness and support critical literacy? How does awareness deepen, and is it reflected in students' written and oral analysis of texts?
- How can SFL-informed instruction support student achievement on high-stakes tests?
- How does a linguistically based approach fulfill the requirements of the CCSS?

In the following discussion, I frame the answers to each question in turn. In order to avoid repetition, this section will not detail interpretations of student work found in Chapters 6, 7, and 8, but instead, puts the evidence into the larger context of the research questions.

Students' Response to Using SFL and Discourse Analysis

My first conclusion is that students' use of discourse analysis tools to code language encourages students to see language as a system of choices, not a set of rules. This finding supports my original goal: to show my students how grammar analysis is subjective and "flexible and open ended," encouraging the mentality that discourse analysis is "a tool kit for working on semiotic activities, not a formalism to be applied to them" (Cope & Kalantzis, 2000, p. 24). This observation is supported by many examples.

First, students recognized that words could be coded differently depending on one's personal interpretation, and, eventually, they even became comfortable in coding one word under multiple titles, showing their understanding of how a single word could play multiple social roles in a text. For example, Tyler coded the word "villain" as both a judgment and identification, recognizing that the word not only renamed Iago but also judged him according to the social norms of decency.

Oftentimes, students would also consider the other linguistic choices available to the author in order to analyze why they made the selection they did and analyze the social purpose. For example, Winnie considered Rowling's options when naming the troll, leading her to recognize that calling it "something" was a choice that she made to create a specific effect on the reader. Similarly, Clara also stated, "She could have used any other word in that place, but she is 'pushed' to signify maybe the anger underneath to show the tone of the passage" (Clara, *Harry Potter* protocol analysis). Here, Clara recognized language as a "pliable repertoire of choices" (Harman, 2008, p. 8) available to Rowling and that her choice of the word "push" had an effect on the emotion emitted from Hermione's action.

Furthermore, this linguistically informed approach also encourages students to recognize not only the language the author chose to use but also what was left out. Similar to Fairclough (1995), Tyler recognized that what can be assumed from what is unsaid might be as important as what is said. Tyler suggested that Obama could have said that his job was to protect all people, instead of just American people. Looking at the word Obama selected after considering his choices, Tyler was able to problematize the meaning of specifying that Obama's job is to protect "American" people, not "all" people, showing his growth in analyzing both the *said* and *unsaid* in text.

In a protocol analysis interview, Parvesh told me, "I like identification analysis because I feel like identification analysis can lead to a lot of my judgment statements. I see appraisal as a triangle of emotion that shows what the author is trying to say. I didn't find any modality in this one, so that analysis didn't really help me much. It wasn't the best choice for this section" (Parvesh, *Othello* protocol analysis). This statement effectively shows Parvesh's growth in using discourse analysis because he suggests the overlapping nature of discourse semantics and how language serves multiple purposes. He also recognized that not all analyses are equally beneficial in specific passages and that the analyst should be discerning in which analysis they should use to get the most data to analyze from the passage. The more linguistic tools in their toolbox, the more options they have to choose from when analyzing texts.

Discourse Analysis to Support Critical Literacy

In addition, discourse analysis instruction supports the critical questioning of language and provides students with linguistic evidence to support critical claims. According to Martin (2000a), this is the reason why many discourse analysts choose SFL as their method: it allows analysts "to ground concerns with power and ideology in the detailed analysis of texts as they unfold, clause by clause, in real contexts of language use" (p. 275). Based on the evidence from this language curriculum, students were able to use the results of their appraisal, identification, and modality analyses to question the social purpose behind specific language choices. When questioning an author's or a character's language choices, students often commented on what their discourse analyses revealed about characters' feelings toward one another, power relationships, and the inclusive or exclusive nature of the language choice.

For example, the dialogue surrounding Winnie and Andrew's *Harry Potter* presentation might not have occurred if these SFL-informed methods had not been introduced. If students had not coded the language, they might not have noticed Kreacher's use of the third person, and the discussion that questioned the social purpose of Rowling's linguistic choice, concluding with the observation that Kreacher might be resisting his subjugation and the valuing of Kreacher's possible native language, might not have taken place. What a loss that would have been.

Similarly, Clara's group was able to use their discourse analysis to discuss the shifting power relationships in the play *Othello*. Creating discussion questions on class and race based on their findings, Clara's group indeed made their discourse analysis *critical* because they focused on how Shakespeare's choices "enact, confirm, legitimate, reproduce, or challenge relations of *power* and *dominance*" (van Dijk, 2003, p. 353). Furthermore, the class discussion that stemmed from their questions exemplified critical dialogue about language in relation to these critical issues. It included multiple students sharing their experience with language in relation to class and race and even concluded with a student who was presumably unaffected by disempowering language to understand how both her classmates and Othello were "othered."

It is important to note that not all critical discussions directly assessed an author's language use. However, every critical discussion originated from an initial CDA based on students' findings. One such case was when Grace questioned what aspects of her life encouraged her to assume that most authors were male. In this way, SFL supported CDA and developed an "intervention in the apparently natural flow of talk . . . [in] attempts to interrupt everyday common sense" (Luke, 1996, p. 12).

Another example would be students' discussion of globalization (or lack thereof) and our stereotyped perception of people from the East (*Aladdin*), which stemmed from our original observations about how the East and West were portrayed throughout Obama's speech. Because of the dialogue surrounding the language regarding the East and the West, students were able to problematize our naturalized ideas about the East (Freire, 1970/1986) and then intervene in the perpetuation of harmful ideology and stereotypes (Blommaert & Buclaen, 2000).

In essence, because learners were a part of the practice, once conscious of the ideologies and power relations that shape it, language became a site of struggle that could "be constructed and deconstructed" (McKensie, 1992, p. 226). This assists students in recognizing the "alienating and disabling effects" (Fairclough, 1995, p. 89) that harmful language imposes on them and on others. Through CDA, learners adopt CLA, which "equipped them with the capacities and understanding which are preconditions for meaningful choice and effective citizenship in the domain of language" (Fairclough, 1992a, p. 54).

Differing Responses to the Use of Discourse Analysis Tools

Students' response to analyzing language utilizing discourse analysis tools differs depending on their familiarity with the social context of the text and the linguistic tools to articulate said context. Furthermore, a hedging analysis of focal students' protocol analyses revealed that students seemed to struggle in different stages (description, interpretation, explanation, and problematization), depending on the text and where it fell in the spiraled curriculum. For example, students struggled most in the description stage when coding *Harry Potter*, possibly because it was their first time using their new skills, and they were in the deconstruction stage of Rothery and Stenglin's (1994) learning cycle.

Furthermore, I thought students would be more engaged with the *Harry Potter* text because of (a) their familiarity with it, (b) its place in popular culture, and (c) its removal from "real-world problems" and its fantasy setting. However, I found that the social context in which the characters were located—"school" and "friendships"—were familiar to students, helping them interpret coding based on their own experiences with such situations. For example, coding *Harry Potter* seemed easier for Tyler and Clara because they were able to use their past experiences working with partners and having their feelings hurt to code words correctly.

It was also apparent that students' responses to *Othello* differed from those for *Harry Potter* due to their distance from Shakespeare's language, Elizabethan culture, and the historical context more broadly. These differences made coding more difficult, leading to struggles with interpretation, description, and problematization. Specifically, it seemed that while the language in *Othello* deserved critical discussion, students' distance from Shakespearian language made it more difficult for them to problematize language. This is shown through students' ability to problematize words used in their identification analysis of *Othello* only after I constructed a hypothetical situation. Once this was introduced, dialogue on the social effect of the words "Moor" and "black ram" took place.

In addition, while students found the coding of Obama's speech easier than that of *Othello*, due to his use of contemporary English, their distance from Eastern culture and their Americanized view on the issues faced by the Middle East affected their ability to interpret, explain, and problematize their discourse analysis results.

Developing Critical Awareness and Understanding of Social Meaning of Language

Based on student work, interviews, and class dialogue, students' ability to discuss the social meaning of language with the use of their linguistic tools can deepen over a relatively short period of time. While there is limited quantitative proof that students' critical awareness developed over time, the analyses of student work and discourse does insinuate that students' confidence in using their discourse coding and pointing out linguistic resources to support their critical observations did develop over time. As was evident in my analysis of Tyler's modality in each text (see Table 6.6), it is clear that, as students practice using discourse analysis tools, their confidence in their coding and interpretation of their coding increases.

Furthermore, such discussion about language leads not only to problematization, but also to suggestions for change. The spiraled curriculum (Macken-Horarik, 1996; Rothery, 1996), helps students move from questioning characters to questioning society to making suggestions to transform social norms (see Freire, 1970/1986; McLaren, 2009). By the end of our language study, the focal students were more willing to question their own knowledge about the East and even recognize our own educational shortcoming when it comes to our understanding of Eastern culture, language, and so on.

In fact, students showed attempts at structuring different social formations (Giroux, 1985) by advocating for teachers from the East—a step that was not taken when discussing our analysis results of *Harry Potter* or *Othello*. Students also took action outside of the classroom. Three students decided to take Arabic as their foreign language in college. This development speaks to their desire not only to problematize our lack of knowledge about the East but also to act and become educated in an Eastern language to advocate for true globalization and shape new conventions (Clark, 1992). Considering the fact that these developments occurred over a four-month curriculum plan, I wonder what developments might occur if a linguistically informed critical curriculum were implemented in language arts classrooms for grades 9 through 12? To me, the possibilities are endless.

Furthermore, there is evidence that students' ability to perform discourse analyses transcends the classroom. After students engaged in the language curriculum, I received multiple emails from students who were involved in this curriculum informing me of how they were able to apply their new language knowledge and analysis methods to their college classes. For example, Clara wrote the following:

> We recently turned in our first essay in English, and I wrote about the Declaration of Independence, Frederick Douglass's "What to the Slave is the Fourth of July?", as well as Whitney Houston's rendition of the national anthem. It was really interesting because, while reading Douglass's speech, I would catch highly modal verbs or phrases, so it reminded me of your class and the work we did. (Clara, email communication)

Other students wrote, "I already blew my professor's mind with my knowing of SFL analysis" (Mary, email communication), and "I feel like my writing technique improved so much during your class because you taught me how to dissect passages on a whole new level. I've even impressed some of my professors by looking at things with SFL; it's practically ingrained in my conscience!" (Eve, email communication) (Simmons, 2018, p. 87). These emails reinforce the idea that discourse analysis tools serve students both academically and personally and extend beyond my classroom.

Language Awareness Reflected in Student Writing

Students also reflect their language awareness in their own writing by making critical observations, using their knowledge of linguistic devices to strengthen their own arguments, and engaging in discourse analyses to answer prompts regarding authors' use of language in AP-style exam passages. First, focal students were more apt to discuss critical topics present in AP passages due to their practice of critically questioning language in texts discussed in class. Grace's response to the Malcolm X prompt was an example of how students were able to recognize critical goals in the writing of others.

However, Parvesh's response to the Drabble prompt showed his critical development, because he did not just observe an author's critical goal but also used historical examples and his own experiences to discuss the harmful effects of not questioning the dominant ideology. It should be noted that this may have been the result of critical discussions that derived from our language study rather than from his knowledge of linguistic tools. Regardless, his choice to question his own role in the perpetuation of social norms reflected his personal critical development in his writing. Furthermore, although students are not usually rewarded for challenging cultural conventions (Rothery & Stenglin, 2000) on high-stakes essay responses, Parvesh showed that students can critically question the status quo and still provide an acceptable response, fulfilling the expectations of exam graders.

Students are also able to apply their knowledge of modality, identification, contrast and concession, and appraisal to strengthen their own arguments. Sandi's application of high modality, strong affect and judgment words, and contrast and concession in her thesis statement for her animal testing essay showed her ability to utilize discourse analysis to enhance the persuasiveness of her own writing. In this way, Sandi recognized the value of persuasive language features and utilized them in her own writing (Macken-Horarik, 2006; Schleppegrell, 2011). This finding also supports previous research from Humphrey et al. (2011, p. 159):

> Students who can draw on resources such as modality, contrast and concession are better able to negotiate deliberate relationships with their listeners; and . . . those who have knowledge of how attitude is encoded, both implicitly and explicitly, are better able to read and create more analytical texts whose evaluations are more nuanced.

This also bolsters findings from Harman (2008) that concluded that familiarity with the functionality of language leads to improved writing.

Students can also use discourse analysis tools to analyze authors' linguistic choices in AP-style passages. When analyzing the Shadd Cary passage to answer the prompt:

> Read the passage carefully, considering the circumstances in which it was written. Then, in a carefully written essay, analyze the techniques Mary Ann Shadd Cary uses to establish the necessity of her newspaper. (College Board, 2008, p. 23)

Both Grace and Clara found that language analysis tools provided a means for discussing how Shadd Cary's linguistic patterns support her writing purpose. In other words, enhanced awareness of specialized language is evident in analyses of Grace and Clara's writing (Christie & Macken-Horarik, 2007).

Furthermore, by comparing Isabelle's essays before and after discourse analysis instruction and utilization, you can see how this curriculum helped focus Isabelle on Oliver's use of language by using analysis tools that strictly identified and addressed Oliver's use of language. Unlike her first essay, where she struggled to analyze language and instead compared the theme of "Owls" to other works of literature, discourse analysis methods helped Isabelle by encouraging her to move beyond a plot summary (Rothery & Stenglin, 2000) and focus on interpreting the passage through an analysis of Oliver's language choices. Therefore, her language analysis supported her observation that Oliver's stylistic choices reflect how she fears nature due to its ability to terrorize and immobilize her, as represented by the owls and the roses.

I believe that these results lead to some interesting possibilities for future research. While this study shows how students used discourse analysis tools to analyze and write about the language use in the works of others, it would be interesting to see how the same language tools could be used by students to analyze their own writing. Since students would confront their own writing in a college setting more than literary texts in many college courses, investigating how this language instruction can inform their own post-secondary writing practices would do much to support the findings that this curriculum transcends the classroom and enables students to use language responsibly and effectively in various writing contexts.

Application of the CCSS

Throughout the book, I hope you have noticed how the curriculum supports many facets of the CCSS—not just the language standards but also reading and writing. However, I want to reiterate how this curriculum especially focuses on the language standards, which are often viewed as "secondary" to reading and writing, making language skills a primary focus of ELA curriculum.

First, in order to conduct the various analyses presented in this curriculum, students use basic knowledge of English conventions and parts of speech (CCSS.ELA-LITERACY.L.1). For example, identifying nouns and pronouns is paramount to conducting an identification analysis and understanding the functions of adverbs and adjectives help with conducting appraisal analyses. Furthermore, understanding verbs is necessary to complete a modality analysis. Next, the more students understand how language reveals relationships, they will be more able to recognize how authors use punctuation to reveal those relationships and use punctuation such as semicolons and colons in their own writing to do the same (CCSS.ELA-LITERACY.L.2). Understanding genre, context of culture, and context of situation helps students "understand how language functions in different contexts" (CCSS.ELA-LITERACY.L.3).

Examples in this book also show how this curriculum helps students recognize how language can hold different meanings depending on who wields it and when. When writing, linguistic knowledge provided by SFL and discourse analysis also assists students in making appropriate language choices based on the writing purpose. As shown in the *Othello* protocol analyses, the analysis methods introduced in this curriculum help students use context clues and tone to determine unknown vocabulary (CCSS.ELA-LITERACY.L.4). Furthermore, conducting an appraisal analysis requires students to understand the nuances of language in order to understand the purposes of indirect/invoked affect, judgment, and appreciation words (CCSS. ELA-LITERACY.L.5). And, finally, SFL and discourse analysis provides students with the metalanguage to talk about language so that we can fully achieve CCSS.ELA-LITERACY.L.6 by providing "domain-specific words" to independently demonstrate their knowledge of how language functions in each expression. Therefore, as Maune and Klassen (2014) point out, SFL-based pedagogy offers "explicit language that can be applied to the CCSS framework without conflicts" (pp. 122–124).

While the curriculum supports the CCSS, it also focuses on the two standards in the Australian national curriculum that I find so progressive and desperately needed in American classrooms (see also Chapter 1). The curriculum looks at language as a social process that can be inclusive or exclusive and empower and disempower people accordingly (Australian Curriculum, Assessment and Reporting Authority, 2020a), and this social process is influenced by a person's value system, purpose, and mode of communication (Australian Curriculum, Assessment and Reporting Authority, 2020b). By focusing on these two elements, we deepen students' ability to use the skills focused on in the CCSS.

Example of an Alternative Implementation

Earlier in the book, I told you that I would provide some other options on how to apply this language study in your classroom. True to my word, Table 9.1 is a list of multiple texts that I think would work nicely in their fields of fantasy, canonical, and nonfiction texts as you apply the scaffolded curriculum presented in Chapter 4. Of course, you are not limited to these—the list is just to jumpstart your creative energy. You'll see that I've expanded each category a bit. For example, I include science fiction texts in the fantasy list, classics typically taught in US schools in the canonical list (as well as texts from the global canon, not just British), and nonfiction from history as well as the modern era in the nonfiction list.

TABLE 9.1. Possible Texts for Spiraled Language Curriculum

Fantasy/Science Fiction Texts	Canonical/Classic Texts	Nonfiction Texts
• *Children of Blood and Bone* by Tomi Adeyemi • *Divergent* trilogy by Veronica Roth • *Dune* by Frank Herbert • *Ender's Game* by Orson Scott Card • *His Dark Materials* trilogy by Philip Pullman • *The Hunger Games* trilogy by Suzanne Collins • *The Iremonger* trilogy by Edward Carey • *The Lord of the Rings* by J. R. R. Tolkien • *Parable* series by Octavia E. Butler • *Watchmen* by Alan Moore	• *Animal Farm* • *Anna Karenina* • *The Bluest Eye* • *Candide* • *Fahrenheit 451* • *Frankenstein* • *The Great Gatsby* • *Gulliver's Travels* • *Heart of Darkness* • *Huckleberry Finn* • *Merchant of Venice* • *Metamorphosis* • *Moby-Dick* • *1984* • *The Odyssey* • *Oliver Twist* • *A Tale of Two Cities* • *The Tempest* • *Things Fall Apart*	• Aung San Suu Kyi "Freedom from Fear" [Essay] • Chief Joseph "I Will Fight No More Forever" [Speech] • Elizabeth I "Speech to the Troops at Tilbury" [Speech] • Frederick Douglass "What to the Slave is the Fourth of July?" [Speech] • Gloria Steinem "Address to the Women of America" [Speech] • Hillary Clinton "Women's Rights are Human Rights" [Speech] • John F. Kennedy "Inauguration Address" [Speech] • Mahatma Gandhi "Quit India" [Speech] • Martin Luther King Jr. 'I Have a Dream" [Speech] and "Letter from a Birmingham Jail" [Open letter] • Patrick Henry "Speech at the Virginia Convention" [Speech] • Thomas Paine "The Crisis #1" [Pamphlet] • Sojourner Truth "Ain't I a Woman?" [Speech] • Theodore Roosevelt "Duties of American Citizenship" [Speech] • Winston Churchill "Blood, Toil, Tears, and Sweat" [First speech to the House of Commons] and "This was Their Finest Hour" [Speech]

Many of these texts have similar themes of inequality, stereotyping, oppression, war, and discrimination—all ripe for language analysis and critical discourse. All you have to do is pick a theme that is a focus in each text type.

A. J. Jackson, a middle school instructional coach, did just that in an eighth-grade English language arts class (Jackson et al., 2017). After beginning the curriculum cycle with *Harry Potter*, they moved on to critically analyze the ways that Thomas Jefferson was portrayed on two different web pages, one from the Smithsonian and one from the Monticello museum website. Applying what students learned from doing identification and appraisal analyses, students found that pages on the Monticello website downplayed Jefferson's role as an enslaver and defender of slavery while also acknowledging it as an evil practice. Later, the eighth-grade language arts teacher decided to weave in the Declaration of Independence, so they did a genre analysis with students to help them understand the document as a legal argument. The class also looked at original letters written by Thomas Jefferson that showed how he identified African Americans in his personal writings, which was in dehumanizing ways, just as in *Harry Potter*. The language curriculum presented in this book also informed the teaching of the *March* trilogy (Lewis et al., 2013, 2015, 2016), which spiraled to articles that presented the Civil Rights Movement in different ways based on their cultural context (southeastern United States, New York, and the United Kingdom).

All of this happened in a year, and, while A. J. and the teacher would have taught some of these texts without the language curriculum or use of discourse analysis, the transferability presented with the *Harry Potter* lesson propelled their focus on CLA. It provided the tools they needed to cultivate a critical gaze to counteract the predominantly normative and dominant perspectives with which the students entered class. Here, you can see how A. J. and an eighth-grade teacher adapted the curriculum to fit the needs of their students and classroom, succeeding in building students' critical awareness and skills required by the CCSS by using elements of this linguistically informed approach.

Implications for Teaching and Research

Martin (2000a) stated that "not much progress has been made with bringing discourse analysis and register analysis into schools by way of mediating and connection between grammatical meaning and genre" and that the next step in the development of a functional language curriculum is addressing "the problem of constructing functional grammar, discourse analysis, and register analysis as tools for teachers and students to use when relating language to the social, whether as part of literacy programs, or as subject-specific learning across the curriculum" (p. 120). The approach and results presented in this book have several implications for educators and scholars, like Martin, who are actively seeking ways of constructing a curriculum that focuses on the relationship between language and society.

While this book details one teacher's experiences implementing a linguistically informed curriculum with students, the approach shows how students are capable and willing to utilize a metalanguage to discuss the social implications of language choices. It supports the hypothesis that implementing such a study of language would provide students with grounding for their critical observations, allowing them to revisit the language of a text to check to see if their interpretation of the social meaning of language is correct in a specific instance. In addition, students' discourse analysis and coding grounded classroom dialogue in language analysis, keeping the discussion focused on the critical questioning of the social effect of language choices and leaving little room for debate or off topic discussion that often defeats the goals of meaningful dialogue.

This language curriculum also serves as a way to "systematize awareness" (Fairclough, 1995) by providing the resources to see and change discourse in society—helping me answer that bewildered student's question mentioned in Chapter 1: "How do we stop it? How do we change it?" Using different analyses and coding language helps students name language and therefore "name the world" (Freire, 1970/1986). By rejecting the "ideal reader" (Janks & Ivanic, 1992), and questioning the written word and interrogating reading positions (Macken-Horarik & Morgan, 2008), this linguistically informed curriculum guides students to connect meanings with word (Christie & Macken-Horarik, 2007), find patterns in language, and empower themselves (Talbot, 1992) by problematizing their finding through dialogue. In essence, discourse analysis gives students the evidence to see what they need to resist, becoming aware of the dominant ideology and its effects (Freire & Faundez, 1989).

Furthermore, my experiences reveal that performing language analysis with students is a form of emancipatory education because it allows students to see how language is used against them and to resist their enslavement (Christie & Mission, 1998) while looking after their own interests and identity (Ivanic & Simpson, 1992). While not as fundamental as the paradigm shifts such as translingualism and code-meshing, according to Fairclough (1992a) and my observations, the linguistically informed curriculum presented in this book is a way of supporting responsible citizenship, especially for those who are already native Standard English speakers. Not only do students learn grammar, metalanguage, and analysis tools, but through their language study, they also gain an awareness of how language positions others, giving power to some and taking it away from others, in multiple genres and texts—fantasy, fiction, and nonfiction—giving them an understanding for the need for such paradigm shifts.

Adding linguistic methods and tools such as SFL and CDA to the high school ELA curriculum does not require the reinvention of the wheel. Instead, it is a much-needed spoke that can help support the implementation of Common Core mandates and strict standards.

Finally, adding linguistic methods and tools such as SFL and CDA to the high school ELA curriculum does not require the reinvention of the wheel. Instead, it is a much-needed spoke that can help support the implementation of Common Core mandates and strict standards. While developing critical literacy was a personal goal for my classroom, student work and dialogue showed growth in their literary analysis skills and writing skills—both standards in the Common Core.

Final Reflection and Closing

Reflecting on my experience engaging in critical language analysis with my students using a linguistically informed curriculum, I always wonder if the experience was as rewarding for them as it was for me when I first became aware of how discourse analysis and SFL could support my critical analysis of language choices—could help me see what before I could not see and therefore change what I once thought was unchangeable. As I thought about a way to ask for my students' unbiased opinions of the experience, I found that a formal questionnaire or survey was unnecessary. Unprompted and unasked, students have shared their feelings about what they learned through notes, emails, and even gifts.

As the end of the year approached and this group of seniors was busy with senior picnics, prom, AP exams, finals, and other activities, I would occasionally find notes on my desk. While I have received thank-you notes from students before, *these* notes all had a common theme: they referenced our study of language and the impact it had on how they viewed the word and the world.

Comments from Students

- "You taught me new approaches not only to literature, but to life."
- "I learned so much about life, literature, and the effect language has on society."
- "I hope you continue teaching future classes the importance of questioning society and stereotypes."
- "You treated us as if what we had to say actually mattered and that we could actually form our opinions and speak up. What I learned in your class, I have applied to other classes."
- "I cannot tell you how much this class has helped me grow in my writing and thinking."
- "SFL has been such a wonderful tool to take away from this class."
- "SFL is ingrained in my conscience."
- "I have learned a tremendous amount about style, symbols, and the reasons behind authors' writing, and I feel like a critic when I read other novels."

What stands out to me and makes me most proud as an educator is that the language education we engaged in together helped these students think

What stands out to me and makes me most proud as an educator is that the language education we engaged in together helped these students think differently not only about what they read on paper but also what they see in the world.

differently not only about what they read on paper but also what they see in the world. In addition, in reading students' comments, it seems as though they, in a way, have overcome what Fairclough (1989) called "a sense of impotence." Students now felt as though they had a tool to help them "demythologize reality" (Freire, 1970/1986) and become conscious of the social implications of language that is at work in all texts and instances—every day (Luke, 1996; Talbot, 1992).

A month and a half into the summer, while I was in the throes of writing the first draft of this book, I received the following email from Grace, one of my focal students:

> Okay, so, at my Intern Company's National Leadership Forum, we had a student panel. And they asked some questions about my experiences thru school. And I talked about how frightened I was to take APs, but finally buckled down and took some! I also talked about how SFL revolutionized the way I look at books/life. Intrigued, I had teachers come up to me and ask me about SFL and one middle school teacher was so interested. I gave her my contact info and I told her I would put her in contact with you if you were interested to email her some of the materials or explain it. If so, I didn't want to give her your home email then, because I wasn't sure if the school email was better/if you had time. Just let me know! . . . (Grace, email communication)

This email confirms that Grace viewed SFL as a valuable tool for language analysis and that it revolutionized not only how she looks at books/language but at *life*. Based on her email, she now saw language as inseparable from society. This revelation proves to me that a linguistically informed approach to language study does help students gain confidence in critically questioning language and the world around them. It also provides hope that they would continue to use it in their lives.

As a second comment about this email, I want to point out that a middle school teacher was interested in including this in her own classroom, showing that there is a desire to teach language as a social process and that this curriculum can support teachers in their attempts to engage students in language study and in developing CLA. While Macken-Horarik and Morgan (2008) were correct in stating that many teachers are overwhelmed with the complexity of grammar,

I believe that teachers also recognize the power it holds and want to empower themselves and their students by incorporating it into their curriculum.

At the end of the year, I also received a splendid gift (see Figure 9.1): a piece of student-created artwork that depicted a memorable quote about the power of language from one of the Harry Potter novels.

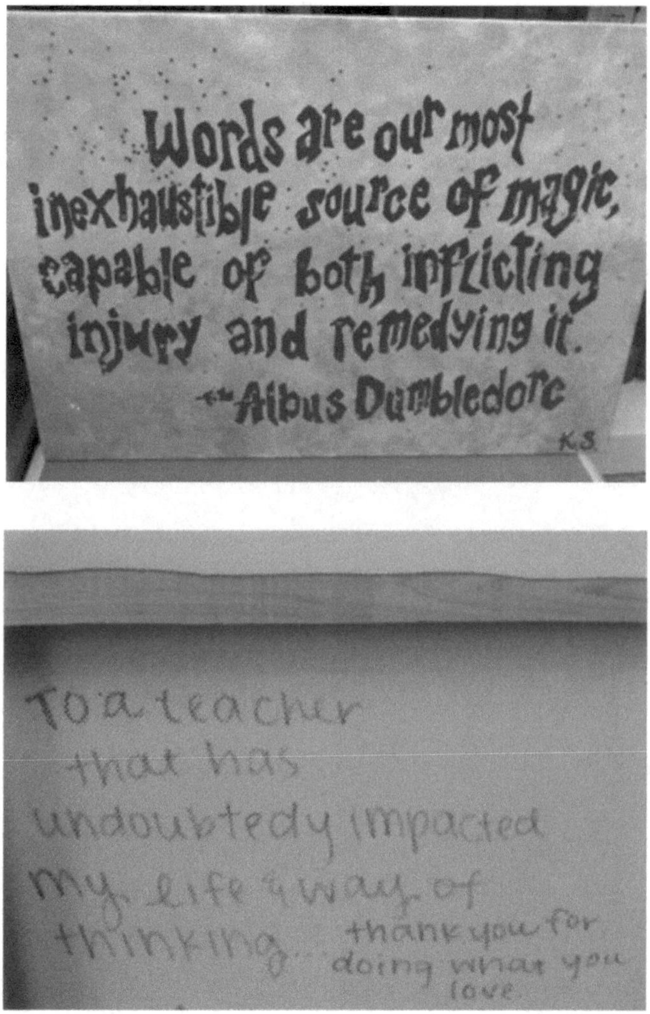

FIGURE 9.1. Student artwork.

This gift is a testament to this particular student's awareness of how language can both empower and disempower as well as a recognition of her responsibility to use language with care. The fact that she chose a quote from Dumbledore to articulate what she took away from the class also suggests that the Harry Potter novel might have been the most effective text in guiding her toward this critical realization. The touching inscription on the back is the most authentic representation of this student's newfound ability and *desire* to question the world around her, the words that she reads, and the language that she uses.

Inspired by my students' growth and development throughout their language study, as the seniors whose work is represented in this book walked out the door for the last time, I watched their hands—hands that high fived, waved, blew kisses, patted each other on the backs, wadded up that last piece of paper to throw in the trash—and I remembered Toni Morrison's Nobel Lecture that inspired my quest in developing a linguistically informed language curriculum. Like the blind woman in her story, once my students left my classroom, I would be blind to how they would use language in their future. However, with infinite hope and trust, I thought to myself, "The bird is now in their hands—the *word* is now in *their* hands."

Appendix: Resources

Harry Potter Appraisal Analysis Exercise

- affect—words that focus on *feelings* of characters, narrators, and/or readers
- judgment—words that focus on the *judgment* of characters, narrators, and/or readers
- appreciation—those that focus on *assessing feelings* about objects, setting and appearance

Appraisal Category	**Code**
affect	
judgment	
appreciation	

From *Harry Potter and the Sorcerer's Stone*, Chapter 12: "The Mirror of Erised":

"So—back again, Harry?"

Harry felt as though his insides had turned to ice. He looked behind him. Sitting on one of the desks by the wall was none other than Albus Dumbledore. Harry must have walked straight past him, so desperate to get to the mirror he hadn't noticed him.

"I—I didn't see you, sir."

"Strange how nearsighted being invisible can make you," said Dumbledore, and Harry was relieved to see that he was smiling.

"So," said Dumbledore, slipping off the desk to sit on the floor with Harry, "you, *like hundreds before you*, have discovered the *delights* of the Mirror of Erised."

"I didn't know it was called that, sir."

"But I expect you've realized by now what it does."

"It—well—it shows me my family—"

"And it showed your friend Ron himself as head boy."

"How did you know—?" (Rowling, 1997, pp. 212–213)

Appraisal Category	Positive		Negative	
affect (feelings of characters, narrators, and/or readers)	Harry	Dumbledore	Harry	Dumbledore
judgment (judgment of characters, narrators, and/or readers)	Ron			
appreciation (assessing feelings about objects, setting, and appearances)	Mirror of Erised			

Appraisal Analysis Reflection Questions

What did the appraisal analysis reveal about the feelings of the characters during this scene?

Based on your chart, how do you think the characters feel toward one another? What is their relationship?

Are any judgments made? If so, how do they reveal the feelings the characters have for others, or how does the judgment shape your feelings toward a specific character?

Harry Potter Modality Practice

Directions: Circle the modal words used by Harry and Dumbledore

"So—back again, Harry?"

Harry felt as though his insides had turned to ice. He looked behind him. Sitting on one of the desks by the wall was none other than Albus Dumbledore. Harry must have walked straight past him, so desperate to get to the mirror he hadn't noticed him.

"I—I didn't see you, sir."

"Strange how nearsighted being invisible can make you," said Dumbledore, and Harry was relieved to see that he was smiling.

"So," said Dumbledore, slipping off the desk to sit on the floor with Harry, "you, *like hundreds before you*, have discovered the *delights* of the Mirror of Erised."

"I didn't know it was called that, sir."

"But I expect you've realized by now what it does."

"It—well—it shows me my family—"

"And it showed your friend Ron himself as head boy."

"How did you know—?"

. . .

"The Mirror will be moved to a new home tomorrow, Harry, and I ask you not to go looking for it again. If you ever do run across it, you will now be prepared. It does not do to dwell on dreams and forget to live, remember that." (Rowling, 1997, pp. 212–213)

Modality Practice Reflection Questions

On the polarity scale, are the words that the characters used mostly *high*, *medium*, or *low*?

Harry:

Dumbledore:

Why do you think this is?

Can a power relationship between the characters be determined based on your analysis? Explain.

Overall, what does this analysis reveal and how does it determine how we continue to read the text/series?

Harry Potter Identification Analysis

Harry Name	Number of times the identification is repeated	Dumbledore Name	Number of times the identification is repeated

Identification Analysis Reflection Questions

Can you determine anything about the power relationship between Harry Potter and Dumbledore based on this analysis?

If so, is the power relationship positive or negative? How can you tell?

What else did the identification analysis reveal?

Identification Analysis

Directions: Choose a scene in the novel where the majority of these characters are either interacting with one another or being talked about. Do an identification analysis and then discuss with a partner what you learned about how each character is presented.

Harry Potter		Ron/Weasleys		Draco/Malfoys		Crabbe and Goyle		Hermione Granger	
Name	#	Name	#	Name	#	Name	#	Name	#

Othello Discourse Analysis Practice

- affect—words that focus of feelings of characters, narrators, and/or readers
- judgment—words that focus on the social or moral judgment of characters, narrators, and/or readers
- appreciation—those words that focus on assessing feeling about objects, setting, and appearance

Appraisal Category	Code
affect	
judgment	
appreciation	

Act 2, Scene 1

OTHELLO
O my fair warrior!

DESDEMONA
My dear Othello!

OTHELLO
It gives me wonder great as my
content
To see you here before me. O my
soul's joy!
If after every tempest come such calms,
May the winds blow till they have
waken'd death! And let the
laboring bark climb hills of seas
Olympus-high, and duck again as
low
As hell's from heaven! If it were now
to die,
'Twere now to be most happy; for I
fear

They kiss.
That e'er our hearts shall make!

IAGO *Aside.*
O, you are well tun'd now! But I'll
set down the pegs that make this
music, as honest as I am.

OTHELLO
Come; let us to the castle.
News, friends: our wars are done; the
Turks are drown'd.
How does my old acquaintance of this
isle?
Honey, you shall be well desir'd in
Cyprus,
I have found great love amongst
them. O my sweet,
I prattle out of fashion, and I dote
In mine own comforts. I prithee, good
Iago,

My soul hath her content so absolute
That not another comfort like to this
Succeeds in unknown fate.

Desdemona
The heavens forbid
But that our loves and comforts should increase Even as our days do grow!

Othello
Amen to that, sweet powers!
I cannot speak enough of this content,
It stops me here; it is too much of joy.
And this, and this, the greatest discords be

Go to the bay and disembark my coffers.
Bring thou the master to the citadel;
He is a good one, and his worthiness
Does challenge much respect. Come, Desdemona, Once more, well met at Cyprus.

Othello's Lines in Act 3, Scene 3

Othello
Excellent wretch! Perdition catch my soul, But I do love thee! and when I love thee not, Chaos is come again.

Othello
What dost thou mean?

Othello
Why, why is this?
Think'st thou I'ld make a lie of jealousy,
To follow still the changes of the moon
With fresh suspicions? No; to be once in doubt is once to be resolved: exchange me for a goat, When I

And live upon the vapour of a dungeon,
Than keep a corner in the thing I love
For others' uses. Yet, 'tis the plague of great ones; Prerogatived are they less than the base; 'Tis destiny unshunnable, like death:
Even then this forked plague is fated to us
When we do quicken. Desdemona comes:
If she be false, O, then heaven mocks itself! I'll not believe't.

Othello
Villain, be sure thou prove my love a whore, Be sure of it; give me the

shall turn the business of my soul To such exsufflicate and blown surmises, Matching thy inference. 'Tis not to make me jealous

To say my wife is fair, feeds well, loves company, Is free of speech, sings, plays and dances well; Where virtue is, these are more virtuous: Nor from mine own weak merits will I draw The smallest fear or doubt of her revolt; For she had eyes, and chose me. No, Iago; I'll see before I doubt; when I doubt, prove; And on the proof, there is no more but this,--

Away at once with love or jealousy!

OTHELLO

No, not much moved:

I do not think but Desdemona's honest.

OTHELLO

And yet, how nature erring from itself,—

OTHELLO

Why did I marry? This honest creature doubtless Sees and knows more, much more, than he unfolds.

OTHELLO

This fellow's of exceeding honesty,

And knows all qualities, with a learned spirit, Of human dealings. If I do prove her haggard, Though that her jesses were my dear ocular proof: Or by the worth of man's eternal soul, Thou hadst been better have been born a dog Than answer my waked wrath!

OTHELLO

By the world, I think my wife be honest and think she is not; I think that thou art just and think thou art not. I'll have some proof. Her name, that was as fresh

As Dian's visage, is now begrimed and black As mine own face. If there be cords, or knives, Poison, or fire, or suffocating streams, I'll not endure it. Would I were satisfied!

OTHELLO

Give me a living reason she's disloyal.

OTHELLO

I'll tear her all to pieces.

OTHELLO

O, that the slave had forty thousand lives!

One is too poor, too weak for my revenge. Now do I see 'tis true. Look here, Iago; All my fond love thus do I blow to heaven. 'Tis gone.

Arise, black vengeance, from thy hollow cell! Yield up, O love, thy crown and hearted throne To tyrannous hate! Swell, bosom, with thy fraught, For 'tis of aspics' tongues!

heartstrings, I'ld whistle her off and let her down the wind, To pray at fortune. Haply, for I am black

And have not those soft parts of conversation That chamberers have, or for I am declined Into the vale of years,—yet that's not much— She's gone. I am abused; and my relief Must be to loathe her. O curse of marriage, That we can call these delicate creatures ours, And not their appetites! I had rather be a toad,

OTHELLO

Damn her, lewd minx! O, damn her!

Come, go with me apart; I will withdraw,

To furnish me with some swift means of death

For the fair devil. Now art thou my lieutenant.

Othello Appraisal Analysis Practice

Appraisal	**Act 2**		**Act 3**	
	Positive	Negative	Positive	Negative
Affect				
Judgment				
Appreciation				

Othello Identification Analysis Practice

Act 2		**Act 3**	
Name	#	Name	#

Othello Modality Practice

Grammatical Resource	High Modality		Medium Modality		Low Modality	
	Act 2	Act 3	Act 2	Act 3	Act 2	Act 3
Modal verbs						
Modal adverbs						
Modal adjectives						
Modal nouns						

Othello Discourse Analysis Reflection

Appraisal Analysis

What did the appraisal analysis reveal about Othello's feelings for Desdemona in Act 2?

What does the appraisal analysis reveal about Othello's feelings for Desdemona in Act 3?

Are any judgments made? If so, how does the judgment shape your feelings toward a specific character?

What are the differences between the appraisal analysis for Act 2 and Act 3? What can account for these differences?

Identification Analysis

Can you determine anything about the relationship of Othello and Desdemona based on this analysis?

If so, is the relationship positive or negative? How can you tell?

What else did the identification analysis reveal to you about the changing nature of the relationship in Act 2 and Act 3?

Modality Analysis

What did the modality analysis reveal?

On the polarity scale, in Act 2, are the words that Othello uses mostly *high*, *medium*, or *low*? Why do you think this is?

On the polarity scale, in Act 3, are the words that Othello uses mostly *high*, *medium*, or *low*? Why do you think this is?

Based on the modality analysis, what grammatical resource did Shakespeare utilize the most and what was the effect?

Do you have any other observations or interpretations you would like to share?

Obama Speech Discourse Analysis Practice

Appraisal Category	Code
affect	
judgment	
appreciation	

Finally, I want to discuss economic development and opportunity. I know that for many, the face of globalization is contradictory. The internet and television can bring knowledge and information, but also offensive sexuality and mindless violence into the home. Trade can bring new wealth and opportunities, but also huge disruptions and change in communities. In all nations—including America—this change can bring fear. Fear that because of modernity we lose control over our economic choices, our politics, and most importantly our identities—those things we most cherish about our communities, our families, our traditions, and our faith.

But I also know that human progress cannot be denied. There need not be contradictions between development and tradition. Countries like Japan and South Korea grew their economies enormously while maintaining distinct cultures. The same is true for the astonishing progress within Muslim-majority countries from Kuala Lumpur to Dubai.

Appraisal	Positive	Negative
affect		
judgment		
appreciation		

Obama Speech Citation Exercise

Citation to support or challenge positions: citations are used to strengthen arguments by providing supporting evidence or evidence that challenges an alternate position.

Citation	Purpose *(to support or challenge)*	Status of Source	Effect
EXAMPLE: "the Arab peace initiative . . . of their responsibilities"	To support	Political agreement	Appeals to politically active and law-based mindset to understand and agree with his point for peace
EXAMPLE: "children of Abraham"	To support	Religious text	Reference to all three groups of people, gives feeling of inclusion and a sense of understanding

Obama Speech Contrast and Concession Practice

Contrast and concession is effective because it positions the speaker as open minded and willing to negotiate by *conceding* to the opposing side about an issue, but then the speaker immediately provides a *contrast* to support the speaker's own position.

This device is made visible through the use of *concessive conjunctions* and *prepositional phrases*.

Some Examples

Concessive Conjunctions (transitions)	Prepositional Phrases or Opening Preposition Words
however; but; still; yet; while; nevertheless; although; even though; whereas	in contrast; on the other hand; in spite of; one could also say; despite; instead of

Concession	Contrast	Grammatical resource used to show relationship
And I consider it part of my responsibility as president of the United States to fight against negative stereotypes of Islam wherever they appear.	But that same principle must apply to Muslim perceptions of America.	But: concessive conjunction
The Arab–Israeli conflict should no longer be used to distract the people of Arab nations from other problems.	Instead, it must be a cause for action to help the Palestinian people . . . choose progress over a self-defeating . . . past.	Instead

Socratic Seminar

A *Socratic seminar* is an academic discussion, based on a text, in which participants ask one another open-ended questions. Within the context of the discussion, students listen closely to the comments of others, thinking critically for themselves, and articulate their own thoughts and their responses to the thoughts of others (Israel, 2002).

Good Socratic seminar questions often begin with or include the following verbs: categorize, classify, compare, contrast, construct, describe patterns and relationships, discover cause and effects, evaluate, explain, generalize, hypothesize, illustrate, infer, integrate, interpret, paraphrase, predict, synthesize.

In preparation for our Socratic seminar, create three open-ended discussion questions:
1. 2. 3.

Harry Potter Discourse Analysis Project

STEP 1: Read your selected critical article. Make notes on the major claims the author is making about the series and the examples they are using to make those claims.

STEP 2: Find examples from the book that are relevant to the author's claims. Perform a discourse analysis using an appraisal analysis, identification analysis, and modality analysis to see if J. K. Rowling's language supports or disproves the author's claims.

STEP 3: Present your finding to the class to stimulate discussion.

Requirements for the Presentation

Your presentation should provide:

1. A synopsis of the author's claims.
2. Your original reaction to the author's claims.
3. If your author is working within a particular theory (feminist, queer, critical race theory, etc.), provide an overview of how the author defines the theory.
4. For each claim, choose one or two examples from the text on which to perform a discourse analysis. Please use all three types of analysis: appraisal, identification, and modality. You do not have to use all three on each example; choose the analysis for each example that you think will best support or disprove the author's claim. However, you need to have performed all three by the end of your presentation.
5. Show your work. When you do an appraisal analysis, create a code that shows the different elements: affect, judgment, and appreciation (see examples from your notes). Then, create a chart like we did with the examples. When you do an identification analysis, underline all nouns and pronouns used to refer to the individuals in question. Create a chart that lists each name per character and how many times it occurs in your selected passage. When you do a modality analysis, underline the words and identify where the words fall on the polarity scale.
6. Discuss with the class what each analysis reveals. Some examples of what you can talk about include:
   - What does the analysis mean?
   - How does it affect your views or interpretation of the novel?
   - What does it mean for the larger genre of children's fantasy literature?
   - What message is being taught?
   - How can it be changed?

You can also address other questions that come up.

Harry Potter Project Rubric

Row	Needs Improvement	Meets Expectations	Exceeds Expectations
Discussion of claims	Identifies a few of the author's major claims, misidentifies claims, or identifies thesis but not the claims that support the thesis	Correctly identifies many of the author's major claims	Correctly identifies all of the author's major claims
Use of appraisal, identification, and modality analysis	Uses one of the three discourse analysis methods to analyze the author's claims	Uses two of the three discourse analysis methods to analyze the author's claims	Uses all three of the discourse analysis methods to analyze the author's claims
Depth of analysis	Lacking in evidence and coding charts; the presentation provides little insight into what the analyses/charts reveal or mean in the larger context of the author's argument	Evidence and coding charts are present but uneven, inconsistent, or incomplete; the presentation provides some insight into what the analyses/charts reveal or mean in the larger context of the author's argument	Coding charts are accurate and discussion of evidence is thorough and directly related to the larger context, providing new insight into the author's argument
Class dialogue	Little to no class engagement; presenters dominate discussion portion of the presentation	Some class engagement; questions are posed, but they do not actively encourage the class to engage in dialogue	Majority of the class in engaged in the conversation (many voices); questions stimulate dialogue and new questions from the audience
Creativity and clarity	Technical errors; disorganized presentation of material; writing errors that interfere with understanding	Clear presentation of material although it might not be creatively inspired; some writing errors, but they do not interfere with understanding	Visually appealing slides that present material in a clear and cohesive manner; few or no errors in writing

Othello Discourse Analysis Project

1. Each group will be **assigned an act (1–5)**.
2. Each group will **perform an identification analysis, appraisal analysis, and modality analysis for their act**. There are many ways you can divide the work: for instance, by type of analysis, by scene, by character (for identification analysis), or by appraisal mode (affect, judgment, and appreciation).
3. Your group will **create the appropriate charts** and share them via Google Docs.
4. After conducting their analysis, your group will **make a handout** summarizing the results and give a brief interpretation of their meaning. The handout must include:
   - a summary of the identification analysis and a critical interpretation of what it means
   - a summary of the appraisal analysis and a critical interpretation of what it means
   - a summary of the modality analysis and a critical interpretation of what it means
   - three Socratic discussion questions for the class, based on your findings

Note: "Summary" DOES NOT mean copies of all of your charts for everyone. Synthesize your data. What are the most obvious or most important findings?

Make sure your handout is clear and easy to read. *It must be confined to one page front and back (so two pages front only).*

Your data will be presented during a Socratic seminar, so be prepared to informally share your data.

Othello Project Rubric

Row	Needs Improvement	Meets Expectations	Exceeds Expectations
Use of appraisal, identification, and modality analysis	Uses one of the three discourse analysis methods to analyze the assigned act	Uses two of the three discourse analysis methods to analyze the assigned act	Uses all three of the discourse analysis methods to analyze the assigned act
Depth of analysis	Lacking in evidence and coding charts; the presentation provides little insight into what the analyses/charts reveal or mean in the larger context of the play's meaning, themes, or character development	Evidence and coding charts are present but uneven, inconsistent, or incomplete; the presentation provides some insight into what the analyses/ charts reveal or mean in the larger context of the play's meaning, themes, or character development	Coding charts are accurate and discussion of evidence is thorough and directly related to the larger context, providing new insight into the play's meaning, themes, or character development
Class dialogue	Little to no class engagement; presenters dominate discussion portion of the presentation	Some class engagement; questions are posed but, they do not actively encourage the class to engage in dialogue	Majority of the class in engaged in the conversation (many voices); questions stimulate dialogue and new questions from the audience
Creativity and clarity of handout	Technical errors; disorganized presentation of material; writing errors that interfere with understanding	Clear presentation of material although it might not be creatively inspired; some writing errors, but they do not interfere with understanding	Visually appealing and presents material in a clear and cohesive manner; few or no errors in writing

Obama Speech Discourse Analysis Assignment

1. Each group will be **assigned an issue that is discussed within the speech**.
2. Each group will **perform an identification analysis, appraisal analysis, and modality analysis, contrast and concession analysis, and citation analysis for their issue**.
3. Your group will **create and complete the appropriate charts** and email them in to the teacher who will make copies of your completed analysis/charts for each student in the class.
4. After conducting your analysis, your group will need to present your findings, informally, to the class, referring the class to their copy of your completed charts that support your analysis.
5. Think about our discussion questions and reflection topics. Was there anything in your results that helped you address, question, or answer one of those questions/topics? If so what and how? Explain to the class and encourage the class to share their interpretation of your results.

Choose to discuss three of the following reflection and discussion questions on Barack Obama's (2009) speech at Cairo University:

1. Does your identification analysis show a dichotomy of "them" versus "us"? Explain your findings and their effect on your feelings toward the subject and people being discussed.

2. Citations are used to strengthen arguments by providing supporting evidence that challenges an alternate position. How does Obama use citations to strengthen his argument? Do his citations play a role in how the audience views the West and the East? Explain.

3. Contrast and concession is effective because it positions the speaker as open minded and willing to negotiate by conceding to the opposing side about an issue, but then the speaker immediately provides a contrast to support the speaker's own position. Does Obama utilize this effectively? How does it impact you as an audience member?

4. Does Obama's modality assist in his persuasive goal to make arguments by laying out the facts of "how it is"?

5. Does Obama use language to suggest that the "Muslim world" (a term he uses to refer to over forty-five countries with little in common aside from the fact that the majority of the population identifies as "Muslim") is a whole different "world"?

6. Based on your SFL analysis, does Obama label Western values as "human," "modern," "civil," and all things "good"?
7. Based on Said's list of harmful "Oriental" stereotypes, looking at your analysis, does Obama's language—and even talking points—majorly support or counter such stereotypes? Does it do both? Does he focus on some more than others? Intentionally or unintentionally? Explain.
8. How does Obama use language to align the West with all that is "rational" and the East with the "irrational"?
9. How does Obama identify Muslim communities in America? What is the implication and effect of this linguistic choice?
10. Ambiguity is a key aspect of political speeches, because it allows the orator to avoid obvious contradictions with what they have said before. Are there places in this speech where Obama is intentionally ambiguous? Why?
11. Often, "what is 'said' in a text always rests upon 'unsaid' assumptions, so part of the analysis of texts is trying to identify what is assumed" (Fairclough, 2003, p. 11). What are some unsaid assumptions in this speech?
12. Is there a *universal* logic or science that allows all "humans" to be able to sit down at a table and discuss issues through "objective" reasoning that is untainted by cultural norms/ assumptions of good, bad, etc.?
13. One could say that *globalization* is the "widening, deepening, and speeding up of worldwide interconnectedness in all aspects of contemporary social life, from the cultural to the criminal, the financial to the spiritual" (Crossley & Watson, 2003, p. 53). A colleague of mine once said, "To be blunt, while education and media in the Muslim world has been dramatically Westernized over the last twenty years, I have to ask how Western education/media have been changed to reflect Muslim or 'Eastern' values in the last twenty years for us to accept this interpretation of 'mutual' global exchange?" As a student in a Westernized culture, do you think your education has been "globalized" to reflect Muslim or "Eastern" values?

14. How does Obama define "progress"? How does he suggest that "tradition" opposes "progress"?
15. Obama is giving a speech that, while primarily addressed to "Muslims around the world," will be heard by the non-Muslim population of the planet as well—not unimportantly, US citizens: how does this simultaneous addressing affect his language choices?
16. Obama is often attacked for "over-identifying" with the "East" and not being "American enough" (birth certificate, middle name, etc.). Based on your analysis of this speech, with whom does he identify most: the "West" or the "East"? How does he make this evident through his language choices?

Obama Speech Discourse Analysis Rubric

Row	Needs Improvement	Meets Expectations	Exceeds Expectations
Coding of charts	Provides completed coding/charts for a few of the discourse analysis methods: appraisal, identification, modality, concession and contrast; citations. Charts contain typos, are unclear, and/or incomplete	Provides completed coding/charts for most of the discourse analysis methods: appraisal, identification, modality, concession and contrast; citations. Charts are adequately completed, relatively clear, and contain few errors	Provides completed coding/charts for all five of the discourse analysis methods: appraisal, identification, modality, concession and contrast; citations. Charts are thoroughly completed, accurate, and easy to understand and read
Socratic discussion	Chose at least one discussion/reflection question that clearly related to their section of the speech/ topic that stimulated dialogue with some of the class	Chose at least two discussion/reflection question that clearly related to their section of the speech/ topic that stimulated dialogue with most of the class	All three of the selected discussion/ reflection questions clearly related to their section of the speech/ topic and stimulated dialogue with the majority of the class

Works Cited

Accurso, K., & Gebhard, M. (2020). SFL praxis in US teacher education: A critical literature review. *Language and Education, 34*(3), 1–27. https://doi.org/10.1080/09500782.2020.1781880

Airasian, P., & Madaus, G. (1983). Linking testing and instruction. *Journal of Educational Measurement, 20*(2), 103–118.

Allen, J. (2007). *Creating welcoming schools: A practical guide to home-school partnerships with diverse families*. Teachers College.

Amberg, J. S., & Vause, D. J. (2009). *American English: History, structure, and usage.* Cambridge University Press.

Anatol, G. L. (2003). The fallen empire: Exploring ethnic otherness in the world of Harry Potter. In G. L. Anatol (Ed.), *Reading Harry Potter: Critical essays* (pp. 163–178). Greenwood.

Anderson, J. (2006). Zooming in and zooming out: Putting grammar in context into context. *English Journal, 95*(5), 28–34. https://doi.org/10.2307/30046585

Applebee, A. N. (1974). *Tradition and reform in the teaching of English: A history*. National Council of Teachers of English.

Applebee, A. N. (1991). *A study of high school anthologies* (Report series 1.5). Office of Educational Research and Improvement.

Appleman, D. (2000). *Critical encounters in high school English: Teaching literary theory to adolescents*. Teachers College.

Aronowitz, S. (1998). Introduction. In P. Freire, *Pedagogy of freedom: Ethics, democracy, and civil courage* (P. Clarke, Trans.; pp. 1–20). Rowman & Littlefield.

Aull, L. L., & Lancaster, Z. (2014). Linguistics markers of stance in early and advanced academic writing: A corpus-based comparison. *Written Communication, 31*(2), 151–183. https://doi.org/10.1177/0741088314527055

Australian Curriculum, Assessment and Reporting Authority. (2020a). *Curriculum content descriptions: ACELA1564*. Australian Curriculum (version 8.4). https://www.australiancurriculum.edu.au/ACELA1564

Australian Curriculum, Assessment and Reporting Authority. (2020b). *Curriculum content descriptions: ACELA1565*. Australian Curriculum (version 8.4). https://www.australiancurriculum.edu.au/ACELA1565

Berry, M. (2017). Stratum, delicacy, realisation and rank. In T. Bartlett & G. O'Grady (Eds.), *The Routledge handbook of systemic functional linguistics* (pp. 66–79). Routledge.

Berthoff, A. E. (1987). Foreword. In P. Freire & D. Macedo (Eds.), *Literacy: Reading the word and the world* (D. A. Koike, Trans.; pp. xi–xxiii). Bergin & Garvey.

Bhatt, A., & Martin-Jones, M. (1995). Whose resource? Minority languages, bilingual learners and language awareness. In N. Fairclough (Ed.), *Critical language awareness* (pp. 185–301). Longman.

Biber, D. (2003). Variation among university spoken and written registers: A new multi-dimensional analysis. In P. Lestyna & C. F. Meyer (Eds.), *Corpus analysis: Language, structure, and language use* (pp. 47–70). Rodopi.

Blommaert, J., & Bulcaen, C. (2000). Critical discourse analysis. *Annual Review of Anthropology, 29*(1), 447–466. https://doi.org/10.1146/annurev.anthro.29.1.447

Brause, R. S., & Mayher, J. S. (2003). Who really goes to school? Teaching and learning for the students we really have. In J. Flood, D. Lapp, J. R. Squire, & J. M. Jensen (Eds.), *Handbook of research on teaching the English language arts* (pp. 285–229). Erlbaum.

Brown, D. W., & Aull, L. L. (2017). Elaborated specificity versus empathic generality: A corpus-based comparison of higher- and lower- scoring advanced placement exams in English. *Research in the Teaching of English, 51*(4), 394–417.

Brown, P., & Levinson, S. (1987). *Politeness*. Cambridge University Press.

Bruner, J. S. (1963). *The process of education*. Knopf.

Bruner, J. S. (1968). *Towards a theory of instruction*. W. W. Norton.

Caffarel, A. (2009). Systemic functional grammar and the study of meaning. In B. Heine & H. Narrog (Eds.), *The Oxford handbook of linguistic analysis* (pp. 883–914). Oxford University Press.

Carey, B. (2003). Hermione and the house-elves: The literary and historical contexts of J. K. Rowling's antislavery campaign. In G. L. Anatol (Ed.), *Reading Harry Potter: Critical essays* (pp. 103–115). Greenwood.

Chappell, D. (2008). Sneaking out after dark: Resistance, agency, and the postmodern child in J. K. Rowling's *Harry Potter* series. *Children's Literature in Education, 39*(4), 281–293. https://doi.org/10.1007/s10583-007-9060-6

Cherland, M. (2009). Harry's girls: *Harry Potter* and the discourse of gender. *Journal of Adolescent & Adult Literacy, 52*(4), 273–282. https://doi.org/10.1598/JAAL.52.4.1

Chouliaraki, L. (1998). Regulation in "progressivist" pedagogic discourse: Individualized teacher–pupil talk. *Discourse & Society, 9*, 5–32. https://doi.org/10.1177/0957926598009001001

Chouliaraki, L., & Fairclough, N. (1999). *Discourse in late modernity: Rethinking critical discourse analysis*. Edinburgh University Press. https://doi.org/10.1515/9780748610839

Christie, F. (2002). *Classroom discourse analysis: A functional perspective*. Continuum.

Christie, F., & Derewianka, B. (2008). *School discourse: Learning to write across the years of schooling*. Continuum.

Christie, F., & Macken-Horarik, M. (2007). Building verticality on subject English. In F. Christie & J. R. Martin (Eds.), *Language knowledge and pedagogy: Functional linguistic and sociological perspectives* (pp. 156–183). Continuum.

Christie, F., & Macken-Horarik, M. (2011). Disciplinarity and the case of school subject English. In F. Christie & K. Maton (Eds.), *Disciplinarity: Functional linguistic and sociological perspectives* (pp. 175–196). Bloomsbury.

Christie, F., & Misson, R. (1998). Framing the issues in literacy education. In F. Christie & R. Mission (Eds.), *Literacy and schooling* (pp. 1–17). Routledge.

Christie, F., & Unsworth, L. (2000). Developing socially responsible language research. In L. Unsworth (Ed.), *Researching language in schools and communities: Functional linguistic perspectives* (pp. 1–26). Cassell.

Clark, R. (1992). Principles and practice of CLA in the classroom. In N. Fairclough (Ed.), *Critical language awareness* (pp. 117–140). Longman.

Coffin, C. (1997). Constructing and giving value to the past. In J. R. Martin & F. Christie (Eds.), *Genres and institutions: Social processes in the workplace and school* (pp. 196–230). Pinter.

College Board. (2001). *AP English language and composition: 2001 free-response questions.* https://secure-media.collegeboard.org/apc/eng_lang_01.pdf

College Board. (2008). *AP English language and composition: Practice exam.* http://havlicek.weebly.com/uploads/6/8/5/2/685209/ap_language_practice_test_2008.pdf

College Board. (2016). *The SAT practice test #5.* https://satsuite.collegeboard.org/media/pdf/sat-practice-test-5.pdf

College Board. (2020a). *English language and composition: Course description.* https://apcentral.collegeboard.org/courses/ap-english-language-and-composition

College Board. (2020b). *English literature and composition: Course description.* https://apcentral.collegeboard.org/courses/ap-english-literature-and-composition

Collins, S. (2008). *Hunger games.* Scholastic Press.

Collins, S. (2009). *Catching fire.* Scholastic Press.

Collins, S. (2010). *Mockingjay.* Scholastic Press.

Common Core State Standards Initiative. (2010). *Common core state standards for English language arts & literacy in history/social studies, science, and technical subjects.* National Governors Association. http://www.corestandards.org/wp-content/uploads/ELA_Standards1.pdf

Cope, B., & Kalantzis, M. (Eds.). (2000). *Multiliteracies: Literacy learning and the design of social futures*. Routledge.

Coutinho, J. (1970). Preface. In P. Freire (Ed.), *Cultural action for freedom* (pp. v–viii). Harvard Educational Review.

Cranny-Francis, A. (1996). Technology and/or weapon: The discipline of reading in the secondary English classroom. In R. Hasan & G. Williams (Eds.), *Literacy in society* (pp. 172–190). Longman.

Crossley, M., & Watson, K. (2003). *Comparative and international research in education: Globalisation, context, and difference*. Routledge.

Crovitz, D., & Devereaux, M. D. (2017). *Grammar to get things done*. Routledge & National Council of Teachers of English.

Csomay, E. (2006). Academic talk in American university classrooms: Crossing boundaries of oral-literature discourse. *Journal of English for Academic Purposes*, *5*(2), 117–135. https://doi.org/10.1016/j.jeap.2006.02.001

Davies, J. (2003). Expressions of gender: an analysis of pupils' gendered discourse styles in small group classroom discussions. *Discourse & Society*, *14*(2), 115–132. https://doi.org/10.1177/0957926503014002853

Derewianka, B. (1990). *Exploring how texts work*. Primary English Teaching Association.

Derewianka, B. M., & Jones, P. (2016). *Teaching language in context* (2nd ed.). Oxford University Press.

Dolch, E. (1933). Testing reading. *The Elementary School Journal*, *34*(1), 36–43.

Durst, R. K. (2014). Geneva Smitherman: Translingualist, code-mesher, activist. *Composition Studies*, *42*(2), 56–72.

Eggins, S. (1994). *An introduction to systemic functional linguistics*. Pinter.

Ehrenhaft, G. (2010). *AP English language and composition*. Kaplan.

Fairclough, N. (1989). *Language and power*. Longman.

Fairclough. N. (1992a). The appropriacy of "appropriateness." In N. Fairclough (Ed.), *Critical language awareness* (pp. 33–56). Longman.

Fairclough, N. (1992b). *Discourse and social change*. Polity Press.

Fairclough, N. (1992c). Introduction. In N. Fairclough (Ed.), *Critical language awareness* (pp. 1–29). Longman.

Fairclough, N. (1995). *Critical discourse analysis*. Trans-Atlantic Publishers.

Fairclough, N. (2003). *Analyzing discourse: Textual analysis for social research*. Routledge.

Fairclough, N. (2006). *Language and globalization*. Routledge.

Fang, Z. (2006). The language demands of science reading in middle school. *International Journal of Science Education*, *28*(5), 491–520. https://doi.org/10.1080/09500690500339092

Fang, Z., & Schleppegrell, M. J. (2010). Disciplinary literacies across content areas: Supporting secondary reading through functional language analysis. *Journal of Adolescent and Adult Literacy*, *53*(7), 597–597. https://doi.org/10.1598/JAAL.53.7.6

Flynn, J. E. (2011). The language of power: Beyond the grammar workbook. *English Journal*, *100*(4), 27–30.

Foucault, M. (1995). *Discipline and punish: The birth of the prison* (A. S. Smith, Trans.). Vintage. (Original work published 1975)

Foucault, M., & Gordon, C. (Ed.). (1980). *Power/knowledge: Selected interviews and other writings, 1972–1977* (C. Gordon, L. Marshall, J. Mepham, & K. Soper, Trans.). Pantheon.

Fowler, R., Hodge, B., Kress, G., & Thew, T. (1979). *Language and control.* Routledge & Kegan Paul.

Frank, A., & McBee, M. (2003). The use of *Harry Potter and the Sorcerer's Stone* to discuss identity development with gifted adolescents. *Journal of Secondary Gifted Education, 15*(1), 33–38. https://doi.org/10.4219/jsge-2003-438

Freadman, A. (1994). "Do as I say": The relationship between teaching and learning new genres. In A. Freadman & P. Medwey (Eds.), *Genre and the new rhetoric*. Taylor & Francis.

Freebody, P. (2007). *Literacy education in school: Research perspectives from the past, for the future*. Australian Council for Educational Research.

Freire, A. M. A., & Macedo, D. (1998). Introduction. In A. M. A. Freire & D. Macedo (Eds.), *The Paulo Freire reader* (pp. 1–44). Continuum.

Freire, P. (1970). *Cultural action for freedom*. Harvard Educational Review.

Freire, P. (1973). *Education for critical consciousness* (M. Bergan Ramos, Trans.). Continuum.

Freire, P. (1985). *The politics of education: Culture, power, and liberation* (D. Macedo, Trans.). Bergin & Garvey.

Freire, P. (1986). *Pedagogy of the oppressed* (M. Bergan Ramos, Trans.). Continuum. (Original work published 1970)

Freire, P. (1994). *Pedagogy of hope: Reliving Pedagogy of the oppressed* (A. M. A. Freire, Notes, R. Barr, Trans.). Continuum.

Freire, P. (1997). *Pedagogy of the heart* (A. M. A. Freire, Notes, D. Macedo & A. Oliveira, Trans.). Continuum.

Freire, P. (1998a). *Pedagogy of freedom: Ethics, democracy, and civic courage* (P. Clarke, Trans.). Lanham, Rowman & Littlefield.

Freire, P. (1998b). *Teachers as cultural workers: Letters to those who dare to teach* (D. Macedo, D. A. Koike, & A. Oliveira, Trans). Westview Press.

Freire, P., & Faundez, A. (1989). *Learning to question: A pedagogy of liberation* (T. Coates, Trans.). Continuum.

Freire, P., & Macedo, D. (1987). *Literacy: Reading the word and the world* (D. A. Koike, Trans.). Bergin & Garvey.

Gallardo-C., X., & Smith, C. J. (2003). Cinderfella: J. K. Rowling's wily web of gender. In G. L. Anatol (Ed.), *Reading Harry Potter: Critical essays* (pp. 191–205). Greenwood.

Gebhard, M., Accurso, K., & Chen, I. (2019). Paradigm shifts in the teaching of grammar in K–12 contexts: A case for a social semiotic perspective. In L. C. de Oliveira (Ed.), *Handbook of TESOL in K–12* (pp. 249–263). Wiley.

Gebhard, M., & Graham, H. (2018). Bats and grammar: Developing critical language awareness in the context of school reform. *English Teaching: Practice and Critique 17*(4), 281–297. https://doi.org/10.1108/ETPC-12-2017-0183

Gebhard, M., Harman, R., & Seger, W. (2007). Reclaiming recess: Learning the language of persuasion. *Language Arts, 84*(5), 419–430.

Gee, J. P. (2004). Discourse analysis: What makes it critical? In R. Rogers (Ed.), *An introduction to discourse analysis in education* (pp. 19–50). Erlbaum.

Giroux, H. A. (1985). Introduction. In P. Freire, *The politics of education: Culture, power, and liberation* (D. Macedo, Trans.; pp. xi–xxv). Bergin & Garvey.

Giroux, H. A. (1987). Literacy and the pedagogy of political empowerment. In P. Freire & D. Macedo, *Literacy: Reading the word and the world* (D. A. Koike, Trans.; pp. 1–28). Bergin & Garvey.

Glasser, W. (1986). *Control theory in the classroom.* Harper and Row Publishers.

Goulet, D. (1973). Introduction. In P. Freire, *Education for critical consciousness* (pp. vii–xiv). Continuum.

The Governor's Office of Student Achievement. (2019). *2018–2019 State of Georgia report card* [CSV file]. https://gosa.georgia.gov/dashboards-data-report-card/downloadable-data

Haas, K. P. (2011) Inspiring an aesthetic appreciation of language. *English Journal, 100*(4), 12–14.

Habermas, J. (1972). *Knowledge and human interests*. Heinemann.

Haladyna, T. (1999). *Developing and validating multiple-choice test items* (2nd ed.). Erlbaum.

Halliday, M. A. K. (1994). *An introduction to functional grammar*. Arnold.

Halliday, M. A. K. (1999). The notion of "context" in language education. In M. Ghadessy (Ed.), *Text and context in functional linguistics* (pp. 1–24). John Benjamins.

Halliday, M. A. K., & Hasan, R. (1985). *Language: Context and text*. Deakin University Press.

Halliday, M. A. K., & Matthiessen, C. M. (2014). *Halliday's introduction to functional grammar* (4th ed.). Routledge. (Original work published 1985)

Harman, R. (2008). *Systemic functional linguistics and the teaching of literature in urban school classrooms* [Unpublished doctoral dissertation]. University of Massachusetts, Amherst.

Harman, R., & Simmons, A. M. (2014). Systemic functional linguistics: Resource to promote critical literacy practices in K–12 classroom contexts. In L. C. de Oliveira & J. Iddings (Eds.), *Genre pedagogy across the curriculum: Theory and application in U.S. classrooms and contexts* (pp. 75–91). Equinox.

Harper, H., & Rennie, J. (2009). I had to go out and get myself a book on grammar: A study of pre-service teachers' knowledge about language. *Australian Journal of Language and Literacy, 33*(1), 22–37.

Hodge, B., & Kress, G. (1988). *Social semiotics.* Polity Press.

Holmes, J. (1995). *Women, men, politeness*. Longman.

Horne, J. C. (2010). Harry and the other: Answering the race question in J. K. Rowling's *Harry Potter* series. *The Lion and the Unicorn, 34*(1), 76–104. https://doi.org/10.1353/uni.0.0488

Humphrey, S. (2011). *Working grammar*. Pearson.

Humphrey, S. (2018). "We can speak to the world": Applying meta-linguistic knowledge to specialized and reflective literacies. In R. Harman (Ed.). *Bilingual learners and social equity: Critical approaches to functional linguistics* (pp. 45–69). Springer.

Humphrey, S., Love, K., & Droga, L. (2011). *Working grammar: An introduction for secondary English teachers*. Pearson.

Hyland, K. (1994). Hedging in academic writing and EAP textbooks. *English for Specific Purposes, 13*(3), 239–256.

Hyland, K. (1998). *Hedging in scientific research articles*. John Benjamins.

Hyland, K. (1999). Talking to students: Metadiscourse in introductory course books. *English for Specific Purposes, 18*(1), 3–26. https://doi.org/10.1016/S0889-4906(97)00025-2

Hyland, K., & Jiang, F. (2016). Change of attitude? A diachronic study of stance. *Written Communication, 33*(3), 251–274. https://doi.org/10.1177/0741088316650399

Hymes, D. (1977). *Foundations of sociolinguistics: An ethnographic approach*. Tavistock Press.

International Reading Association & National Council of Teachers of English. (1996). *Standards for the English language arts*. http://www.ncte.org/library/NCTEFiles/Resources/Books/Sample/StandardsDoc.pdf

Israel, E. (2002). Examining multiple perspectives in literature. In J. Holden & J. S. Schmit (Eds.), *Inquiry and the literary text: Constructing discussions in the English classroom* (pp. 89–103). National Council of Teachers of English.

Ivanic, R., & Simpson, J. (1992). Who's who in academic writing? In N. Fairclough (Ed.), *Critical language awareness* (pp. 141–173). Longman.

Jackson, A. J., Baker, N., & Crippen, M. (2017, October 21). *SFL praxis in eighth-grade English language arts classrooms* [Paper presentation]. Graduate Student North America Systemic Functional Linguistics Association symposium, University of Georgia, Athens, GA, United States.

Jackson, H. (1990). *Grammar and meaning: A semantic approach to English grammar*. Longman.

Janks, H., & Ivanic, R. (1992). CLA and emancipatory discourse. In N. Fairclough (Ed.), *Critical language awareness* (pp. 305–331). Longman.

Jorgensen, M. W., & Phillips, L. J. (2002). *Discourse analysis as theory and method*. SAGE.

Keely, K. A. (2011). Dangerous words: Recognizing the power of language by researching derogatory terms. *English Journal, 100*(4), 55–60.

Kellner, R. T. (2010). J. K. Rowling's ambivalence towards feminism: House-elves—women in disguise—in the *Harry Potter* books. *The Midwest Quarterly, 51*(4), 367–385.

Knapp, P., & Watkins, M. (2005). *Genre, text, and grammar: Technologies for teaching and assessing writing*. New South Wales Press.

Lakoff, G. (1972). Hedges: A study in meaning criteria and the logic of fuzzy concepts. In P. Peranteau, J. Levi, & G. Phares (Eds.), *Papers from the eighth regional meeting* (pp. 183–228). Chicago Linguistics Society.

Lakoff, R. T. (1975). *Language and woman's place*. Oxford University Press.

Lancaster, L., & Taylor, R. (1992). Critical approaches to language, learning, and pedagogy: A case study. In N. Fairclough (Ed.), *Critical language awareness* (pp. 256–283). Longman.

Lewis, J., Aydin, A., & Powell, N. (2013). *March: Book One.* Top Shelf Productions.

Lewis, J., Aydin, A., & Powell, N. (2015). *March: Book Two.* Top Shelf Productions.

Lewis, J., Aydin, A., & Powell, N. (2016). *March: Book Three.* Top Shelf Productions.

Lindbolm, K., & Dunn, P. A. (2006). Analyzing grammar rants: An alternative to traditional grammar instruction. *English Journal, 95*(5), 71–77. http://doi.org/10.2307/30046592

Love, K. (2006). Appraisal in online discussions of literary texts. *Text & Talk, 26*(2), 217–244. https://doi.org/10.1515/TEXT.2006.010

Luke, A. (1996). Genres of power? Literacy education and the production of capital. In R. Hasan & G. Williams (Eds.), *Literacy in society* (pp. 308–338). Longman.

Macken-Horarik, M. (1996). *Construing the invisible: Specialized literacy practices in junior secondary English* [Unpublished doctoral dissertation]. University of Sydney.

Macken-Horarik, M. (2003). Appraisal and the special instructiveness of narrative. *Text, 23*(2), 285–312. https://doi.org/10.1515/text.2003.012

Macken-Horarik, M. (2004). Interacting with the multimodal text: Reflections on image and verbiage in ArtExpress. *Visual Communication, 3*(1), 5–29. https://doi.org/10.1177/1470357204039596

Macken-Horarik, M. (2006). Knowledge through "know how": Systemic functional grammatics and the symbolic reading. *English Teaching: Practice and Critique, 5*(1), 102–121.

Macken-Horarik, M. (2009). Navigational metalanguages for new territory in English: The potential of grammatics. *English Teaching: Practice and Critique, 8*(3), 55–69.

Macken-Horarik, M., & Morgan, W. (2008). Getting "meta": Reflexivity and literariness in a secondary English literature course. *English Teaching: Practice and Critique, 6*(4), 22–35.

Malinowski, B. (1968). *A diary in the strict sense of the term.* Routledge.

Martin, J. R. (1984). Language, register and genre. In F. Christie (Ed.), *Language studies: Children writing reader* (pp. 21–30). Deakin University Press.

Martin, J. R. (1992). *English text: System and structure.* John Benjamins.

Martin, J. R. (2000a). Close reading: Functional linguistics as a tool for critical discourse analysis. In L. Unsworth (Ed.), *Researching language in schools and communities: Functional linguistic perspectives* (pp. 275–302). Cassell.

Martin, J. R. (2000b). Design and practice: Enacting functional linguistics. *Annual Review of Applied Linguistics, 20,* 116–126. https://doi.org/10.1017/S026719050002007X

Martin, J. R., & Rose, D. (2003). *Working with discourse: Meaning beyond the clause.* Continuum.

Martin, J. R., & White, P. R. R. (2005). *The language of evaluation: Appraisal in English.* Palgrave Macmillan.

Maune, M., & Klassen, M. (2014). Filling the gaps: Genre as scaffold to the text types of the Common Core State Standards. In L. C. de Oliveira & J. Iddings (Eds.). *Genre pedagogy across the curriculum: Theory and application in U.S. classrooms and contexts* (pp. 107–124). Equinox.

McCreight, J. (2016). *Celebrating diversity through language study: A new approach to grammar lessons.* Heinemann.

McKensie, M. (1992). "What I've always known but never been told": Euphemisms, school discourse, and empowerment. In N. Fairclough (Ed.), *Critical language awareness* (pp. 223–237). Longman.

McLaren, P. (2009). Critical pedagogy: A look at the major concepts. In A. Darder, M. P. Baltodano, & R. D. Torres (Eds.), *The critical pedagogy reader* (2nd ed., pp. 61–83). Routledge.

Merriam-Webster. (n.d.). Caitiff. In *Merriam-Webster.com* dictionary. Retrieved November 11, 2020, from https://www.merriam-webster.com/dictionary/caitiff

Meyer, P. G. (1997). Hedging strategies in written academic discourse: Strengthening the argument by weakening the claim. In R. Markkanen (Ed.), *Hedging and discourse* (pp. 21–44). De Gruyter.

Moll, L. C., Amanti, C., Neff, D., & Gonzalez, N. (1992). Funds of knowledge for teaching: Using a qualitative approach to connect homes and classrooms. *Theory into Practice, 32*(2), 132–141.

Morrison, T. (1993, December 7). *Nobel lecture* [Speech transcript]. Nobel Prize. http://www.nobelprize.org/nobel_prizes/literature/laureates/1993/morrison-lecture.html

Murphy, B., & Rankin, E. (2002). *5 steps to a 5: AP English language.* McGraw-Hill.

Myhill, D. (2010). Rhythm and blues: Making textual music with grammar and punctuation. In D. Wyse, R. Andrews, & J. Hoffman (Eds.), *The Routledge international handbook of English, language and literacy teaching* (pp. 170–181). Routledge.

National Council of Teachers of English. (1994). *Resolution on language study* [Position statement]. https://ncte.org/statement/languagestudy

Neary-Sundquist, C. (2013). The use of hedges in the speech of ESL learners. *Estudios de Lingüística Inglesa Aplicada, 13,* Article 5, 149–174. http://doi.org/10.12795/elia.2013.i13.05

Noel, M. W. (2011) A cold manipulation of language. *English Journal, 100*(4), 50–54.

Nylund, D. (2007). Reading Harry Potter: Popular culture, queer theory and the fashioning of youth identity. *Journal of Systemic Therapies, 26*(2), 13–24.

Obama, B. (2009, June 4). *A new beginning* [Speech transcript]. The White House. https://obamawhitehouse.archives.gov/the-press-office/remarks-president-cairo-university-6-04-09

Oliver, M. (1995). Owls. *Blue pastures.* Harcourt.

Ostry, E. (2003). Accepting Mudbloods: The ambivalent social vision of J. K. Rowling's fairy tales. In G. L. Anatol (Ed.), *Reading Harry Potter: Critical essays* (pp. 89–102). Greenwood.

Park, J. (2003). Class and socioeconomic identity in Harry Potter's England. In G. L. Anatol (Ed.), *Reading Harry Potter: Critical essays* (pp. 179–189). Greenwood.

Pearson, D., & Dole, J. (1987). Explicit comprehension instruction: A review of research and a new conceptualization of instruction. *The Elementary School Journal, 88*(2), 151–165.

Pease, J. [@joshuadpease]. (2020, June 10). *If you're a white person who thinks all this racism is getting out of hand* [Tweet]. Twitter. https://twitter.com/joshuadpease

Pullman, P. (1995). *The golden compass.* Knopf.

Pullman, P. (1997). *The subtle knife.* Knopf.

Pullman, P. (2000). *The amber spyglass.* Knopf.

Rana, M. (2009). *Creating magical worlds: Otherness and othering in Harry Potter.* Peter Lang.

Rana, M. (2011). "The less you lot have ter do with these foreigners, the happier yeh'll be": Cultural and national otherness in J. K. Rowling's *Harry Potter* series. *International Research in Children's Literature, 4*(1), 45–58. https://doi.org/10.3366/ircl.2011.0006

Robinson, A., Faraone, V., Hittleman, D., & Unruh, E. (1990). Reading comprehension in America: 1910–1987. In J. Fitzgerald (Ed.), *Reading comprehension instruction 1783–1987: A review of trends and research* (pp. 66–89). International Reading Association.

Rogers, R., Malancharuvil-Berkes, E., Mosley, M., Hui, D., & O'Garro Joseph, G. (2005). Critical discourse analysis: A review of literature. *Review of Educational Research, 75*(3), 365–416. https://doi.org/10.3102/003465430750033

Roth, V. (2011). *Divergent.* HarperCollins.

Roth, V. (2012). *Insurgent.* HarperCollins.

Roth, V. (2013). *Allegiant.* HarperCollins.

Rothery, J. (1986). *Teaching writing in the primary school: a genre based approach to development of writing abilities* [Writing Project report: Working papers in linguistics]. Department of Linguistics, University of Sydney.

Rothery, J. (1994). *Exploring literacy in school English* [Part of the "Write it Right" English resource pack]. Disadvantaged Schools Program, Metropolitan East Region, NSW Department of School Education.

Rothery, J. (1996). Making changes: Developing an educational linguistics. In R. Hasan & G. Williams (Eds.), *Literacy in society* (pp. 86–123). Longman.

Rothery, J., & Stenglin, M. (1994). *Spine-chilling stories: A unit of work for junior secondary English* [Part of the "Write it Right" English resource pack]. Disadvantaged Schools Program, Metropolitan East Region, NSW Department of School Education.

Rothery, J., & Stenglin, M. (2000). Interpreting literature: The role of appraisal. In L. Unsworth (Ed.), *Researching language in schools and communities: Functional linguistic perspectives* (pp. 222–243). Cassell.

Rowling, J. K. (1997). *Harry Potter and the sorcerer's stone.* Scholastic.

Rowling, J. K. (1998). *Harry Potter and the chamber of secrets.* Scholastic.

Rowling, J. K. (1999). *Harry Potter and the prisoner of Azkaban*. Scholastic.

Rowling, J. K. (2000). *Harry Potter and the goblet of fire*. Scholastic.

Rowling, J. K. (2003). *Harry Potter and the order of the phoenix*. Scholastic.

Rowling, J. K. (2005). *Harry Potter and the half-blood prince*. Scholastic.

Rowling, J. K. (2007). *Harry Potter and the deathly hallows*. Scholastic.

Rupp, A., & Lesaux, N. (2006). Meeting expectations? An empirical investigation of a standards-based assessment of reading comprehension. *Educational Evaluation and Policy Analysis, 28*(4), 315–333. https://doi.org/10.3102/016237370280043

Rymes, B. (2008). The relationship between mass media and classroom discourse. *Working Papers in Linguistics, 23*(1), 65–88.

Rymes, B. (2009). *Classroom discourse analysis: A tool for critical reflection.* Hampton Press.

Said, E. W. (1979). *Orientalism*. Vintage Books.

Schleppegrell, M. J. (2004). *The language of schooling: A functional linguistics perspective.* Erlbaum.

Schleppegrell, M. J. (2011). Supporting disciplinary learning through language analysis: Developing historical literacy. In F. Christie & K. Maton (Eds.), *Disciplinarity: Functional linguistic and sociological perspectives* (pp. 197–216). Bloomsbury.

Schleppegrell, M. J., & Achugar, M. (2003). Learning language and learning history: A functional linguistics approach. *TESOL Journal, 12*(2), 21–27. https://doi.org/10.1002/J.1949-3533.2003.TB00126.X

Schleppegrell, M. J., & de Oliveira, L. C. (2006). An integrated language and content approach for history teachers. *Journal of English for Academic Purposes, 5*(4), 254–268. https://doi.org/10.1016/j.jeap.2006.08.003

Schleppegrell, M. J., & Moore, J. (2018). Linguistic tools for supporting emergent critical language awareness in elementary school. In R. Harman (Ed.). *Bilingual learners and social equity: Critical approaches to functional linguistics* (pp. 23–43). Springer.

Segel, D. (1937). A critique of the elementary-school graduation examination. *The Elementary School Journal, 37*(7), 530–535.

Shadd Cary, M. A. (1854, March 25). Why establish this paper? [Editorial]. *Provincial Freeman*, 1.

Shakespeare, W. (2002). *Othello*. In T. R. Arp & G. Johnson (Eds.), *Perrine's literature: Structure, sound, and sense* (8th ed., pp. 1361–1461). Thomson. (Original work published ca. 1604)

Shaull, R. (1986). Foreword. In P. Freire, *Pedagogy of the oppressed* (M. Bergan Ramos, Trans.; pp. 9–15). Continuum. (Original work published 1970)

Simmons, A. M. (2011). Fusing fantasy film and traditional texts to support critical literacy. *SIGNAL Journal, 34*(2), 25–29.

Simmons, A. M. (2016a). In your dreams: Validating the teaching of fantasy novels in the adolescent classroom. *SIGNAL Journal, 39*(1), 8–15.

Simmons, A. M. (2016b). Responsible grammar rebels: Using the Hunger Games trilogy to teach the intentional sentence fragment. *Journal of Adolescent and Adult Literacy, 59*(4), 387–395. http://doi.org/10.1002/jaal.449

Simmons, A. M. (2016c). Supporting critical literacy in high school English by using systemic functional linguistics to analyze fantasy, canonical, and non-fiction texts. *Critical Inquiry in Language Studies, 13*(3), 183–209. https://doi.org/10.1080/15427587.2016.1152475

Simmons, A. M. (2018). Student use of SFL resources on fantasy, canonical, and non-fiction texts: Critical literacy in the high school ELA classroom. In R. Harman (Ed.). *Bilingual learners and social equity: Critical approaches to functional linguistics* (pp. 71–90). Springer. https://doi.org/10.1007/978-3-319-60953-9_4

Simmons, A. M. (2023). Isabelle goes to college: Rethinking grammar instruction in Advanced Placement English. In K. Accurso & M. Gebhard (Eds.), *In pursuit of a multilingual equity agenda: SFL teacher action research.* Routledge.

Simmons, A. M., & Page, M. (2010). Motivating students through power and choice. *English Journal, 100*(1), 65–69. http://doi.org/10.2307/20787693

Smitherman, G. (2000). *Talkin that talk: Language, culture, and education in African America.* Routledge.

Smitherman, G. (2017). Raciolinguistics, "mis-education," and language arts teaching in the 21st century. *Language Arts Journal of Michigan, 32*(2), 4–12. https://doi.org/10.9707/2168-149X.2164

Svarova, J. (2008). *Politeness markers in spoken language* [Unpublished master's thesis]. Masaryk University, Brno.

Swales, J. (2001). Metatalk in American academic talk: The case of "point" and "thing." *Journal of English Language, 29*(1), 34–54. https://doi.org/10.1177/0075424012200518

Symons, C., Palincsar, A. S., & Schleppegrell, M. J. (2017). Fourth-grade emergent bilinguals' uses of functional grammar analysis to talk about text. *Learning and Instruction, 52*(2017), 102–111. https://doi.org/10.1016/j.learninstruc.2017.05.003

Talbot, M. (1992). The construction of gender in a teenage magazine. In N. Fairclough (Ed.), *Critical language awareness* (pp. 174–199). Longman.

thegayby_2015 [@thegayby]. (2016, Oct 16). *How come a girl can wear guys clothes* [Meme]. iFunny. https://ifunny.co/user/thegayby_2015

Thomas, M. (2003). Teaching fantasy: Overcoming the stigma and fluff. *English Journal, 92*(5), 60–64.

Thompson, G. (2004). *Introducing functional grammar.* Arnold.

United States Department of Education. (2020). *Common Core of Data* [CCD data files]. https://nces.ed.gov/ccd/files.asp

Valencia, S., Pearson, D., Peters, C., & Wixon, K. (1989). Theory and practice in statewide reading assessment: Closing the gap. *Educational Leadership, 46*(7), 57–63.

van Dijk, T. A. (2003). Critical discourse analysis. In D. Tannen, H. E. Hamilton, & D. Schiffrin (Eds.), *The handbook of discourse analysis* (pp. 352–371). Blackwell.

Vygotsky, L. S. (1978). *Mind and society: The development of higher psychological processes*. Harvard University Press.

Wallace, C. (2003). *Critical reading in language education*. Palgrave Macmillan.

Weis, L. (1995). Identity formation and the process of "othering": Unraveling sexual threads. *Educational Foundations*, *9*(1), 17–33.

Wennerstrom, A. (2003). *Discourse analysis in the language classroom*. University of Michigan Press.

Wilamová, S. (2005). On the function of hedging devices in negatively polite discourse. *BRNO Studies in English*, *31*(1), 85–93.

Williams, G. (2000). Children's literature, children and uses of language description. In L. Unsworth (Ed.), *Researching language in schools and communities: A functional linguistic perspective* (pp. 111–129). Continuum.

Willinsky, J. (2007). *Of critical theory and critical literacy*. Public Knowledge Project. https://pkp.sfu.ca/files/Critical%20Literacy.pdf

X., Malcolm, & Haley, A. (1965). *The autobiography of Malcolm X*. Grove Press.

Yates, L. (2010). Pragmatic challenges for second language learners. In A. Trosborg (Ed.), *Pragmatics across languages and cultures* (pp. 287–308). De Gruyter.

Zhang, W., & Cheung, Y. L. (2018). The construction of authorial voice in writing research articles: A corpus-based study from an appraisal theory perspective. *International Journal of English Studies*, *18*(2), 53–75. http://doi.org/10.6018/ijes/2018/2/320261

Index

The letter *f* following a page locator denotes a figure, and *t* denotes a table.

Author

Amber M. Simmons has a PhD in language and literacy education from the University of Georgia and seventeen years of teaching experience. She has received a number of awards, including the ISLS Founder Emerging Scholar Award, NASFLA Promising Scholar Award, Atlanta Families' Award for Excellence in Education, Brookwood High School Teacher of the Year, Gwinnett County Public Schools Teacher of the Year (finalist), GCTE Teacher of the Year, and an NCTE High School Teacher of Excellence Award. Her work and previous publications center on supporting student growth and developing language awareness in the high school ELA classroom through the introduction of SFL and social-emotional learning practices. She currently lives in Flowery Branch, GA, with her husband and two children, where she continues to serve as a high school language arts teacher.

This book was typeset in AvenirNext, Myriad Pro, and Palatino by Barbara Frazier.

The typefaces used on the cover include Avenir Next LT Pro and hellogalleriasans.

The book was printed on 50 lb., white offset paper.